NEW PERSPECTIVES IN TRANSATLANTIC STUDIES

Edited by

Heidi Slettedahl Macpherson
and
Will Kaufman

University Press of America,® Inc.
Lanham · New York · Oxford

Copyright © 2002 by
University Press of America,® Inc.
4720 Boston Way
Lanham, Maryland 20706
UPA Acquisitions Department (301) 459-3366

12 Hid's Copse Rd.
Cumnor Hill, Oxford OX2 9JJ

Library of Congress Cataloging-in-Publication Data

New perspectives in transatlantic studies /
edited by Heidi Slettedahl Macpherson and Will Kaufman.
p.   cm
Includes bibliographical references and index.
1. Europe—Relations—America. 2. America—Relations—Europe.
3. America—Ethnic relations. 4. Europe—Intellectual life.
5. European Union. I. Macpherson, Heidi Slettedahl.
II. Kaufman, Will.

D1065. A45 N48 2001   303.48'2407—dc21   2001054034 CIP

ISBN 0-7618-2164-3 (pbk. : alk. paper)

For Diana Duvall and Fumio Fujimoto

Contents

Acknowledgements

This book would not be possible without the hard work and dedication of the Board of Directors of the Maastricht Center for Transatlantic Studies. We especially thank Terry Rodenberg, Diana Duvall, Fumio Fujimoto, Shoko Fujimoto, and Mr. M. Tsuchida. This book results from a successful international conference and their help was invaluable in ensuring its success. We also wish to thank Paul Giles and Susan Castillo their excellent plenary and keynote addresses, to which we make reference, as well as their sustained support for our transatlantic projects. Additional thanks are due to Helen Stoker of Liverpool Tate for supplying us with the correct references for the painting "The Arrival" which we discuss in our introduction. We wish to thank our colleagues at the University of Central Lancashire, who have supported and who continue to support the Maastricht Center, and our spouses, Sarah Keates and Allan Macpherson, who help to make all this possible.

Our thanks go finally to Willard Diaz, director of *APOSTROFE: Revista ppara la Invetigacion en Ciencias Sociales* (Arequipa-PERU), for permission to publish Marcia Loo's chapter. It first appeared in its original Spanish under the title "El Cuerpo Hegemonico" and has been revised for this collection.

Introduction

Transatlantic Studies: Conceptual Challenges

Will Kaufman and Heidi Slettedahl Macpherson

At the Liverpool Tate Gallery in England, one painting among many stands out as representative of the energies of the transatlantic enterprise. Entitled "The Arrival" (1913), this Vorticist/Futurist painting by Christopher Richard Wynne Nevinson (1889-1946) is analogous both visually and culturally to a sense of the transatlantic that this collection of essays endeavors to invoke. The painting retains enough visual clues to let the viewer clearly see the ship at the center, both reaching out to viewers but also refracting away from them. The words "Transatlantic" are stenciled along one plank. The transatlantic is, therefore, embodied in the ship; it *is* the ship. There is no real sense of where the ship is—the *here* of the painting is somewhere in-between; movement (famously celebrated by the Futurists) is forward and relentless. Indeed, the Atlantic itself is only partially represented— the blue swathes either side of the ship could be ocean or sky. Nevinson, according to the display caption, suggested that the painting "represented a state of simultaneous mind." It is important to recall that Nevinson was, with Marinetti, the author of "Vital English Art: A Futurist Manifesto."[1] The display caption also quotes an early reviewer as saying that the painting "resembles a Channel steamer after a violent collection with a pier"—an assertion worth exploring, given the transatlantic tag it clearly wears. A second assertion, that the painting resembles a "melting-pot"—a term that cannot help but be associated, however falsely, with America—also needs to be unpacked.) Consider the many contradictions apparent here: the title is "The Arrival" yet the ship is still obviously at sea; the transatlantic is reinterpreted as a narrower (more local?) site, the English Channel; the multidirectional nature of the images suggests not one arrival, but many, disparate (ongoing?) ones. To which Atlantic shore is the ship arriving? In many ways, it doesn't matter—what matters is the dynamic sense of movement, and the irresistible energy of change.

Its connection with Transatlantic Studies is, one hopes, fairly obvious. As Ian Baucom argues, in relation to Sonia Boyce's *Coloured* but equally applicable here, the artwork "demonstrate[s] that the cross-Atlantic territory it thus maps refuses stasis; that, like the work itself, it is perpetually in motion, perpetually assembling, disassembling, and reassembling itself." Similarly, Paul Giles argues that "there is an analogy to be made between transnationalism [a term with close though by no means coterminous connections to the transatlantic, as we shall see], which twists national identity in new directions, and cultural forms of surrealism which have, because of their rebarbative and manifestly iconoclastic dimensions, worked to twist the national imaginary into strange and unfamiliar shapes."[2]

Like the painting, Transatlantic Studies suggests an evolving (though increasingly theorized) space. It shares its position with other, similar (though not equivalent) terms, such as circum-Atlanticism, or, more widely, transnationalism, internationalism, globalization. These (contested) terms furnish the basis on which Transatlantic Studies defines itself—both with and against. As James Clifford reminds us, "Every focus excludes; there is no politically innocent methodology for intercultural interpretation."[3] It is, therefore, imperative to unpack the terms that compete or collide with Transatlantic Studies. Circum-Atlanticism is the term used by scholars who wish to suggest that their particular vision of the Atlantic is one which is more inclusive and all-embracing, yet the circum- prefix, suggesting "around, surrounding, or on all sides," appears to us to be "inclusive" only in the respect of blurring localities—a criticism also lobbied at scholars who embrace a non-specific globalization which denies the particularized space that remains so important to individuals, if even on a mythic level. The geographers Martin W. Lewis and Kären Wigen, for example, are perturbed by "a vague 'globalism' that avoids place-, culture-, and language specificity"[4] The prefix trans-, on the other hand, implying both "across" and "beyond," allows for those localities to be simultaneously interconnected and separate.

This is not to suggest that any classification is definitive. Consider, for example, the ways in which scholars debate the merits of the other terms in our list. Stephen Owen suggests that the terms "global" or "international" are "sweeter" terms than the term "transnational" which he prefers because of its connection to a "corporate model, with historically local links across particular national boundaries, with clear centers of power, hierarchies of subordination, and routes of circulation that pass through those centers of power." Owen argues that the other terms imply a sort of global equality which patently does not exist, a "universalist" perspective through the back door, as it were. His example of transnationalism comes in the form of market forces:

> For the work of a contemporary Greek poet to get to Romania, it probably must go first to New York ... where its value is weighed against other work coming in through particular lines of distribution. If the Greek poet's work is judged valuable for the world market in those centers, it may be translated and only then exported to Bucharest.[5]

Other critics invoke the term transnational but with significantly different emphases. Consider, for example, Paul Giles's work, in which he defines transnationalism as that which "serves to reveal the parameters of national formations and thus to hollow out their pressing, peremptory claims to legitimacy." For Giles, transnationalism "positions itself at a point of intersection ... where the coercive aspects of imagined communities are turned back on themselves, reversed or mirrored, so that their covert presuppositions and ideological inflections become apparent." In this respect, transnationalism is less a market-driven, hegemonic totality than an idea which can "empty out the power relations that lurk ominously within these kinds of imaginary identification, interrupting the self-perpetuating circuit which tries simply to appropriate the authenticity of the land to underwrite certain forms of social authority or aesthetic closure."[6]

Henry Louis Gates, Jr., in an article nominally focused on "Planet Rap" and the internationalization and hybridization of African-American hip hop music, quotes T. S. Eliot's skeptical musings on the future of a "world culture": "'so long as there exist cultures which are beyond some point antagonistic to each other, antagonistic to the point of irreconcilability, all attempts at political-economic affiliations will be in vain.'" Gates, however, modifies Eliot's sentiments: "But one can be skeptical, as Eliot of course was, of the prospect of both such things and still recognize the value of some measure of intercultural tolerance."[7] Transatlantic Studies goes beyond "intercultural tolerance," of course, and engages, to some extent, with all of the contested terms of transnationalism, internationalism, and globalization. In his plenary address at the Transatlantic Studies conference that gave birth to this collection of essays, Giles offered his own definition of the field as one which is "cutting across established disciplines and geographical areas, not as seeking in a globalizing way to transcend difference or local particularity, but to look at them as from an unfamiliar perspective[8]

Transatlantic Studies found its basis in more localized area studies such as American Studies, but grows out of the bounded nature of such disciplines. It reflects the momentous shift towards some sort of "globalization" in thought that the new millennium has provoked. Such a shift has not been without its problems. Indeed, the founding of the Maastricht Center for Transatlantic Studies (MCTS) in 1995 was one of many international responses to what has been termed the "crisis" in area studies. In England, area studies have won recognition in the national Research Assessment Exercises and in the newly-formed "Subject Centres" that examine teaching practices and arenas—if only in relation to other disciplines. (Some critics argue that their very inclusion in such nationally-recognized institutions suggests their inculcation of suspect agendas.) But at the same time that interdisciplinarity is being hailed as the way forward for scholars in the humanities and social sciences, student numbers on courses such as American Studies have been falling, and questions about the relevance of nationally-based disciplines inevitably arise. It is in this caldron of diverse and potentially divisive interests that Transatlantic Studies comes to the fore. The prevailing *Zeitgeist* is clearly moving away from artificially constructed geographical entities to areas which had been previously overlooked as significant sites in and of themselves.

The founders of MCTS, an international study center with transatlantic partners which is also redefining itself as a center for transatlantic research, have found themselves grappling with these crucial ideas. They are dealing with the same dilemmas, challenges and unexpected arenas as a conspicuous group of scholars who had, in the closing decades of the 20th century, sited the Atlantic as a crucial point of historical, cultural, political and economic interrogation. Marcus Rediker's *Between the Devil and the Deep Blue Sea* appeared in 1987, digging through the surface and perimeters of the British and American nation-states to explore the working world of 18th-century

Atlantic seafarers and pirates. Paul Gilroy published *The Black Atlantic: Modernity and Double-Consciousness* in 1993, also looking beyond the category of "nation" to that of African "peoples" and their diasporic impact on both sides of the Atlantic. Three years later, Joseph Roach's *Cities of the Dead* introduced the concept of "Circum-Atlantic Performance" in a study of "the social foundations of aesthetic forms." Peter Linebaugh published a number of essays that led to his publication, with Rediker, of *The Many Headed Hydra: Sailors, Slaves, Commoners, and the History of the Revolutionary Atlantic*[9] in 2000. One could list many more texts that broaden out, in the English language at least, from that extensive but—in disciplinary terms— narrow body of studies devoted to literary or historical connections between, say, the United States and England, Spain and Latin America, or Africa and the United States.

The proliferation of these and other separate, Atlantic-focused studies occurs at a time when area studies—like nation-states themselves—face challenges to the perimeters that have hitherto defined them. In the preface to our earlier collection of essays, Susan Castillo acknowledged the "difficulties encountered in defining Area Studies and ... the practical and institutional problems this might create in terms of the disciplinary affiliations of individual researchers."[10] The crisis in area studies may in fact be an ethical as well as a practical one. One might ask a difficult question: have such conceptions as "American Studies," African Studies," "European Studies" (as well as national sub-designations) led to willfully closed intellectual enterprises—Americocentric, Afrocentric, Eurocentric, Hispanocentric? Such a question was critical enough for the Ford Foundation to inject massive funds into its celebrated initiative "Crossing Borders: Revitalizing Area Studies" in 1997. As Lewis and Wigen explain in their "Maritime Response to the Crisis in Area Studies," the Ford Foundation project grew out of a University of Chicago white paper entitled *Area Studies: Regional Worlds* (1997):

> One of its key recommendations was to move away from static "trait geographies" (in which East Asia was defined as the land of ideographic writing, Confucianism, chopsticks, and the like) toward "process geographies," in which regions could be conceptualized as both dynamic and interconnected."[11]

Lewis, Wigen and their colleagues at Duke University secured a Ford Foundation grant to establish an important initiative: "Oceans Connect: Culture, Capital, and Commodity Flows Across Basins." The title of their project can in some ways be seen as representative of the energies and direction of Transatlantic Studies: "flows" can be read as a verb as well as a noun, though of course such a reading is going against the (grammatical) grain. The dual nature of the word implies its protean state, and images of flux and change are incorporated into the title, even as the optimistic "Connect" may suggest otherwise. The Duke University team have been among the first to articulate the theoretical foundations of the scholarly approaches undertaken by Roach, Gilroy, Giles, Linebaugh and Rediker (among others) and the pedagogical approach followed at MCTS. As they rightly argue, "One useful alternative ... reframes area studies around ocean and sea basins. Putting maritime interactions at the center of vision brings to light a set of historical regions that have largely remained invisible on the conventional map of the world." In explaining the objectives of Duke's "four basin-centered working groups," focusing on the Atlantic, the Eurasian seas, the Indian Ocean and the Mediterranean (a Pacific group is in formation), Lewis and Wigen point to some of the lapses inherent in the traditional, "static" configurations of area studies:

> Shifting the maritime realm from the margins to the center of discussion has had a variety of implications. In the first place, it has brought the world's major seas into focus as lively zones of contact (and conflict). This in turn has highlighted the role of littoral societies, not merely as the peripheries of one or another territorial civilization but as diverse, cosmopolitan communities in their own right.[12]

A focus on the Atlantic, with "its foregrounding of movement and flux," does indeed provoke "a challenge [to] static modes of thinking about place-based identity."[13] But Lewis and Wigen also emphasize the element not only of "contact," but also of "conflict"—and, for Transatlantic Studies, a major point of conflict is national identity, which, like the separate foci of area studies, refuses to give up the ghost. This is perhaps ironic, given the chimerical nature of what is conventionally recognized as the "nation." Eric Hobsbawm, Benedict Anderson, Ian Baucom, David Hewison, Patrick Wright and Linda Colley, among others, have all originated or drawn on theories of "inventing tradition" and "imagining communities" in their explorations of national identity—in particular, English/British national identity.[14] In this they are enlarging the processes with which many American Studies scholars are already familiar; the catalogue of titles bearing the phrases "Inventing America" or "Imagining America" is too long to innumerate. But linking all these earlier and later explorations is the process that Baucom (after Ernst Renan) carefully articulates with regard to British identity: the mixture of "compulsory forgetting" and "selective memory" in the construction of a national identity.[15] Obviously, what colors such theorizing is the implied or explicit suggestion of artificiality.

Such artificiality can be at once applauded and derided in the same utterance, or in two utterances with opposing intentions. The US historian, Arthur Schlesinger, Jr., for instance, can roundly damn American Afrocentrism as "the invention of tradition" while still approving of Ernest Gellner's high valuation of nationalism—"[inventing] nations where they do not exist"—in order to "give individual lives meaning in an increasingly baffling universe."[16] And while Schlesinger undoubtedly sees the melting pot as the great American accomplishment, his polar opposite in this regard, the British conservative MP Enoch Powell, famously appealed to the "invention of tradition" in order to maintain the dubious myth of English racial purity, as he obliged his fellow politicians in 1946 to "offer [their] people good myths and to save them from harmful myths."[17] Nowhere is Antony Easthope's argument that "a sense of national identity comes about when a set of signifiers are endowed by fantasy with meaning"[18] more clearly, and problematically, realized than here.

However, these questions beg others: if national identity is so "imaginary," if it relies to such an acknowledged degree on "invention," why is it so intractable—so static? What is it that allows even the most cynical individualists or idealistic globalists to identify themselves with "nation," what Easthope calls "the most powerful collective identity to emerge with modernity"?[19] Declan Kiberd writes in relation to the acknowledged myths of Irish national character that "if huge numbers of people believed in them, then they also must be accorded their place as decisive agents of history."[20] Easthope is even more categorical: "Any theoretical opposition which would contrast some notion of authentic identity with the inauthenticity of national identity has to be rejected."[21] There is no shortage of criticism against the pure "inventors and imaginers of nationhood" (Hobsbawm, Anderson, Gellner and others): as Miguel Angel Centeno warns, "This new literature, while a corrective on the old essentialism, may have gone too far in its social-constructivism."[22] In agreement, Montserrat Guibernau writes about the power of the nation "to be a provider of identity for individuals conscious of forming a group based upon a common culture, past, project for the future and attachment to a concrete territory."[23] According to Lawrence Buell, "nations are utopian social fictions that are at once epistemologically suspect, economically obsolete, politically potent (since world order continues to recognize the sovereign nation as primary unit), territorially determinate (except in wartime), and culturally porous."[24] And, lest we forget, Henry Louis Gates, Jr. reminds us that "'Nationalism' has historically been the banner under which the annihilation or conquest of ethnic particularity has proceeded"[25] Yet at the same time, individuals are encouraged to "call their nation" and to align themselves solely with it (the difficulty of claiming dual-nationality is but one example of the fraught nature of such claiming.)

Underlying the measured interrogations of nationalism and national culture by the likes of Baucom, Easthope, Kiberd, Guibernau and others, is the acknowledgement of the central place of desire—in Easthope's words, a "thirst for unity."[26] With all respect to Paul Gilroy's hopes of "the postmodern eclipse of the modern nation-state,"[27] the very fractures, disintegrations and proliferations of both globalism and localism that might characterize just such a "postmodern eclipse" may in fact assist the opposite—that is, the further entrenchment of national desire. As Giles notes, our "positivistic belief in the viability of the nation" is "inflected by a deeply romanticized image of the nation as a site of immanent rather than merely projected significance, whose meaning we might ultimately grasp if only we could give ourselves access to enough of its linguistic and cultural riches."[28]

The persistence of the "nation" as an object of desire is the source of one of the greatest challenges to Transatlantic Studies as a viable intellectual project. Area studies, like nations, do not willingly self-destruct. Fortunately or not, Transatlantic Studies demands no such thing. One must recognize, as Lawrence Buell does, that despite a widening of its intellectual borders, American Studies (for instance) will "continue to center on the United States,"[29] just as Canadian Studies focuses on Canada (despite its colonial ties to France and England). This is where Transatlantic Studies moves beyond the nation, even as a concept, in order to embrace the tracings that link the various nations of the Atlantic seaboard and beyond. Giles points out the necessary ability to acknowledge "the hollowing out of national identity while simultaneously admitting its capacity to shape cultural forms in a spectral way."[30] Giles explores the conflict and the points of stasis surrounding the Atlantic contact, which Transatlantic Studies must be able to accommodate rather than attempt to elide in the equally necessary "foregrounding of movement and flux." It is worth returning to Giles's foreword to our earlier collection:

> All these authors are concerned with the increasingly problematic status of the nation-state and with the tendency of conceptual categories to exceed national boundaries. At the same time, they do not find themselves impelled to abandon the signifying capacity of the nation

entirely; indeed, Transatlantic Studies might be said to situate itself at that awkward, liminal place where the national meets the global.[31]

Giles reminds us of "the frictions and disjunctions brought about by the slow but inexorable erosion of national formations along with the various reactions and tensions which this process produces." He asks us to engage with "the paradoxical (and sometimes apparently incongruous) points of convergence, divergence and traversal between local interests and global imperatives"—in short, to acknowledge that "Transatlantic Studies takes its impetus from an uncomfortable, highly contested situation where traditional identities find themselves traversed by the forces of difference."[32] An element of unease, of restlessness, appears naturally germane to Transatlantic Studies: it cannot, then, be a critical panacea in the service of some smooth transition towards globalism. As these essays demonstrate, both resistance and confluence are built into most, if not all, interrogations of the Atlantic contact.

A useful indication of such incongruity lies in the recent work on transatlantic colonial literatures by Susan Castillo and Ivy Schweitzer. In her keynote address to the "Transatlantic Studies: New Perspectives" conference, Castillo explored the concept of "ekphrasis" as she related the experience of co-editing the landmark anthology, *The Literatures of Colonial America*:

> I was fascinated to observe the edgy, fragmented, plurivocal character of the texts I encountered. First of all, I observed a recurring ekphrastic tension between texts describing transatlantic interactions and the images which accompany them. In conventional definitions, the phenomenon of ekphrasis is characterized as the translation of certain properties from one medium (the visual) into another (the verbal). In colonial texts, however (and, I would argue, transatlantic texts in general), ekphrasis is in essence a cultural practice, given that mediation is occurring not only between the visual and verbal realms but between differing modes of cultural experience and indeed between differing historical traditions of the representation of cultural experience.[33]

Students and practitioners of translation will be aware that theirs is a highly contestatory exercise, one that defies the surety of closure and resolution: publishers' blurbs to the contrary, there is no such thing as a definitive translation. In relating ekphrasis and translation to the practice of Transatlantic Studies, Castillo introduces a useful critical tool that prepares one for the battle between flux and stasis in the transatlantic engagement. Castillo's own work on the Peruvian writer,

Guaman Poma de Ayala (c. 1525-c.1615) is a rich exploration of transatlantic ekphrasis and resistant translation. As she notes, this supposedly colonized Native author was able to appropriate

> the technology (i.e. writing and print culture), the language, and the literary/historiographic conventions of the imperial Spanish conquerors in order not only to bear witness to the injustices committed against his people but also to subvert European codes of visual and textual representation and use them to his own advantage.[34]

Transatlantic Studies is about engagement, not about the wholesale imposition of one force or body upon another. Castillo and Schweitzer make this clear in the preface to their anthology, which could just as easily be referring to the contemporary Atlantic as to the colonial:

> [T]he process of colonization was not a one-way street in which Europeans imposed their ideologies and social structures upon a passive continent, but rather, as Fernando Ortiz, Mary Louise Pratt and Michel de Certeau have suggested, an intricate series of interactions of power and resistance in which the individuals and groups concerned produced lasting effects upon one another.[35]

II

The present collection is drawn from papers presented at the "Transatlantic Studies: New Perspectives" conference held at MCTS, The Netherlands, in October 2000. Either explicitly or implicitly, the authors of the essays have explored a variety of transatlantic engagements with an eye to the dynamism and resistance hitherto discussed. Divided into 5 sections, the collection begins by examining the context of the transatlantic in the 16th and 17th centuries. "Oceans Apart? Setting the Transatlantic Context" thus nods to the Duke University title of "Oceans Connect" but suggests that its optimism could perhaps be tempered slightly. Melanie Perrault sets the nature of these engagements with the opening chapter, "Waterways in the Atlantic World: Contact and Cultural Negotiations Across a Liquid Landscape." The fluidity of her title is not meant to imply a smoothly flowing engagement: as she argues, "waterways were places in which no single group could gain hegemony." Her siting of the Atlantic as a point of contact between peoples from England, West Africa, Guiana and Virginia in the late 16th and early 17th centuries reveals the ocean basin as both a "physical" and a "socially constructed space" where conflict and negotiation between humans and nature could be played out. Elvira Vilches's "The Economy of the Marvelous" explores the way that Columbus used the bodies of Amerindians as visual representations of "wonder" and "gold" in order to "represent the myth of the New World as a wonderland of untapped wealth so real it denied even strongly apparent symptoms of colonial disappointment." Milissa Ellison-Murphree's chapter, "End-Time and Exorcism in England," establishes a continuity between "England's" two witch-hunts—in 17th-century East Anglia and Salem—as well as the points of conflict in which "local tensions" were sparked by the "predestinarian eschatology" of the Puritan Commonwealth.

In Section 2, "Racial Encounters in the Contact Zone," contributors explore the ways that bodies and discourses about them inform narratives of the transatlantic. Gates argues that "an honest account of ethnic dynamism gives full weight to the forces of assimilation and convergence as well as those of differentiation and divergence,"[36] a sentiment explored in different ways by each of the authors in this section. Lars Ivar Owesen-Lein Borge shifts the transatlantic phenomenon of witch-hunting into the area of race and linguistic slippage in his chapter, "Mulattos Accused of Witchcraft and Sorcery in Late Colonial New Spain." Borge explores the ambiguities of Spain's system of racial terminology and classification as it was imposed upon the shifting, local concept of *mulatto* in colonial Mexico. Richard Milton Juang's "A Taste for Flesh" examines the ironic conflict between "the imagining of European interiorities and European bodies" and "the discursive 'shaping' of slave bodies and the imagining of slave interiorities," upon which the promotion of the transatlantic slave trade rested. In "Spirits of the Earth and Sky," Michael C. Wilson explores the collision between two ethnic cultures "in the same natural landscape," focusing on the diverse meaning of the land for the First Nations people of Canada and the US and their European rivals for it.

Artistic exchanges across the Atlantic are also sources of "friction and disjunction" as well as "movement and flux." Indeed, the Atlantic Studies group at Duke takes as one of its tasks the examination of "the role of the visual and performing arts in shaping a circum-Atlantic cultural imaginary."[37] This important role is explored in Section 3, "Transatlantic Artistic Exchanges." Phillippe Mahoux-Pauzin's "A Transatlantic Case of Romanticism" draws, on the one hand, a line between the British and American romantic modes, and on the other, a picture of resistance to modernity through a study of the English painter-poet Thomas Cole's encounter with the American landscape. In "European Modernity-Awareness and Transatlantic Intertextuality," Steve Brewer and Martin Jesinghausen construct one more Atlantic triangle trade, with Edgar Allan Poe as the disruptive source of value for Charles Baudelaire, Walter Benjamin and Michel Foucault. María Dolores Narbona Carrión focuses on the relationships between the US writer, Elizabeth Stuart Phelps, and European women writers who established a fellowship designed to challenge the transatlantic network of literary patriarchy. Marcia Loo's "The Hegemonic Body" analyzes the politics of *El Alcatraz*, the Black Peruvian dance enacting rituals of resistance against Spanish colonial instrumentalization.

Dynamism and resistance characterize transatlantic economies no less than they do artistic exchanges, cultural negotiations, racial encounters and ideological contests; thus Section 4, "Transatlantic Economies," explores the ways that industry and monetary systems interact in a transatlantic environment. Sharron Schwartz's chapter, "Exporting the Industrial Revolution," sets up a particularly intriguing illustration of the transatlantic as a point of "convergence, divergence and traversal between local interests and global imperatives." Schwartz's study of the 19th-century migration of Cornish mining technology to Latin America demonstrates that local or regional identity will assert itself even amidst the momentous scale of international industrial exchange. Examining the effects of a "transatlantic network" on the other side of the Atlantic, Brigitte Leucht's chapter follows a group of people who "to varying degrees and for varying reasons, shared a belief in European integration." Her focus on the friendship between the US lawyer, George W. Ball, and the French statesman, Jean Monnet, raises the question of the extent to which supra-national imperatives such as European integration can be founded on the most fragile of relationships between individuals. Saturnino Aguado's speculative analysis of the dollar and the euro charts the possibility of a bipolar struggle for global influence between what may well become the world's last two supercurrencies.

The struggle for transatlantic influence dominates the final section, "Politics, Philosophy, and Security: Revisiting International Relations." Anthony Marasco's study of Pragmatism challenges the conventional wisdom about its apparently American origin. In "Old Orders, New Orders and Third Ways," Philip Davies assesses the impact of British-American "Third Way" philosophy on the major political parties of both nations, questioning whether "it may, in the end, be the best ... that transatlantic social democratic forces can expect." Roberta Glaspie, Lesley Hodgson, Andrew Thompson and Donald Wallace offer disturbing evidence of the impact of US resistance to the establishment of an International Criminal Court, as a further reminder of the tenacious hold of national sovereignty on transnational enterprises. In "The Trauma of a Nuclear Pearl Harbor," Susanna Schrafstetter examines the ways that the US confidently viewed the Atlantic as a physical barrier against attack. She explores US fears over the loss of its historical invulnerability and the impact of those fears on the fate of the North Atlantic Alliance and beyond—to "the real beginning of the globalization of conflict." Sven Biscop's concluding chapter focuses on what remains another unresolved transatlantic power struggle: that between the US and the European Union over the development of a European defense force.

In the aggregate, these essays demonstrate the continuing international interest in the exploration of the transatlantic engagement. When our first collection, *Transatlantic Studies*, was published, we were pleased to see that the Cataloging Data described it as "Essays based on on-going discussions at the Maastricht Center for Transatlantic Studies." The discussions are still on-going, not only at Maastricht but, as we have seen, elsewhere—in Duke University's "Oceans Connect" project; in a host of transatlantic conferences and conference panels (their number has increased exponentially in the last two years particularly); in the forthcoming (2002) launch of the *Journal of Transatlantic Studies* from the Edinburgh University Press; and in the many works from a growing body of scholars captivated by the continuing reverberations of the Atlantic explorations.

---

[1] Interested readers can find a copy of the painting on the web at http://www.tate.org.uk/servlet/AText?id=10234&type=caption and can read more about vorticism on http://users.senet.com.au/~dsmith/vorticism.htm

[2] Ian Baucom, "Hydrographies," *The Geographical Review* 89, no. 2 (1999): 301-313 (313); Paul Giles, "Trans Atlantique" (plenary address at the "Transatlantic Studies: New Perspectives" conference, Maastricht, October 2000), 16.

[3] James Clifford, "Travelling Cultures" in *Cultural Studies*, eds. Lawrence Grossberg, Cary Nelson and Paula Treichler (London: Routledge, 1992), 96-166 (97).

[4] Martin W. Lewis and Kären Wigen, "A Maritime Response to the Crisis in Area Studies," *Geographical Review* 89, no. 2 (April 1999): 161-68 (162).

[5] Stephen Owen, "National Literatures in a Global World? Sometimes—Maybe," in *Field Work: Sites in Literary and Cultural Studies*, eds. Marjorie Garber, Rebecca L. Walkowitz, and Paul B. Franklin (New York: Routledge, 1996), 120-24 (121).Ibid.

[6] Paul Giles, "Transnationalism in Practice" (paper presented at the "Dislocations: Transnational Perspectives on Postnational American Studies" conference, the University of Birmingham, February 24, 2001), 1-2, 10.

[7] Henry Louis Gates, Jr., "Planet Rap: Notes on the Globalization of Culture," in *Field Work: Sites in Literary and Cultural Studies*, eds. Marjorie Garber, Rebecca L. Walkowitz, and Paul B. Franklin (New York: Routledge, 1996), 55-66 (61-62).

[8] Giles, "Trans Atlantique," 15.

[9] Marcus Rediker, *Between the Devil and the Deep Blue Sea: Merchant Seamen, Pirates, and the Anglo-American Maritime World, 1700-1750* (Cambridge: Cambridge University Press, 1987); Paul Gilroy, *The Black Atlantic: Modernity and Double-Consciousness* (Cambridge, MA: Harvard University Press, 1993); Joseph Roach, *Cities of the Dead: The Social Foundations of Aesthetic Forms* (New York: Columbia University Press, 1996); Peter Linebaugh and Marcus Rediker, *The Many-Headed Hydra: Sailors, Slaves, Commoners, and the History of the Revolutionary Atlantic* (Boston: Beacon Press, 2000).

[10] Susan Castillo, preface to *Transatlantic Studies*, ed. by Will Kaufman and Heidi Slettedahl Macpherson (Lanham: University Press of America, 2000), xiii.

[11] Lewis and Wigen, 165.

[12] Ibid., 161, 165.

[13] Ibid., 165.

[14] Benedict Anderson, *Imagined Communities* (London: Verso, 1991); Ian Baucom, *Out of Place: Englishness, Empire, and the Locations of Identity* (Princeton: Princeton University Press, 1999); Linda Colley, *Britons: Forging the Nation, 1707-1837* (London: Yale University Press, 1992); Robert Hewison, *The Heritage Industry: Britain in a Climate of Decline* (London: Methuen, 1987); Eric Hobsbawm and Terence Ranger, eds, *The Invention of Tradition* (Cambridge: Cambridge University Press, 1992); Patrick Wright, *On Living in an Old Country: The National Past in Contemporary Britain* (London: Verso, 1985).

[15] Baucom, *Out of Place*, 52.

[16] Arthur Schlesinger, Jr., *The Disuniting of America* (London: W. W. Norton, 1992), 47, 85.

[17] Enoch Powell, speech at Trinity College, Dublin, 1946. Quoted in Tom Nairn, *The Break-up of Britain* (London: Verso, 1981), 266.

[18] Antony Easthope, *Englishness and National Culture* (London: Routledge, 1999), 22.

[19] Ibid., ix.

[20] Declan Kiberd, *Inventing Ireland* (London: Vintage, 1996), 646.

[21] Easthope, 10.

[22] Miguel Angel Centeno, "War and Memories: Symbols of State Nationalism in Latin America," *European Review of Latin American and Caribbean Studies* 66 (June 1999): 75-106 (75).

[23] Montserrat Guibernau, *Nationalisms* (Cambridge: Polity Press, 1996), 3.

[24] Lawrence Buell, "Are We Post-American Studies?" in *Field Work: Sites in Literary and Cultural Studies*, eds. Marjorie Garber et al (New York: Routledge, 1996), 87-93 (89).

[25] Gates, 61.

[26] Easthope, 49.

[27] Quoted in *Cultural Studies*, eds. Lawrence Grossberg, Cary Nelson and Paula Treichler (London: Routledge, 1992), 188.

[28] Giles, "Transnationalism in Practice," 8.

[29] Buell, 89.

[30] Giles, "Trans Atlantique," 15.

[31] Paul Giles, foreword to *Transatlantic Studies*, eds. Will Kaufman and Heidi Slettedahl Macpherson (Lanham: University Press of America, 2000), x.

[32] Ibid., x.

[33] Susan Castillo, "A Different Mirror: Ruses of Resistance in Guaman Poma de Ayala's *Letter to a King*" (keynote address at the "Transatlantic Studies: New Perspectives" Conference, Maastricht, October 2000), 1.

[34] Ibid., 2.

[35] Susan Castillo and Ivy Schweitzer, preface to *The Literatures of Colonial America*, eds. Susan Castillo and Ivy Schweitzer (Oxford: Blackwell, 2001), xvi.

[36] Gates, 64.

[37] Lewis and Wigen, 167.

Part One:
Oceans Apart? Setting the Transatlantic Context

Chapter 1

Waterways In the Atlantic World: Contact and Cultural Negotiation Across a Liquid Landscape

Melanie Perreault

Walter Raleigh's dream of finding fame and fortune in the "discovery" of Guiana seemed at great risk as his disheartened crew searched desperately for a sense of direction and the Orinoco River that would return them to the rest of the English party. The Indian guide the men had forcibly abducted earlier was as confused as the English visitors, and panic began to set in as the exploration party became hopelessly lost. The situation was so desperate, Raleigh wrote, that "if God had not sent us another help, we might have wandered a whole year in that labyrinth of rivers, ere we had found any way, either out or in ... for I know all the earth doth not yield the like confluence of streams or branches ... and so like one to another, as no man can tell which to take."[1] Raleigh's experience illustrates an often overlooked aspect of the early contact period—much of the action took place on or around water, a medium with ambiguous meaning for both the English and the people they encountered.

When European sailors set sail for long-distance voyages in the 16th century, they transformed the oceans that had long been seen as a barrier to cultural diasporas into a rapid transport system that facilitated and mediated cultural contact. Water was movement, a source of life, a potential source of wealth, a religiously imbued object that figured prominently in creation stories. But water also occupied a less benevolent place in the minds of overseas travelers. Death by drowning was a constant fear, sea monsters haunted the imagination of the most timid adventurers, and murky waters often held the hidden danger of disease to those who drank or bathed in deceptively welcoming pools. Water was also a cultural touchstone for the peoples the Europeans met after crossing the oceans. Here, too, water was at the center of creation stories, religious beliefs, and popular imagination. Significantly, water offered native peoples a rare opportunity to demonstrate mastery and exert tremendous power during the contact period, and even more importantly, to have this mastery recognized by the often ethnocentric European visitors. Superior knowledge of the methods to harness water, to wrest subsistence from the depths, and to traverse even the most convoluted river system was a crucial component of the effort to resist domination. The eventual loss of this source of power for native peoples ushered in a significant shift in the evolving relationship between increasingly demanding English colonists and traders, and the peoples and environments they intended to master in the 17th century.

It is vital to examine the creation of "waterways" as a medium of cultural negotiation in the Atlantic encounter. Like Richard White's notion of a "middle ground," waterways were places in which no single group could gain hegemony. Constantly under development, waterways brought together humans and nature in the contact period and offered both a physical space for encounters, and a socially constructed space with which to frame and understand the various peoples involved. Like the complex river systems that only reluctantly ushered the English into the inner recesses of Guiana, the English experience was full of twists and turns, dangerous rocky outbreaks and smooth-flowing currents, with the potential for disaster or great reward seemingly just around the next bend. Unfortunately for the English, optimism gave way to disappointment after they repeatedly traveled around the "next bend" only to find another twist in the turgid river.[2]

In the mid-16th century, English men (and later women) embarked upon a series of long-distance expeditions across the seas. The purpose of these journeys varied; some were intended as reconnaissance voyages to map and learn about dimly understood lands. Others were designed to foster trade or make preliminary efforts to establish permanent colonies in the New World. Whatever the intent, the members of overseas voyages had at least one experience in common—to get to their destination, they had to spend weeks or even months confined aboard waterlogged wooden vessels, surrounded by a seemingly endless expanse of water. Exhausted sailors often were confronted with the ultimate irony of running out of potable drinking water even as briny seas pitched and rolled their ships. In the 1550s, the trading centers of coastal West Africa were the focal point for many of these journeys for the English and other European competitors. By the 1580s, English attention to the Americas grew, as first Roanoke and then Virginia began to occupy the minds of those who envisioned colonial settlements. By the 1590s, serious attention shifted to more exotic opportunities for trade and colonization in the river systems of Guiana.[3]

Water occupied a central place in the mythic worlds of 16th-century Europeans and the peoples they would encounter after traversing the seas. Not surprisingly, coastal and riverine cultures in West Africa often included water in their creation stories. The Ijebu of coastal Nigeria for example, claimed to be descendants of people once sacrificed to the sea.[4] Water was alive with active spirits who played an important role in the daily life of West Africa. Residents of Igbuzo were careful not to offend the stream goddess Oboshi, who jealously guarded her children, the fish.[5] Although the particular spirits varied, belief in animism and natural spirits who occasionally needed to be mollified was widespread throughout the Americas before contact with Europeans. In Guiana, the coastal Warrau peoples recognized water spirits divided into those who resided in rivers, oceans, and the bottom of the water. And further north, John Smith reported that when "the waters are rough in the rivers and sea coasts" the religious leaders of the Powhatan Indians of Virginia "run to the water sides ... after many hellish outcries and invocations, they cast tobacco, Copper, *Pocones* or other such trash in the water, to pacifie that God whom they thinke to be very angry in those stormes." Dependent on good weather for the survival of their harvest, the Powhatan Indians sought to remedy any perceived slight of the powerful natural spirits.[6]

Christians could point to Genesis for an explanation of the expansive waters of the oceans. Here, God transformed an unformed earth on the second day of creation with a single decree: "Let the waters under the heavens be gathered into one place, and let the dry land appear." The goal of long-distance sailing was to find the regions in which dry land met the water, yet this conjunction also presented significant dangers for European ships. And while sailors could find comfort in their belief that God was responsible for stocking the waters with fish and other sea creatures, the fear that malevolent monsters swam side-by-side with harmless dolphins in the deepest reaches of the oceans could not be ignored. Readers of Genesis could also not help but note the cataclysmic flood created by an angry God who used the deluge to destroy "every living thing that was on the face of the ground, man and animals and creeping things and birds of the air."[7] While Christians could reassure themselves that God would not destroy the world with water again, the story served to remind them of the raw power of water to bring disaster in the form of floods or abundance in the gentle showers necessary for crops.

However ambiguous the spiritual symbolism of water in the Christian mind, England itself seemed to be particularly blessed with benevolent waters. After describing foreign waters that allegedly caused symptoms ranging from uncontrollable laughter to undesirable effeminacy in their consumers, William Harrison noted that in England "we have ... no hurtful waters amongst us, but all wholesome and profitable for the benefit of the people." Harrison was skeptical about the attribution of effeminacy to drinking particular waters, arguing instead that the condition was due to "superfluous wealth and inconstancy of living and behavior."[8] Fish inhabited all interior streams and rivers in England, Harrison reported confidently, and the coastal waters were particularly rich with resources from oysters to haddock. Surely, one of the greatest attributes of the English environment was its local waterways. Nonetheless, in the 16th century, the English were increasingly called to leave the familiar rivers and streams of their own land to confront less welcoming waters.

As members of an island nation, the English placed a considerable portion of their identity in mastering long-distance sailing. But this identity was being challenged in the 16th century as other European nations entered the oceans with increasing frequency. Richard Hakluyt lamented the sense of decay he sensed in England, and suggested that overseas voyages would challenge the English to greatness once again, "For in this action we are not to cut over the narrow seas in a day or a night between Flanders, France, or Ireland in small Barkes of twenty or thirty tons, but we are to pass over the breast of the main Ocean and to live at sea a month or six weeks together."[9] Men who forged their character in the boot camp atmosphere of the cramped quarters and windswept decks of creaking wooden vessels might be a little rough around the edges, Hakluyt suggested, but were certainly not at risk for joining the growing population of slothful beggars.

For many Europeans involved in overseas voyages, the prospect of crossing large expanses of water was a frightening proposition. Navigation was still a crude science in the 16th century, making long-distance travel particularly perilous. Despite advances in celestial navigation, coastal observation remained a key component of reckoning locations. Reports of overseas voyages often contained detailed descriptions of local landmarks, such as John Lok's account of Cape Mensurado in West Africa, which "may be known by reason that the rising of it is like a porpoise-head. Also toward the south-east there are three trees, whereof the easternmost is the highest and the middlemost is like a hay stack and the southernmost like unto a gibbet."[10] By relying on coastal features, expeditions to West Africa increased the risk of running aground in the notoriously dangerous coastline. Crossing unfamiliar open water presented its own challenges and could frighten even the most experienced sailors. Faced with a potential mutiny on the Chesapeake Bay in 1608, John Smith addressed his men: "as for your fears, that I will lose myself in these unknown large waters, or be swallowed up in some stormy gust, abandon these childish fears, for worse than is past cannot happen."[11] Smith's motivational message was not exactly the cheerful vote of confidence his men may have wanted to hear, but it served to rally the sailors around their leader. After overcoming navigational difficulties and hostile weather patterns, English sailors were confronted with the inhabitants of unfamiliar lands.

Many of the first meetings between English and natives took place on the culturally neutral space of coastal waters rather than land. William Towerson's first meeting with Africans took place when "we, being far into the sea, met with diverse boats of the country, small, long, and narrow, and in every boat one man and no more."[12] Perhaps aware of the ambiguity inherent in such water meetings, the visitors sought to engage the native inhabitants in an environment that was more clearly defined as English space whenever possible. When Arthur Barlowe's men first met a resident of Roanoke Island in 1584, they brought the Indian man aboard ship and quickly gave him a shirt, a hat, and some food, all clear markers of English culture. Upon returning to land, however, the man immediately began fishing, leaving a gift of fish on the bank. The fish were not simply an offering of reciprocity, but a symbolic statement identifying the primary sources of power each side would have as the encounter continued. Just as the Indian man had to enter into an alien environment to receive the English gifts, the sailors would have to leave their ship, a tangible remnant of English identity and security, to step onto unfamiliar soil.[13]

The stalemate on Roanoke Island was replicated in other coastal areas. In West Africa, the rocky coastline forced an uneasy truce between Africans and the English, even as various Europeans chased each other in a futile attempt to establish control over the waters. The physical setting of the trade on the water rather than land was an important part of the increasingly rancorous debate between the English and Portuguese over territorial claims. When a Portuguese ambassador complained that an English voyage in 1553 violated Portuguese sovereignty, the English merchants responded that they "entered not into the land with any force, but tarried only in their ships, abiding there the resort of the people to them, who came to them in their ships, bringing such commodities as their country had." Without military conquest as a viable option, the Europeans "had to abandon the time-honored tradition of trading and raiding and substitute a relationship based more or less completely on peaceful regulated trade." But while the ocean coasts may have offered a relatively neutral space from which to negotiate cultural interactions, during the early contact period the riverine systems belonged largely to the native peoples themselves.[14]

Long before any European arrival, the riverine systems of West Africa and the Americas shaped daily life and trade. In West Africa, the Niger, Senegal, and Gambia Rivers offered relatively easy access to the interior and the coast. Trade flourished along the rivers, rewarding those with expertise in water travel with economic and political advantages. Dominance over the water of the lower Niger system through war canoes allowed some African groups to collect tribute from traders, protect their villages, and gain prestige.[15] In Virginia, Algonquian life centered closely around the rivers and streams that linked the Chesapeake Bay to the inner reaches of the mainland. Whereas Europeans often used rivers to mark boundaries between towns, counties, and even entire countries, the Algonquians formed political units around rivers, setting up housing on each side of a stream.[16] This settlement strategy marks an important cultural difference between European and Indian—while for the Europeans, water was a barrier, the demarcation line between countries or towns, or something to be conquered, for Indians it was a central gathering point. Familiarity with the local waterways proved to be a significant source of power for native peoples as they struggled to maintain cultural integrity in the post-contact world.

Given the convoluted geography and the confusing number of native groups, it is not surprising that native informants were more important in Guiana than in any other region during the first contact period. In the late 16th century, the search for the riches of the mythical El Dorado as well as less exotic sources of wealth led English explorers into the tangled river systems between the Amazon and the Orinoco rivers. Try as they might, the English often found it impossible to distinguish one turn in a river from another. Lost exploring expeditions risked becoming separated from the main group, exposing themselves to potential attack from the Spanish or Guianan enemies. During Lawrence Keymis's 1596 reconnaissance mission, a pinnace that had been separated from the group off the coast of England eventually made it to Guiana, only to become lost searching for the predetermined meeting place on the Orinoco. After struggling for four weeks, the sailors in the pinnace "were enforced to borrow a [native] pilot against his will" to direct the Englishmen to the river. Without the native guide, the pinnace would have been forced to attempt to return to England alone, a dangerous proposition given the prevalence of privateers in the Caribbean.[17]

In areas where navigation was not as complicated as Guiana, the English still found themselves at the mercy of the Indians when trying to utilize the bounty of the waters. In Virginia, the biggest danger was not in getting lost, so much as it was difficulty wresting subsistence from the waterways. English visitors to the region encountered an environment defined by major rivers such as the James, the Rappahanock, and the Potomac, each penetrating the land from the Chesapeake Bay to the Piedmont of the Appalachian Mountains. During Ralph Lane's exploration trip up the Roanoke River, the Indians along the route abandoned the river to force the English to feed themselves. Intentional abandonment was a way for the Indians to attack the English without resorting to military force, and was oftentimes a more successful strategy. Lane acknowledged that the tactic was clever, since "at that time, we had no weirs for fish, neither could our men skill of the making of them." The English failure to construct fishing weirs was remarkable since Thomas Harriot included a description of the Algonquian device and John White made detailed drawings of the native traps. "Doubtless," Harriot wrote, "it is a pleasant sight to see the people, sometimes wading, and going sometimes sailing in those rivers, which are shallow and not deep, free from all care of heaping up riches for their posterity." More than twenty years later, John Smith led an expedition in the Chesapeake Bay during which the hungry Englishmen found "in diverse places that abundance of fish lying so thick with their heads above the water, as for want of nets ... we attempted to catch them with a frying pan, but we found it a bad instrument to catch fish with."[18] The English inability to master the available resources of local waters not only made them vulnerable to periods of hunger, but called into question one of the fundamental justifications for overseas voyages—the hope for wealth at the other end.

After crossing dangerous seas of the Atlantic, water was often transformed in English reports from an obstacle to a tantalizing source of potential wealth. The sailors aboard Arthur Barlowe's 1584 voyage to the North Carolina Outer Banks were thrilled to find "shoal water, which smelled so sweetly, and was so strong a smell, as if we had been in the midst of some delicate garden."[19] For proponents of colonization efforts, the description of an ideal environment became a central theme of their reports. The presence of a winding river was an important component of the idealized European image of a pastoral scene. Walter Raleigh described a Guianan Arcadia, with "hills so raised here and there over the valleys, the river winding into diverse branches."[20] Clearly, prospective colonists might not be tempted to relocate into a land of alligator infested, flood-swollen rivers. Raleigh's description was a careful balance between the exotic and the paradisiacal; the gentle waters offered an ideal place to settle, while the sense of the unknown environment held out hopes for riches. The potential wealth to be extracted from the water became particularly important in Virginia, where the prospects for gold quickly became dim. Barlowe expected that pearls would eventually become an important source of wealth. And if all else failed, the English held out hope that water could transport them to the known riches of the Far East.[21]

While colonial promoters touted the valuable commodities of exotic waters from a safe distance, the men who actually confronted foreign rivers and streams were often overwhelmed by the fear of what was hidden underneath the surface. Despite the presence of sea monsters on early maps of the oceans, the English reported no encounters with the beasts while sailing the oceans. Instead, "monsters" seemed to inhabit interior waterways. One group of Englishmen attempting to navigate a river in West Africa "saw a great many monsters like unto horses ... up in the water, sometimes above, sometime beneath." The "monsters," most likely hippopotamuses, proceeded to attack the English pinnaces, knocking 26 men into the water and causing the disappearance of 2 men, who "it is thought the monsters did [carry away], for they [the sailors] could swim very well and yet never [were seen]." Other ships rescued the remaining men and the sailors decided to abandon their ventures after the monsters seemed to follow them around.[22] Walter Raleigh confronted another dangerous water animal in Guiana when he came across a river teeming with "thousands of those ugly serpents," alligators. One of his men recklessly decided to swim in the river, where he was "in all our sights taken and devoured with one of those lagartos."[23]

As frightening as water monsters could be, the most significant water-borne dangers in the Atlantic world were unseen. West Africa in particular had many tropical diseases associated with water. The coastal tidal swamps and marshes contained pools of standing or brackish water that were perfect breeding grounds for *Anopheles* mosquitoes and the malaria they transmitted. Amoebic dysentery was a particularly debilitating disease in which the swallowed cysts attack the host's intestines and liver, causing severe ulcers in violent cases. One of the major symptoms of the disease is the bloody stools of the victim, causing the English to name the affliction the "bloody flux."[24] Despite repeated warnings from their superiors, sailors sought relief from the oppressive heat by jumping into cool waters whenever they had the opportunity. According to Richard Eden, the sailors "not used before to such sudden and vehement alterations (then the which nothing is more dangerous), were thereby brought into swellings and agues."[25]

The salt-choked waters of the James River estuary system were equally dangerous. In order to facilitate trade, English settlers were advised to establish settlements "at the mouths of those great portable and navigable Rivers" in the New World. Following instructions to the letter, the first colonists noted with little alarm that the surrounding lands were "low marshes" with long grasses that could serve as feed for livestock. Unfortunately, the marshes were also a breeding ground for mosquito-borne diseases. Another danger lurked just offshore in the James River. The river is an estuary system; each summer, salt water invades 30 miles up the river, creating a salt plug on the saltwater-freshwater boundary. The plug traps sediments and organic wastes, making the James an incubator for bacteria. Colonists drank the same water they dumped their waste in, assuming that the pollution would be washed down the river. Typhoid, dysentery, and salt poisoning awaited anyone who consumed the contaminated water. One month after the colonists built their fort at Jamestown, the settlers started dying of "cruel diseases [such] as swellings, fluxes, [and] burning fevers." The source of the illnesses was clear: William Strachey reported that the dying colonists of Jamestown had "no freshwater springs serving the town, but what we drew from a well six or seven fathom[s] deep, fed by the brackish river oozing into it." Convinced that they were living in a land well suited for trade and defense from the Spanish and the Indians, the colonists stubbornly continued to drink the water even as they complained about the bitter taste.[26]

Again, local expertise on avoiding contaminated water often meant the difference between life and death for the visiting English throughout the Atlantic world. As John Smith watched his men die from an epidemic of diseases in 1607, he noticed that the Powhatan Indians did not fall victim to the same illnesses. Careful observation revealed that the Powhatans had adapted to the environmental peculiarity of their waterways by using seasonal migration patterns to avoid drinking the brackish water. Despite the protests of leaders more concerned with military defense rather than water conditions, Smith dispersed the colony in 1609 to mimic the Indians' settlement patterns. The result was a sharp reduction in English mortality until the colonists were once again compelled to live in the saltwater zone in the "starving time" of 1609-10.[27]

Raleigh described a notoriously dangerous river in interior Guiana, whose red-colored waters infected unsuspecting Europeans "with a grievous kind of flux." After asking the locals how they managed to use the water without harm, Raleigh learned that "after the sun was near the middle of the sky, they used to fill their pots and pitchers with the water, but either before that time, or towards the setting of the sun, it was dangerous to drink of, and in the night strong poison."[28] While the Guianans would not have described the phenomenon in such scientific terms, their strategy for safely using water took advantage of a process known as vertical migration, in which phytoplankton and potentially disease carrying microbes rise to the surface of waters in the heat of the day, but retreat at night.[29]

John Wilson's trade mission to interior Guiana 10 years later met with locals who were less cooperative in assisting the struggling English. Wilson reported that that since "they had no comfortable drinks ... diverse of them died of the Flux, which the Indians ... know right well to cure, yet concealed it from our General."[30] While withholding valuable information about waterways was a passive form of resistance against English encroachment, native peoples occasionally took a more aggressive approach to exert power in the early relationship. After describing a series of intense storms in Guiana, John Ley explained that the source of the deluge was revealed to him in a conversation with an Iaos Indian. Ley reported that "one evening I showed my Indian a black Cloud coming threatening a cruel storm, and suddenly he said 'naughty Indian make naughty weather,' and made signs how they did cut the throat of a man."[31] The explicit threat of a slit throat combined with a more mysterious ability to control the weather served to unnerve the Englishman, who knew well how dangerous the rivers of Guiana became when flooded by powerful storms.

For their part, the English attempted to use the waterways as best they could to exert power in the early contact period. Since they could not use familiarity with local waters as a source of power, the English turned to their technological expertise to demonstrate their authority. The large wooden vessels of the visiting English were a source of wonder for peoples more used to canoes than masted ships. When a group of Algonquians met with the English in Jamestown just after the supply ships left the colony, the Indians "enquired after our shipping, which the President said was gone to Croatoan." Recognizing that the question was really an attempt to gauge the strength of the colony, the English leader lied because "they fear much our ships; and therefore he would not have them think it far from us." When the Powhatans and the English began an increasingly violent war in 1610, the rivers ran red with the blood of both sides of the conflict. George Percy described a notorious incident in which a Paspaheghan woman and her children were captured and taken aboard an English boat, where "it was agreed upon to put the children to death which was effected by throwing them overboard and shooting out their brains in the water." Pastoral visions of winding rivers filled with abundant fish and inhabited by friendly locals were replaced with the harsh reality that the waterways of the Atlantic would not easily harbor the visitors and the native peoples.[32]

As more English men (and eventually women) followed John Smith's lead and became familiar with local waterways, the native peoples lost one of the most important sources of power they had in the early encounters with Europeans. The signs of growing English familiarity with foreign rivers are readily apparent on early maps—the Orinoco became the Raleana River, so named by Lawrence Keymis in honor of his superior. Walter Raleigh described the simple logic of renaming waterways when he described entering a river "which because it had no name, we called it the river of the Red crosse, our selves being the first Christians that ever came therein." Powhatan Indians might still be found in the waters of the recently christened James River, while other waterways took names that were Anglicized versions of native words. By taking the prerogative to name the waterways after their own leaders, the English redefined native space and transformed it into their own physical and cultural space, signifying their new relationship as the rightful owners of, rather than visitors to, the Atlantic world.[33]

In West Africa, the rivers became a central highway in the developing slave trade in the 17th century. African canoes and European pinnaces patrolled the waterways in search of captives to transport to larger vessels waiting on the coast. In both Guiana and Virginia, the interior waters received the chained human cargo from the other side of the Atlantic and filled the holds of departing ships with tightly packed barrels of tobacco. In the course of only a few years, the English had transformed the liquid landscape from an unpredictable, alien environment before which they were forced to humble themselves to native authority, into an interconnected medium that eased the exploitation of local resources and peoples

Indeed, by the end of the 17th century, the English had become so comfortable with the waterways of the Chesapeake region that their very identity seemed inextricably linked with the riverine environment. Tobacco plantations dotted the landscape, taking advantage of the eastward flowing waters to move goods quickly to central warehouses for inspection. The debilitating diseases that took such a toll on early English explorers no longer were such a threat, as familiarity transformed the colonists into knowledgeable authorities on the water. In a 1699 letter from Virginia, the Reverend Hugh Jones compared "the many Rivers, Creeks, and Rivulets of Water ... to veins in human Bodies."[34] Symbolically incorporated into English bodies, the estuary system of the Chesapeake provided the lifeblood of a colonial corpus poised to transform the land and the waterways of the Atlantic world.

---

[1] Richard Hakluyt, trans. and comp., *The Principal Navigations, Voyages, Traffiques, and Discoveries of the English Nation*, 12 vols. (Glasgow: University of Glasgow Press, 1903), 10: 380.

[2] See Richard White, *The Middle Ground: Indians, Empires, and Republics in the Great Lakes Region, 1650-1815* (New York: Cambridge University Press, 1991). Douglas Sackman developed the concept of "waterways" as it is used here in his unpublished paper "Pacific Passages: Waterways and Power in the North Pacific Contact Zone," delivered at the American Society for Environmental History Conference, Tacoma, Washington, March, 2000.

[3] For a discussion of 16th-century English voyages, see Kenneth R. Andrews, *Trade, Plunder, and Settlement: Maritime Enterprise and the Genesis of the British Empire, 1480-1630* (Cambridge: Cambridge University Press, 1984).

[4] Robert Smith, *Kingdoms of the Yoruba*, 3rd ed. (Madison: University of Wisconsin Press, 1988), 65.

[5] Don C. Ohadike, *Anioma: A Social History of the Western Igbo People* (Athens, Ohio: Ohio University Press, 1994), 102. The stream orisha (god or goddess) was also central to the Yoruba creation story. See Smith, *Kingdoms of the Yoruba*, 15.

[6] J. H. Steward, ed., *Handbook of South American Indians*, vol. 3 (Washington, D.C: Smithsonian Institution, Bureau of American Ethnology, Bulletin 143, 1946-63), 880; John Smith, *A Map of Virginia [1612]* in Philip Barbour, ed. *The Complete Works of Captain John Smith*, 3 vols. (Chapel Hill: University of North Carolina Press, 1986), 1: 171. For a discussion of Powhatan religious beliefs, see Helen C. Rountree, *The Powhatan Indians of Virginia: Their Traditional Culture* (Norman: University of Oklahoma Press, 1989), 126-152.

[7] *Genesis* 7:23.

[8] William Harrison, *The Description of England [1587]*, ed. Georges Edelen (Ithaca: Cornell University Press, 1968), 272, 323.

[9] Hakluyt was particularly discouraged to note that "though many and sundry rewards were proposed to encourage our people unto the sea, yet I still find complaints of decay in the navy." Richard Hakluyt, *Discourse of Western Planting [1584]*, edited by David B. Quinn and Alison M. Quinn (London: Hakluyt Society, 1993), 67.

[10] Hakluyt, *Principal Navigations*, 6: 158.

[11] Barbour, 1: 227. The fragility of second and third-hand accounts of overseas expeditions is evident in Richard Eden's attempt to explain stories of water spouts in Africa. After a detailed effort to explain the "science" of the natural phenomenon, Eden noted that "Richard Chancellor told me that he heard Sebastian Cabot report, that (as farre as I remember) either about the coasts of Brasile or Rio de Plata, his shippe or pinnesse was suddenly lifted from the sea, and cast upon land, I wot not howe far." Hakluyt, *Principal Navigations*, 6: 158.

[12] John William Blake, ed., *Europeans in West Africa* (London: Hakluyt Society, 1942), 366.

[13] David B. Quinn, ed., *New American World: A Documentary History of North America to 1612*, 4 vols. (New York: Arno Press, 1979): 3, 277.

[14] Blake, *Europeans in West Africa*, 356; John Thornton, *Africa and Africans in the Making of the Atlantic World* (New York: Cambridge University Press, 1992), 38.

[15] Don C. Ohadike, *Anioma*, 39

[16] Rountree, *Eastern Shore Indians*, 33.

[17] Hakluyt, *Principal Navigations*, 10: 477.

[18] Quinn, *New American World*, 3: 301; Harriot, *A Briefe and True Report of the New Found Land of Virginia [1590]* (New York: Dover Publications, 1972), 56; Barbour, 1: 228. Harriot's idealized description of Algonquian fishing techniques erased the actual labor involved and understated the difficulty of spearing fish. Despite his failure to catch fish, Smith assured Powhatan that the Indian strategy to starve the English by abandoning the rivers would be ineffective, "for we have a rule to finde beyond your knowledge." Barbour, 1: 248.

[19] Quinn, *New American World*, 3: 277.

[20] To further assert their authority over Guiana, the English renamed many of the rivers. Lawrence Keymis declared in 1596 that the Orinoco River would henceforth be named "Raleana" in honor of his superior. Hakluyt 10: 476.

[21] A discouraged Ralph Lane declared that "the discovery of a good mine ... or a passage to the Southsea ... and nothing else can bring this country ... to be inhabited by our nation." Quinn, *New American World*, 3: 298. Richard Hakluyt was more optimistic about the potential to use river travel for more local trade. In 1584, he instructed future colonists to settle near rivers so that the English could "at all times send up their ships, barks, barges, and boats into the Inland with all the commodities of England, and return unto the said forts all the commodities of the inlands that we shall receive in exchange, and thence at pleasure convey the same into England." Hakluyt, *Discourse*, 72.

[22] James A. Williamson, *Sir John Hawkins: The Time and the Man* (Oxford: Clarendon Press, 1927), 509-510. On monsters and early maps, see John Friedman, "Cultural Conflicts in Medieval World Maps," in Stuart B. Schwartz, ed., *Implicit Understandings: Observing, Reporting, and Reflecting on the Encounters Between Europeans and Other Peoples in the Early Modern Era* (New York: Cambridge University Press, 1995), 64-95.

[23] Hakluyt, *Principal Navigations*, 10: 388.

[24] Though it is difficult to gauge the precise mortality rates for early English voyages to West Africa due to sketchy information, the rates for later expeditions during the slave trade are staggering. Approximately 1 of 3 Europeans died in their first 4 months in West Africa, and 3 of 5 were dead by the first year. See K. G. Davies, "The Living and the Dead: White Mortality in West Africa, 1684-1732," in Eugene Genovese and Stanley Engerman, eds., *Race and Slavery in the Western Hemisphere: Quantitative Studies* (Princeton: Princeton University Press, 1975), 93.

[25] Hakluyt, *Principal Navigations*, 6: 163.

[26] Quinn, *New American World*, 5: 272, 295; Carville Earle, "Environment, Disease, and Mortality in Early Virginia," *Journal of Historical Geography* 5 (1979): 391-401.

[27] Earle, "Environment, Disease, and Mortality": 106.

[28] Hakluyt, *Principal Navigations*, 10, 370.

[29] K. Salonen, "Hypolimnetic Retrieval by Diel Vertical Migrations of Lake Phytoplankton." *Freshwater Biology, 14*, 431-438.

[30] Samuel Purchas, *Hakluytus Posthumus, or Purchas His Pilgrimes*, 20 vols. (New York: Macmillan, 1906), 16: 342.

[31] Joyce Lorimer, ed., *English and Irish Settlement on the River Amazon, 1550-1646* (London: Hakluyt Society, 1989), 134.

[32] Quinn, *New American World*, 5: 277; George Percy, "A Trewe Relacyon," *Tyler's Quarterly Historical and Genealogical Magazine*, 3 (1922): 272.

[33] Hakluyt, *Principal Navigations*, 10: 381.

[34] Jones, cited in Anne Yentsch, *A Chesapeake Family and Their Slaves* (Cambridge: Cambridge University Press, 1994), 6.

Chapter 2

The Economy of the Marvelous: Columbus's Transatlantic Tokens of Exchange

Elvira Vilches, North Carolina State University

In the documents of discovery, Columbus manipulates the exotic, the erotic, and the outlandish to overvalue the meager cargoes of gold he ships to Spain.[1] Despite the high hopes these texts communicate, it is not gold, but rather the reported presence of alleged cannibals and Amazons that conveys the finding of lands of gold. While Columbus strays from one island to the next, hoping to uncover deposits of gold ore and locate the rich lands of the Great Khan, his writings employ unmistakable signs of the East—man eaters, women warriors, and parrots—with the double purpose of erasing his geographical error and of producing tokens standing for the treasures yet to be found. On the page, the quest for the precious metal becomes a search for alternative ways to represent the worth embodied by gold as the standard of monetary value.

At a time when gold, not paper money, is the norm, Columbus's writing tenders the illusion of hard cash by generating mere tokens with no intrinsic value, such as the New World wonders, which are first depicted on paper and later displayed in Spain. The representative value of wonders relies on a cultural repertoire that establishes an association between fantastic Oriental peoples and wealth. By replacing gold as a "fortune good" with "fortune signs," this resilient mariner constructs a symbolic economy that runs parallel to the development of gold mining and colonial trade.[2] Within this paradigm of symbolic value, the novelty of the Amerindians, the rarity of their gold wares, and their exotic pets stand as bills of exchange that intimate an early rendering of gold. Following the notion of what early modern Europeans valued as wonders—that is, the exotic and the bizarre, and the interest for admiring and collecting objects never seen before—I call this process of substituting gold's intrinsic value with cannibals, Amazons, parrots, and gold wares the "economy of the marvelous." By bringing together the *Journal of the first Voyage, Relation of the Second Voyage,* letters written by members of Columbus's crew, Peter Martyr's correspondence, and royal performances, I describe the different layers of estimation that New World wonders accumulated in their trajectory from the page to the palace. I also include a close reading of the themes that visual texts incorporate from colonial discourse to represent the myth of the New World as a wonderland of untapped wealth so real it denied even strongly apparent symptoms of colonial disappointment.

Before discussing this paradigm of symbolic value that Columbus improvises to cope with the difficulty he had in producing reliable sources of gold, let me summarize some of the issues that I will address in this essay. After a brief account of mining and trade in the Caribbean, I will focus on the ways in which Columbus manages to oversell his first voyage. The spectacle that Columbus stages on his return to Spain, together with a special cargo he sends to show the achievements of his second voyage, are the two central scenes around which I trace the "economy of the marvelous." My argument returns to these scenes in order to understand why New World wonders are tokens of American gold. Columbus's display of captured Amerindians and artifacts exemplifies the effort to bring America to Europe. For those who could not make the trip to the New World and who either were not satisfied merely to read about it or did not trust graphic representations, direct presentations were provided. Specimens of all kinds were greatly admired for their visible and tangible connection with the New World. Each wonder functioned as *pars pro toto*, shards that reconstruct the new continent piece by piece in a carefully edited depiction of the New World. During the Renaissance, the interest in Americana is a manifested extension of the rise of the *kunstkammern* or *Wunderkammern* (*Cámaras del tesoro*). Private collections of curiosities, whether stored in cabinets or put on display for a select public, really emerge in the 17ᵗʰ century. The status of the collectors ranged from monarchs and aristocrats to humanist scholars. Collections of curiosities or wonders were conceived of both as potential source of knowledge and as ostentation of wealth.[3]

"Wonder(s)" is a general term that denotes specimens of all kinds—human, animal, and inanimate—brought as proof of the lands discovered. In Columbus's writing cannibals are the wonders which have the most relevant role. Even though the terms "cannibal" and "Amazon" have very specific meanings—man eater and warrior woman—they are also emblems of otherness that establish European stereotypes of Amerindians. Columbus's texts contrast the Caribs, the group accused of eating human flesh, with the gentle Taino. Yet, this difference is not maintained, since cannibal, Caribs, and Tainos are listed under a general rubric that includes the transgression of all taboos. While the Admiral writes, shows, and sells Caribs, the Amazons are as elusive as the unreachable Cipango. Yet, warrior women become the staple of the marvelous in later texts, and especially in allegories of the New World.

To elucidate how wonders can stand in for gold and why they are able to replace gold's intrinsic value with alternative valences, I draw upon the difference between gold and the role of money as tokens lacking intrinsic value, as well as the correlation between value and desire. The "economy of the marvelous" begins with Columbus's first voyage as he combines written reports with the parade of wonders he displayed on his return to Spain. This symbolic paradigm of value coexists with the Crown's efforts to establish productive mining and trade in the colonies. While transatlantic economic ventures did not succeed because of mismanagement, disease, and the mistreatment of the indigenous population, the "economy of the marvelous" created a mirage of wealth that was more real than the slender monetary gains. The economy of La Hispaniola was never strong; gold production was very slim and succeeded only by imposing a policy of forced labor on the native population. What Frank Moya Pons has described as the "economy of gold" resulted, he argues, in an economy of flesh since selling and renting Indians was more profitable than mining. The production of gold decreased with the rapid decline of the native population and by 1508, gold was so insufficient that mining was soon replaced by sugar plantations cultivated by African slaves.[4] The same economic pattern applies to the colonies that were founded right after the decline of La Hispaniola. By 1510 Puerto Rico, Panama, and Cuba exhausted their gold resources. Although this gold was depleted, the conquests of Mexico and Peru generated a consistent revenue.

However, the overall volume of gold continued to be very modest, since it did not surpass 30 tons.[5]

Columbus's writing, however, tailors economic disappointment carefully so that it seems a minor shortcoming that will postpone briefly the estimated profits. Logs, letters, and accounts repeatedly include lengthy descriptions of gold wares and nuggets, pearls, reports of native informants describing golden lands, and even the price of expensive spices such as almastic, cinnamon, and aloe that Columbus claims he has found. The catalogue-like enumeration of goods goes hand-in-hand with reiterative appearances of cannibals, the slippery ubiquity of Amazons, beautiful naked Indians of both sexes, as well as sporadic manatees, sirens, and griffins. When Columbus reaches Spain, his accounts of the customs and mores of the Amerindians are, for the first time, backed up by the spectacle of Indians, crafts, and exotic animals. Columbus claims he has reached Cipango, where there is abundant gold. He also explains that he has settled a fort with several men who will trade and gather gold. Nevertheless, despite his promises, Columbus brought not gold, but New World wonders never seen before. In Seville, according to the eyewitness report of Las Casas, 7 Indians were displayed under the Arch of Saint Nicolas, along with colorful parrots, masks made with precious stones and gold, pieces of the finest gold, and many other strange items. When Ferdinand and Isabella received the Admiral in Barcelona, they were so impressed that they took all the marvels they saw as samples of the lavish earnings they anticipated.[6]

The news of Columbus's expedition provoked great excitement. Columbus's first letter was printed and published 9 times in 1493.[7] Peter Martyr, the Italian humanist in residence at the Spanish court, writes that Christopher Columbus "has returned safe and sound." Martyr reports that the Admiral has found marvelous things, and that he has produced gold as proof of the existence of mines in those regions.[8] The news of the first voyage spread so quickly and made the West Indies seem so alluring that Columbus and Juan Rodríguez de Fonseca, the archdeacon of Seville, had no difficulty in finding 1200 men to go on the second voyage. Once in La Hispaniola, members of the expedition, such as Pedro Chanca, the royal physician, report that gold is everywhere and that the monarchs are the richest princes in the world. A fellow traveler, Guillermo Coma, writes that gold can be easily removed from rocks, mines, and rivers.[9] After the return of some of the settlers, Martyr describes in *Decades* his fascination with a big nugget of gold weighting 20 ounces that he handles and admires in the royal court.[10]

The excellent prospects for establishing a chain of trading posts along the islands are soon overshadowed by reports of Bernardo Boyl and Pedro Margarite, who, on their return with Torres's relief fleet on February 2, 1494, informed the king and queen that the whole enterprise was a joke, that there was no gold on La Hispaniola, and that the expenditures of the crown would never be recovered.[11] In "Relación del segundo viaje" Columbus declares that he is sending a map, along with several cannibals and their captives, some women and some castrated young males, as well as some parrots which can be given as gifts to different kings as signs of Castile's successful colonial undertaking.[12]

The arrival of Torres's fleet, on the other hand, shows that, despite the supposed gold of Cibao and the wonderful news of the River of Gold, they had to the sell slaves in order to get cash to pay for food, supplies, and cattle. Juan Bardi, a member of the crew, reported that Columbus entrusted Torres with a few gold nuggets and the group of cannibals mentioned above, to which were added 52 parrots, 8 macaws, and some rabbits with no ears and tails.[13] Memoirs of other adventurers who reached La Hispaniola on the second voyage also refer to the exotic and the erotic when hard commodities are scarce. The accounts of Simón Verde and Miguel de Cuneo demonstrate that the colony does not encompass bountiful lands. Verde writes that the spices shipped to Spain were useless, although some believed they had found cinnamon. Cuneo complains about food shortages and the difficulty of finding gold, with the exception of the little obtained through barter. Both travelers cope with their colonial disillusionment with the company of supposed cannibals. Their lengthy descriptions portray the Indians as beasts with degenerate appetites. Coma writes that the local women enjoy seducing white men with their lascivious dances, whereas Cuneo gives lustful portrayals of the concubines of the cannibals sent to Spain. He writes that Columbus gave him a young cannibal woman whom he raped. He also testifies that those slaves who did not fit in Torres's second relief fleet on February 24, 1495 were given to the settlers for nothing.[14]

At the royal palace the Amerindians, along with their parrots and gold wares, stand for the fertile lands, great mines of gold and other metals, and the thousands of valuables that Columbus enumerates in his writings. The textual description and the actual exhibition of New World wonders constitute blank checks for the potential profits to be made. The explorer, as José Piedra contends, is able to advertise failure as success "in lieu of the fabled marketplaces sought out by Spain's imperial aspirations."[15] I suggest that Columbus's persuasive efforts succeed by manipulating the cultural correlation between wonders and gold. Gold is the temptation that lured explorers across the Atlantic. Marvel is the word that fills all gaps, the name given to make comprehensible what remains in the margins. I argue that early modern Europe assimilates the New World through a system of improvised values that, in turn, constructs an illusion of wealth. The relationship between gold and wonders is tripartite since the latter, in addition to being indices of the legendary Orient, function as conceptual signs, related signifiers, and monetary symbols.

Among the collection of wonders that crisscrosses the *Journal of the First Voyage*, the cannibals are mentioned so often that they emerge as the emblem of the New World. Keeping the Amazons at a comfortable distance, the cannibals are not only the sharpest indicators of gold, but also the signifiers that constantly substitute for it, as well as the commodities sold for a price. While the sale of slaves remains secondary, natives are described, displayed, given, and kept as IOUs of transatlantic gold. The promise of future payment that wonders embody encapsulates a waiting game through which Columbus tries to produce expressions of value to supplement his monetary void. Buying time allows Columbus to extend his erratic course while he practices a "semiotics of errancy" so that writing can convert the uncertain Caribbean into the known India.[16] This attempt at translation entails procrastination. Columbus's mistaken landfall implies a considerable delay in complying with the preset goals of the expedition as described in the "Title," "Letter of Credence," and "Articles of Agreement." The imperial aspirations repeated in these documents, to "discover and acquire," are partially completed. Of the two, the action of discovery is the only one that is realized, although it is limited itself to the coastline. Acquisition, on the other hand, depends on the arrival in Marco Polo's Cipango and Cathay and is therefore postponed. The acquisition of "gold, precious stones, pearls, spices, and other things of value" only serves as a "symbolic field of reference," as Rabasa puts it, that charts the proximity of the sought market places.[17] While sailing and writing approach these destinations, the sight, description, and collection of cannibals and other wonders trace the itinerary and fill in the absence of expected assets.

The writing of Columbus traces his approach to Cipango by adapting the native name of Cibao and situating other names like Bohio and Baveque in the itinerary. Yet, these places are not indicated as part of the actual route, but rather as potential destinations that will please the royal sponsors. In the *Journal* the recorded information about fertile and rich locations leads to infinite excuses to keep searching for gold:

These islands are very green and fertile and the air very balmy, and there may be many things that I don't know, for I do not wish to delay but to discover and go to many islands to find gold. And since these people make signs that it is worn on arms and legs, and it is gold all right because they point to some pieces that I have, I cannot fail (with Our Lord's help) to find out where it comes from.[18]

Paradoxically, the growing concern about wasting time causes the consistent delay of his quest for gold. From the moment he sets foot in the Caribbean to the time he sails back to Spain, Columbus has only collected bits and pieces of gold, which he has either traded bells for or found by chance. Just before setting sail for home, he claims he is finally reaching Cipango. At this point the gold he has not acquired is supplanted by tales of cruel one-eyed men with dog faces who cut off the genitals of their victims and drink their blood. Moreover, the so-called Caribs alternate between making war and making love to their harmless Taino neighbors, as well as to the warrior women who live on a nearby island. The depiction of the Caribs' preferences for killing and mating are further enhanced by the fact that cannibals and Amazons live among members of the same gender and that they alternate between queer and straight eroticism and sexuality. The transgression of traditional roles and mores is also complemented with the possession of exceedingly rich mines, which interestingly enough are supposedly located on islands on the route to the Iberian Peninsula.

Cannibals, as well as Amazons, stand as tokens that fully guarantee gold by combining and accumulating different valences. Within Columbus's circle of Caribbean exchanges, the cruelty and bestiality attributed to the cannibals constitute the most valuable chip when negotiating with Taino caciques. Whereas in a Western cultural context the threat of being eaten and consumed culinary or erotically construes the Caribs as the monstrous gatekeepers who prevent all sorts of mobility, following the logic of the metonymic association between the monster and the forbidden, the presence of cannibals implies the finding of treasures.[19] Furthermore, the repeated themes of nudity and alternative sexualities represent, as Piedra contends, "libidinally created islands" that make cannibals, Amazons, and Amerindians "consolation prizes."[20]

The Caribs are sold in Spain as slaves in order to pay for food, cattle, and supplies urgently needed in La Isabella, the first colony in La Hispaniola. Although the frequent sale of slaves becomes the only reliable source of income, it is ironic that only the Indians presented as wonders are able to communicate the dream of wealth that Spain's imperial aspirations project to the other side of the Atlantic. Once American subjects and objects are displayed in Spain, their bodies expose the land of pleasure that writing has created. Dazzled by the spectacle of people and things never heard of, Ferdinand and Isabella see through New World wonders everything else that remains at the other side of the Atlantic. For Peter Martyr, the humanist reporting Columbus's adventures, wonders amplify the samples of gold and pearls he has seen at the royal palace; whereas for Miguel de Cuneo, a crew member of the second voyage, naked natives replace gold with uninhibited libido. Somehow this third layer of estimation, the one that underwrites the Other as pleasure, becomes the currency of travel accounts, royal chronicles, and allegories of the New World.

The link between wealth and libido comprises not only the understanding of gold as the means to obtain and enjoy all pleasures, but also economic spheres that assimilate value and desire. Culturally, as Jean-Joseph Goux observes, there is an imaginary set through which gold is viewed as the object that possesses all fantasies in potentiality. The yellow metal is the polyvalent substitute that either is worth all gratifications or contains them in pose, in a general concentrated form.[21] Likewise, wonders by virtue of being gold's tokens embody all the desires that gold may purchase.

The uninterrupted connection between wonders and gold becomes more apparent if one takes into account the context in which wonders circulate. The most important factor contributing to the vogue of the marvelous in early modern Europe is the discovery of the Americas. Explorers recreate their adventures by shipping trophies of their discoveries. In Europe exotic peoples, pets, and wares circulate among the family and friends of monarchs as recognizable signs of overseas advances. Within this exclusive circle, the consumers of wonder quench their appetite for the bizarre by hoarding all kinds of specimens.[22] At the other end of the chain are avid readers who devour travel accounts. The series of letters that Martyr wrote from the Spanish court to cardinals and popes is a case in point. What may seem like ephemeral court spectacles are, thanks to writing and printing, coveted readings for men of letters and princes.

The avid curiosity for New World wonders delineates a realm in which use value has been displaced by desire. Taking into account the ideas of the marginalist movement and specifically Karl Menger, Goux looks at the relationship between economic value and desire in order to define economic utility as the subject's desire to procure a given item at a given time. To create value, then, all that is necessary is to create a sufficient intensity of desire.[23] In the specific case of Columbus, such intensity of desire derives from his ability to offer cannibals, Amazons, and naked Indians as perverse supplements of the real thing. By promising gold and displaying New World wonders, Columbus produces the scarcity that automatically increases the desire to enjoy both. The interstice that the spectacle of Amerindian subjects creates between abundance and scarcity, satisfaction and desire produces a "metaphoric thirst" which seeks satisfaction in comparable things and signs.[24] The yearning for something else is consequently associated with lack and disappearance, since they are effective means to entice desire. Gold is always insufficient; New World wonders are equally scarce. Transplanted into a strange environment, people, pets, and crafts are exclusive specimens to be admired and collected. Their uniqueness, their status as fragments of the wealthiest lands, along with an imposed exotic and erotic cachet displace economic value with attraction value.

The disruption that desire imposes on value also affects the function of wonders as means of exchange. The problem set up by the marvelous is that despite the fact that it functions like hopeful coins for transatlantic gold, wonders cannot stand as method of payment. Offered as blank checks or IOUs for the riches to come, wonders keep expanding their credit at the risk of losing their value as instruments of circulation. The gold coin is ostensibly exchangeable for something hard and real, whereas wonders only have symbolic value and work as nominal money. In a time when gold, not paper money, is the norm, wonders bring about the dissociation of the functions filled by gold as money: the standard, a medium of exchange, and the treasury.

The gold piece is at once an ideal standard of economic value, a symbolic instrument of circulation, and finally a real value that can be placed in reserve. This remarkable conjunction is undone by New World wonders. The tokens that the "economy of the marvelous" puts into circulation have the purely symbolic function of being instruments of exchange. While "fortune-signs" replace "fortune-goods," writing tries to guarantee wonders' hard value by repeating fictions that will ultimately accumulate a stock of representations. The combination of colonial texts and the visual appreciation of specimens creates a thesaurus of representations through which Europe sees the New World. By "thesaurus" I mean both a treasure trove of words and images as well as a storage space for exhibiting and collecting.

In the end, the overlapping of texts, images, and collections construes the New World as a wish horizon that conjures up an illusion of wealth more powerful than colonial frustration and discontent. Among travel accounts, diaries, chronicles, and maps, the texts that explain most directly the "economy of the marvelous" are the New World allegories that were so popular during the 16th and 17th centuries.[25] If earlier colonial texts use the cannibals as the most welcome staple of exoticism and libido, the New World allegories shift their emphasis to the Amazon. The images that this allegoric genre portrays conflate traits of unruly nature and riches in the female body. Thus the colonial dream of gold is translated into metaphors of sexuality that convey wealth by demonstrating all the pleasures and violations that gold can buy. The overlapping of the monetary and the erotic constitutes an economy of infinite largess, whose currency and medium of exchange are bodies of pleasure. This register of estimation has a contradictory effect because it gives all without expecting anything in return. The absolute gift of lands, riches, and bodies imposes the desire to possess and the fear of being dispossessed, for the New World is so boundless that it makes the colonizer feel insignificant.

One of the larger-than-life characters representing this New World economy is the warrior woman. The Amazon has always been the central mediator in the representation of imperialist ideology. From the time of the Roman empire onward, the warrior woman has represented difference, exchange, accumulation, and commodification.[26] Depicted as an Amazon, America offers the invitation to be conquered, while she posits the threat of engulfing and devouring her suitor. This dark side becomes apparent by the amalgamation of cannibalism and the unruled sexuality that America as a naked woman represents. Both elements are the norm in scenes that portray America as a warrior woman bearing weapons and holding decapitated heads, surrounded by other body parts. Set against a background depicting cannibal banquets, the cruelty of America is aggravated by the exotic animals that accompany her. In the earliest allegories, such as Crispin de Passe's *America* (1564), a jaguar, a dog, big birds, and a winged snake are crafted in a mannerist fashion with the intent to convey savagery and sinister bestiality.[27] The aggregation of nudity, consumption of flesh, and animality demonstrates the explicit association between excess and wealth in this allegory. Indeed, it is by virtue of this chain of fantasies and fears that the jewels that dress America and the treasure trove that lies under her feet embody the rich continent that offers gold, labor, and love for the taking.

As chaotic nature, as the space of the feminine, the New World is not concerned with property. It constitutes what Hélène Cixous calls the "realm of the gift," where giving is a disinterested act of generosity whose goal is the other's pleasure.[28] America, the dark continent, the woman, can give all because she has nothing to lose, because she does not wear out. During the financial and political crisis of the 17th century, these images of feminine largess emerge in plays that re-enact the conquest of America as the consequence of love affairs between Spanish soldiers and Indian queens. These plays disclose the dealings of the "economy of the marvelous" as a means to evoke the illusion of wealth by conjuring up the myth of the Americas as a golden land. Portrayed as wealthy and powerful Amazons, the Indian queens' beautiful bodies are described as lavish treasure troves whose gold will provide the necessary riches so that the *vellón*, the copper coin intentionally overvalued, can shine as if it were gold. The representations of ancient imperial vigor and old wealth, just like copper money, are void; their worth is a chimera because it exists only as paper: bills of exchange, contracts, and promissory notes. Gold can no longer be consider as store of value, but rather as a conventional symbol of wealth. At this time of crisis, the means of exchange are a mere promise, just as Columbus's tokens. Both the wealth written on paper and that inscribed in the body of wonders stand as promissory notes that can never be redeemed.

---

[1] These documents include the "Tittle," "Letter of Credence," and "Articles of Agreement," all of which are collected in the *Capitulations of Santa Fe* (April, 1492); the *Journal of the first voyage*, as edited by Las Casas; the "Letter to the Monarchs" (March 1493); and the "Letter to Santángel" (February 1493). I also include *Relación del segundo viaje*. For a discussion on the editorial role of Las Casas and the interrelation between these documents see Margarita Zamora, *Reading Columbus* (Berkeley: U of California P, 1993). I am indebted to Stuart Day for his comments and editorial advice.

[2] I borrow these terms from Jean Joseph Goux, "Banking on Signs," *Diacritics* 18 (1988): 20, 15-25.

[3] Peter Mason, "From Presentation to Representation: *Americana* in Europe," *Journal of the History of Collections* 1 (1994): 6, 1-20.

[4] Frank Moya Pons, *Después de Colón: trabajo, sociedad y política en la economía del oro* (Madrid: Alianza Universidad, 1986).

[5] Murdo Macleod, "Spain and America: the Atlantic Trade, 1492-1470," in *The Cambridge History of Latin America*, ed. Leslie Bethell (Cambridge: Cambridge UP, 1984), 368.

[6] Bartolomé de Las Casas, *Historia de las Indias*, ed. Agustín Millares Carlo, vol. 1 (México: Fondo de Cultura Económica, 1951), 332-334.

[7] Columbus's "Letter to Santángel" reached 20 editions by 1500. For the diffusion of news about Columbus's first voyage, see S. E. Morison, *Christopher Columbus, Mariner* (Boston: Brown, 1955), 108; Charles Verlinden and Florentino Pérez-Embid, *Cristóbal Colón y el Descubrimiento de América* (Madrid: Ediciones Rialp, 1967), 91-94.

[8] "Epistolario de Pedro Mártir de Anglería," trans. José López Toro, in *Documentos inéditos para la historia de España*, vol. 9 (Madrid: Góngora, 1953), letters 133, 242.

[9] *Cartas de particulares a Colón y relaciones coetáneas*, eds. Juan Gil and Consuelo Varela (Madrid: Alianza Editorial, 1984), 177-203.

[10] Peter Martyr, *De Orbe Novo*, trans. Francis Augustus Macnutt, vol. 1 (New York: Burt Franklin, 1912), 109.

[11] Willam D. Phillips and Carla Rahn Phillips, *The Worlds of Christopher Columbus* (Cambridge: Cambridge UP, 1992), 208.

[12] *Cristóbal Colón: textos y documentos completos*, ed. Consuelo Varela (Madrid: Alianza, 1995), 241.

[13] Gil and Varela, *Cartas de particulares a Colón*, 214.

[14] Ibid., 202, 242.

[15] José Piedra, "The Game of Critical Arrival." *Diacritics* 19 (1989): 40, 34-60.

[16] José Rabasa, *Inventing America: Spanish Historiography and the Formation of Eurocentrism* (Norman: University of Oklahoma, 1993), 54-55.

[17] Ibid., 71.

[18] Samuel Eliot Morison, *Journals and Other Documents on the Life and Voyages of Cristóbal Colón* (New York: Heritage Press, 1963), 70.

[19] Jeffrey Jerome Cohen, "Monster Theory (Seven Thesis)," in *Monster Theory*, ed. Jeffery Jerome Cohen (Minneapolis: University of Minnesota Press, 1996), 12.

[20] José Piedra, "Loving Columbus," in *Amerindian Images and the Legacy of Columbus*, eds. René Jara and Nicholas Spadaccini (Minneapolis: University of Minnesota Press, 1992), 237-9.

[21] Jean-Joseph Goux, *Symbolic Economies After Marx and Freud*, trans. Jennifer Curtiss Gage (Ithaca: Cornell UP, 1990), 204.

[22] Joy Kenseth, "The Age of the Marvelous: An Introduction," in *The Age of the Marvelous* (Hanover: Hood Museum of Art, Darmouth College, 1991), 1-61.

[23] *Symbolic Economies*, 200-201.

[24] Ibid., 201.

[25] Honour Hugh, *The New Golden Land: European Images of America from the Discoveries to the Present Time* (New York: Pantheon Books, 1975).

[26] Laura Brown, "Amazons and Africans: Gender, Race, and Empire in Daniel Defoe," in *Women, Race, and Writing in the Early Modern Period*, eds. Margo Hendricks and Patricia Parker (London: Routledge, 1994), 118-137.

[27] *America*, Amsterdam, Rijskprentenkabinett. 188 x 220 mm

[28] Hélenè Cixous, *La Jeune Née* (Paris: UGE, 1975), 147.

Chapter 3

End-Time and Exorcisms in England: Witch-Hunting and Salvation in the 17th Century[1]

Milissa Ellison-Murphree

Seventeenth-century England saw but two large witch-hunts. During the English Civil War, 7 contiguous counties north and east of London hosted an enormous hunt lasting from 1645 to 1647.[2] A half-century later and across the Atlantic, the celebrated Salem witch-hunts began in 1692 and lasted for nearly 20 months. Each of these events was characterized by local leaders exhorting the godly to separate themselves from spiritual contaminants.[3] From pulpits and in print, the Saints of East Anglia and those of Salem Village were urged to avoid divine wrath and rejection by casting from their midst those apostates who acted against God and Commonwealth.[4] In both hunts, this call for an exorcism of the community was the spark that local tensions and predestinarian eschatology fueled when searching for the ungodly was redefined as witch-hunting. Many of these similarities are due to extensive reliance by the leaders of both hunts upon the writings of Richard Bernard, whose Jacobean ministry included experience of both exorcism and witchcraft.

In June 1645, King Charles I suffered his decisive defeat at Naseby. Triumphant at last, the victorious Puritans turned to transforming

England—the new Israel—into a nation pleasing unto God. "They are all cursed that help not the Lord," Essex minister Stephen Marshall had proclaimed from his Finchingfield pulpit, "and so our Saviour will say *Goe yee cursed into everlasting fire, prepared for the Divell and his Angels*."[5] Matthew Newcomen of Dedham agreed, declaring tersely, "All the visible enemies of the Church of God are but the *Emissaries* of Satan."[6] The Rule of the Saints had begun.

One of its first manifestations came just a month after Naseby, when the Chelmsford Summer Sessions in Essex tried and hanged 19 women for the crime of witchcraft.[7] Over the next 18 months, courts in 6 other East Anglian counties ordered the executions of nearly 150 more men and women.[8] Ninety-two local people in Essex alone participated in the hunts and trials.[9] Remarkably, these people ranged from the poorest seamen and laborers through landholding yeomen, 3 local ministers, 2 Cambridge Divines and even Robert Rich, 2nd Earl of Warwick and one of the principal leaders of Parliament's Puritan party.[10] Witch-hunting was "an acceptable service before God," explained Jonathan Stearne in his 1648 defense of the events. "[For] doth not the Lord by the prophet *Micah* promise to cut off Witchcraft out of the land ... in the time that he intended to blesse a Nation?"[11] This logic and language neatly intersected with ideas of national purification and salvation already given widespread currency and credibility by the clergy. Polarized by their fears of damnation, the people of East Anglia responded by hanging 168 of their neighbors as the enemies of God.[12]

There has been no extensive scholarly study of the 1645-47 East Anglian witch-hunts. Historians thus have been at a loss when attempting to make sense of what Jim Sharpe has characterized as "one of the most remarkable episodes in the history of English, and indeed European, witchcraft."[13] The prevailing interpretation was first aired in 1911, when Wallace Notestein's work on English witchcraft argued that two professional witch-hunters, Matthew Hopkins and Jonathan Stearne, profited from the post-war "judicial anarchy" by inciting a sort of mass hysteria with foreign ideas about witches.[14] Eighteen years later, the versatile George Lyman Kittredge's study of transatlantic witchcraft enlarged upon Notestein's explanation without challenging it in any substantive way.[15] In 1970, however, Alan Macfarlane published a study of Tudor and Stuart witchcraft, advancing the argument that Hopkins's and Stearne's "Continental ideas" sparked hunts fueled by the ingrained animosities of small-town politics.[16] A year later, impressed by his student's assertions, Keith Thomas married all these conceptions. In his tremendously influential *Religion and the Decline of Magic,* Thomas argued that the war caused a "delay in the resumption of normal judicial machinery" which Hopkins and Stearne exploited with the aid of local people eager to bring down their enemies.[17]

However, these explanations fail to account for the long-term involvement of actors from every level of society, the sheer physical size of East Anglia, and the rather conventional knowledge of witchcraft demonstrated by the witch-finders. Moreover, the eastern region retained reasonably adequate legal structures after the war (which, indeed, had barely touched it)—there was no "judicial anarchy."[18] Most importantly, however, these explanations ignore the fact that the years just prior to and during the war saw religious and political insecurities open the way for an increasingly influential clergy to deliver its message of an imminent Apocalypse presaged by a struggle between the godly and their foes.

Long before the war, clerical eschatological thought was systematically overlaid upon popular thaumaturgical beliefs in East Anglia, resulting in the intermingling of familiar English notions of magic with some particular conceptions of salvation. For decades prior to the arrival of the witch-hunters, prominent voices in the regional ministry claimed that the godly had spiritual enemies who had assailed God's people in the past and would continue to do so in future. Moreover, many prescribed a set of actions to be taken against the ungodly so as to ensure God's favor.

Between 1621 and 1630, East Anglia suffered periodic depressions in the cloth trade. The resultant hardships were exacerbated by the disastrous harvests in 1629 and 1630. The clergy explicitly identified the people's suffering as God's reactions to the nation's sins: Laud's Arminian program; toleration of recusants; the Catholicism of the king's wife; and their own failure to reform the church.[19] "England was being chastised for her apostasy," noted William Hunt, "as the kingdom of Judah had been punished for the idolatry of King Manasseh."[20] God manifested his wrath with England by destroying the harvests, ensuring the popularity of the new draperies, bringing back the plague in 1636, allowing Laud his successes, and, almost inevitably, bringing the country to war.

During the uncertainties of the war years, the sermons of the "painful preachers" offered messages of reform and salvation—even hope—to a troubled people. Faced with the fact that many people might regard a civil war as an improbable element of salvation, these ministers interpreted England's history as holy history. The ambiguous nature of the struggle with Charles became intelligible by seeing it as part of God's overall plan for England, a plan that included a long period of strife and turmoil for the true church. Influential Essex minister

Stephen Marshall argued that, in this struggle, only the godly were fit defenders of "the Lord's cause."[21] Sir Harbottle Grimston of Bradfield Hall, near Manningtree, believed that the Church was under assault by "Vipers and Monsters of all sorts," and exhorted the Commons to practice humbleness and trust in God.[22] Such men believed that the troubles of the present were to be understood through providences: those physical manifestations of the divine will that, correctly interpreted, would guide the godly toward a blessed future on earth.

As the Civil War progressed, however, an increasing number of ministers turned their gaze towards the godly themselves in an attempt to understand the war. It now seemed that God brought about the war because the English people had failed to honor the terms of their covenant with him. This apocalyptic interpretation of the war continued to operate within the general framework of providential models such as Marshall's and Grimston's, but it required godly action beyond general church reform or patient individual suffering. It consequently emphasized entirely different themes. The Eastern ministers began to pursue a more self-conscious and public program of national regeneration. The war, they said, was planned by God to bring the sins of the nation to its attention. Thus, the long-pursued reformation of the church was explicitly linked with the fate of the nation. The nation was defined as part of the kingdom of Christ, who "is by designation of his Father, appointed ... to rule and governe all those whom hee hath redeemed to be a people for himself."[23]

This ancient struggle between the godly and their foes traced back to the days when "Pharaoh and his Councellors" led the Egyptians in "burdening and destroying [the faithful until they] had no heart to mind Religion or any thing". Admittedly, this early attack by the paramount idolaters of divinely engineered history had failed. In the 17th century, however, Satan's legions had other weapons at hand. The enemy now sought to destroy the new Israel from within, "by procuring matches [between] some of the members of the Church and some of their owne." Even if the godly managed to avoid "mixing with unbelievers," the threat remained. "There is danger," Matthew Newcomen of Essex exhorted in 1643, for a "conspiracie of men bound by a curse to destroy us [might] counterfeit ... a friendly compliance with the Church." Clearly, though, "they intended nothing more than to overthrow [it]." Thus, he concluded, all future generations of the godly "[were] indammaged [if] ... the unbelieving party doth survive."[24] The message was clear: to be safe, to retain their special and covenanted relationship with God, the godly of England must identify and eliminate the ungodly.

It was precisely such enemies that the people of East Anglia and Salem sought to destroy in the witch-hunts of the 17th century. Jonathan Stearne was one of two witch-hunters who led the mid-century events in East Anglia. By 1648, the hunts had drawn sharp criticism in the region, and Stearne defended them in a long tract, *A Confirmation and Discovery of Witch-Craft*. Stearne struck familiar themes, emphasizing that God would retract England's divine covenant if the ungodly—witches—were not exorcised from the communities of the godly. "[These are] perilous times," he argued. In order to be saved, "we must learn to follow the Lord, and hate Witches [for they are] in league with Satan and abominable idolaters, inticing people from their faith in God ... They are therefore worthy to die."[25]

Aside from mirroring the language of the clergy, Stearne's tract was also heavily indebted to Richard Bernard's 1627 *Guide ... to the Prosecution of Witch-Craft*.[26] Concerned by the proliferation of witchcraft accusations, Bernard's book began by counseling judicial moderation in the conviction of witches. He proceeded, though, to devote the remaining three-quarters of his book—nearly 200 pages—to a tightly-constructed argument leading inexorably to the conclusion that "Being therefore in league with Satan, being abominable Idolators, enticing people from their faith in God, [witches] are therefore worthy to die."[27] Following Bernard's lead, Stearne largely disregarded the early calls for circumspection and engaged instead in "an outstanding instance of extensive and peculiar plagiarism ... [by copying] page after page from Bernard ... following the phraseology [of the latter part of the book] almost or quite word for word."[28] Stearne's use of Bernard is beyond question. It is, in fact, Bernard's voice we hear whenever the witch-hunter turned to the task of defining a witch.

In 1692, Richard Bernard spoke once more.[29] Samuel Parris, minister of Salem Village, was one of the most visible and consistent actors in the infamous 1692-1693 trials that began when Parris's daughter and niece launched accusations of witchcraft against Parris's household slave, Tituba. An examination of the effects of his activities during the years prior to the witch scare—namely, between 1689, when Parris first came to Salem Village and January 1692, when Tituba was accused—suggests that the connection between his ministry and his actions during the trials has been oversimplified. Moreover, Parris's ministerial statements propagated a particular sort of religious doctrine that, when overlaid on the strife and uncertainty already existing in the community, have heretofore been associated in a simple correspondence that does not reflect the more awkward and complicated reality.

In 1993, the Massachusetts Historical Society published Parris's sole remaining sermon notebook.[30] This book contains lengthy outlines of the 27 Sacrament Day sermons Parris prepared and delivered between his ordination in September 1689 until May 1694, a year after the last of the witch trials.[31] Analyzing Parris's sermons in light of the English moral and theological context exemplified by the East Anglian witch-hunting phenomenon allows a fresh series of questions to be asked of the Salem Village events. It also links them directly to the writings of Richard Bernard. Parris's sermon notes reveal several things. As the initial two years of his ministry passed, the fledgling minister became embroiled in personal and political difficulties within the community. Bedeviled by his struggles, Parris became increasingly divisive and accusatory while (not surprisingly for sacrament day sermons) focusing many of his sermons and sermon cycles on the physical and spiritual sufferings of Christ and the hypocrisy, ingratitude, and sinfulness of man. Within this framework, Parris gave significant prominence to select themes: betrayal, physical suffering, hypocrisy, spiritual war, the necessary separation of the election from the damned, the cleansing of the church, and the inevitable onslaught of the godly by Satan's minions (which, he noted, included the traitors within his own congregation).[32] Judas had betrayed Christ, he reminded his listeners, and there could be similar betrayers—what he later called "dissembling Judases"—whose existence was hinted at by the continued failure of the congregation to honor its contract with him. "Cursed be he," he said in September 1691, "that doeth the work of the Lord deceitfully."[33] In December, Parris returned to these ideas. "Deceitful doers of the Lord's work," he proclaimed, "set themselves directly under God's curse.... Look to Saul, who as an effect of that curse became haunted with an evil & wicked spirit and ran in his distress to a witch."[34] Three weeks later, 9-year-old Elizabeth Parris and her 11-year-old cousin Abigail accused Tituba of witchcraft. Others may have been surprised at the unveiling of a witch so close to the heart of the gathered, but Samuel Parris was not. "There are such Devils in the church," he proclaimed from his pulpit in March. "Not only sinners but notorious sinners; sinners more like to the Devil than others.... If *ever* there were Witches, Men & Women in covenant with the Devil, here are *multitudes* in New England.... None ought, nor is it possible that any should, maintain communion with Christ, & yet keep up fellowship with devils."[35]

Parris was not an experienced minister. The son of a Barbados merchant, he inherited a substantial portion of his father's estate. He quickly sold his inheritance, however, using the proceeds to move to Boston, where he established himself as a merchant. He entered

Harvard shortly thereafter but did not stay long enough to graduate. When the Salem Village congregation offered him a position, Parris accepted and moved himself and his family to a community already riven by strife.[36] Once settled into his new home, Parris found himself burdened by the regular production of sermons for a scripturally proficient and potentially hostile audience. In order to better handle his ministerial obligations, Parris increasingly relied on ministerial guides, which may be loosely understood as a 17th-century equivalent of ministerial *Cliff's Notes*. The first, John Trapp's *Commentary or Exposition upon All the Books of the Old and New Testaments*, treated the Bible on a verse-by-verse basis. Trapp's work was also replete with learned quotations; Parris used these to ornament his sermons, perhaps to the surprise of a congregation not yet exposed to the recent taste for such rhetorical flourishes. Parris also used *The Bibles Abstract and Epitomie,* [being] *all the Principall Matters in Theologie ...With the Doctrines and Uses compendiously explained.* This work formed the third and final part of the *Thesaurus Biblicus: seu Promptuarium Sacrum, (The Bible's Treasury, or Holy Storehouse).* The *Thesaurus* was a two-part survey of scriptural word usages arranged in alphabetical order. It detailed the various Latin forms of each word, listed the biblical verses in which each word appeared, and recommended translations of important words and phrases. The *Abstract and Epitomie* gathered this material into various topics followed by suggested ministerial uses. It thereby provided the substance of numerous sermons along various themes.[37]

While both the title page and the introduction to the *Thesaurus* were signed by "Richard Bernard," the frontispiece of the *Abstract and Epitomie* was inscribed as "pro Richardo Barnardo." Scholars studying Parris's sermons and the witch-hunts themselves have not realized that "Richardo Barnardo" is simply the Latin ablative form of "Richard Bernard." Perhaps as a consequence of this, scholars also have not consulted the *Thesaurus Biblicus*, of which the *Abstract and Epitomie* formed but a part. Reading the *Thesaurus* is, though, an interesting and profitable exercise. At the entry for "witch," for example, are various appropriate scriptural citations, a list of related terms ("sorcerer, wizard, magician, and soothsayer"), and the striking recommendation to "[s]ee my book of witchcraft, called the guide to grand-jury-men." There is, then, no doubt that the three Richard Bernards are actually one. [38] This is an important unification, revealing as it does that minister Samuel Parris of Salem Village relied upon the scriptural exegeses of a contemporaneously-acknowledged authority on witchcraft. Indeed, this provides a different perspective on Parris himself, the witchcraft events in Salem Village, and the moral and intellectual contexts of English witch-hunting on both sides of the Atlantic.

Bernard's influence on Parris may be seen at a variety of junctures. Parris, like many of his peers, gave great emphasis to the crucial role of the pastorate in community affairs.[39] Almost immediately upon moving to Salem Village, Parris struggled with contract negotiations, his drive to increase congregational membership, what must have been an infuriating dispute over an inadequate firewood supply, the incorrect anticipation of inflationary fluctuations in pork prices in his contract with the congregation, and the daily demands of his family.[40] All the while, he mustered his middling and incomplete education towards understanding and elucidating the demands of a jealous, wrathful, and interfering God as well as the secretive and destructive actions of "the Divell."

Parris concentrated his sermon of January 3, 1692 on the mediating functions of Christ while continuing to assert the central importance of the ministry. Only preaching, he argued, could bring about the "separating of the Elect from the rest of mankind.... And for this purpose Christ hath given his ministers extraordinary, & ordinary [powers], fitten & qualifyed for this work." Bolstered by "the efficacy of his Spirit," ministers worked with the Lord. The Elect learned "Spiritual obedience ... [through] manifold & various troubles.... [The godly were] new-born, new creatures ... different from, yea contrary to the men of the world: Hince ariseth hatred & persecution." Eventually, though, Christ would enact "the punishment of the enemies of the Church: The Devil the grand enemy of the Church ... [along with] Wicked & Reprobate men (the assistants of Satan to afflict the Church) [whom Christ] punisheth."[41]

The confidence placed in these ministerial powers by Samuel Parris (as well as by the East Anglian witch-hunters, although they had extended the franchise so as to include themselves) had been explicitly enunciated by Richard Bernard nearly a century earlier. One need only peruse a few of the titles of Bernard's works to detect themes very appealing to struggling ministers and ambitious witch-hunters—titles such as *The faithfull shepheard...wherein is set forth the excellencie of the ministerie* (1607); *Two twinnes: or two parts of one portion of scripture. I. Is of catechising. II. Of the ministers maintenance* (1613); *The isle of man; or, the legall proceeding in Man-Shire against sinne. Wherein, the chiefe malefactors disturbing both church and state are detected* (1626).[42] Bernard's *Abstract and Epitomie* not only supported Parris's desire to consolidate his position in the community, however; it also provided him with a convenient, easily-grasped method by which he could proceed. The *Bibles Abstract and Epitomie* (as well as the *Guide to Grand-Jury Men)* relied on the simple binary dichotomies and essentialist assumptions of Ramist logical organization. Within this structural approach to exegesis, all aspects of the universe aligned themselves neatly into a sequence of attributes and characteristics whose truth was demonstrated with marginal proof-texts.[43] These proofs Bernard drew from the scriptural citations he had exhaustively compiled and arranged alphabetically in his *Thesaurus Biblicus.*

Once Parris had mastered the use of the *Abstract and Epitomie*, his sermons bristled with Bernard-esque distinctions. His September 28, 1690 consideration of the spiritual and corporal aspects of the Crucifixion provides adequate example. The sermon began with a discussion of Christ's sufferings on the cross, then turned to a delineation of the "two speciall causes of Christs wounds & Bruises, viz: 1. The Efficient Causes. [and] 2. The final Causes." The "Efficient" causes were immediately subdivided into "principal, efficient, or instrumental" ones. The principal cause (God) was then explored in terms of both his "Internal Motions & External Motions." Finishing with a flourish of finely shaded distinctions between internal (or inward) and outward (or moving) causes, Parris left his congregation to mull on their place in such an orderly universe and closed for the day. He surged forward, however, on November 9, 1690 with a listing of the instrumental causes, which he further divided between those caused by animate and inanimate creatures. In triumph, Parris touched lightly on the thoughts of Beza, propounded for a moment in Latin, and concluded by admonishing that "[w]e should now conclude [the] text with application." He realized, however, that "time forbids."[44]

A final, shared tendency between the East Anglian witch-hunters and Samuel Parris was their insistence on the actual wickedness of some people who might deceptively appear to be good. As already observed, Parris was quite concerned by the ramifications and permutations of this possibility, returning to it numerous times between 1689 and 1692. Fifty years earlier, Matthew Hopkins of East Anglia had enjoined his readers to "Observe these generation of Witches, if they be at any time abused by being called Whore, Theefe, &c, ... are the readiest to cry and wring their hands." In a similar vein, Hopkins's colleague Stearne described those who appeared to be "Saints on earth ... and by their carriages seemed to be very religious people ... [such as Anne West, who] prayed constantly ... using these words *Oh my God, my God*, [but] meaning [Satan], and not the LORD."[45] Indeed, that so many of the accused were identified as dissemblers, deceivers and hypocrites was a singular—one might even say defining—characteristic of

England's two witch-hunts. In 1645 and again in 1692, the godly searched for witches amongst their own.

By this point, then, it should not be surprising that Richard Bernard had also mounted a campaign against the so-called "good" witches, arguing in his *Guide* that "[E]very Witch ought to die, the imagined good, as well as the bad."[46] His *Abstract and Epitomie* was comprised of lists—the "Instruments of Gods wrath," "Woes pronounced by God against Sinners," and "A Catalogue of severall sinnes committed, as well by the godly, as by the wicked" being but a few. The "Catalogue of severall sinnes" was exhaustive, noting nearly 200 separate sins, including those committed "perfidiously, secretly, maliciously, deceitfully, craftily, hypocritically, subtilly, [and] deludingly." Emphasizing the secretive nature of sin, Bernard further specified that "Hypocrisie brings forth Dissimulation," and concluded this section with the observation that *They cover with a covering, not with my Spirit:* (saith God) *that they may adde sin to sin.*"[47]

While yet a boy, Richard Bernard's talents impressed the two daughters of Sir Christopher Wray, the Lord Chief Justice of England. As a consequence, they subsidized Bernard's education at Christ's College, Cambridge. At Cambridge, Bernard studied under the great English divine William Perkins, the most eminent exponent of English Calvinism. Perkins's influence on Bernard is clear. Perkins had sponsored the incorporation of Ramist logic into the Cambridge curriculum, those same structures later forming the methodological underpinnings of Bernard's somewhat idiosyncratic Biblical expositions.[48] Perkins himself wrote a work called *A Discourse of the Damned Art of Witchcraft*, which adapted his theological assertions of a covenant between God and man to express the symmetrical idea that witches, as apostates, were likewise bound by a covenant with Satan. Moreover, Perkins argued that good witches were worse than bad ones. In many ways, Richard Bernard simply followed his teacher's lead.[49]

Passing the M.A. in 1598, Bernard held the living of Worksop, Nottinghamshire, by 1601. He wrote a number of his early works while there and was held in high regard, being "*laborious* in the publick exercise of his *Ministery* ... untill they were, by the last *Bishop* of that diocese ... imperiously suppressed."[50] His reputation was damaged when he involved himself in the exorcism of John Fox. Bernard eventually ceded Worksop around 1612, moving from there to Batcombe in Somersetshire, where he wrote both his *Guide to Grand Jury-Men* (which called for the godly to cast out witches, much as Bernard had attempted to cast the demons from John Fox) and his combined *Thesaurus Biblicus/Bibles Abstract and Epitomie*.

It has long been established that Jonathan Stearne of East Anglia borrowed heavily from Bernard's writings. Moreover, with the identification of Richard Bernard as the author of *The Bibles Abstract and Epitomie*, it is here demonstrated for the first time that Samuel Parris was incorporating the Biblical interpretations of the same Richard Bernard, whose work was so durable that it was one of the authorities cited during the Salem Village trials.[51] Surely a great deal of Bernard's appeal was his use of the easily grasped dichotomies of the Ramist logic. By sorting the universe—the plenum—into double columns and proof-texting each entry with sacred Scripture, Ramism allowed the godly to define both themselves and their enemies. In their attempts to reconstruct the simple truths of the Apostolic Past that they sought to recapture,[52] the people of East Anglia and those of Salem Village found themselves besieged by enemies, but this time from within. Once these enemies were defined and identified, the scriptural mandate was simple and clear: *Thou shalt not suffer a witch to live.*[53] In the performance of these community exorcisms, principals on both sides of the Atlantic allowed the voice of Richard Bernard to speak virtually unmodified.

Intellectual influences are tricky things: they are difficult to trace with assurance and are fraught with the hazards of careless reductions leading to insupportably monocausal explanations. Equally untenable, however, are interpretations of the two English witch-hunts that rely on the fiction of historical exceptionalism that draws a watery divide between England and the English colonies. The structural and thematic elements of Bernard's works resonate in the East Anglian and Salem Village tragedies. This identification of Bernard and the centrality of his works establishes what is surely only a partial but nonetheless important bridge between the early modern communities of the godly. It also locates important intellectual sources for England's two witch-hunts in their common past.

---

[1] Aspects of these findings were presented to the 1999 and 2000 gatherings of the Western Conference for British Studies and to the "Transatlantic Studies: New Perspectives" conference (Maastricht 2000). Portions of the Samuel Parris research first appeared in my unpublished essay, "Translating Salem," which received the 1999 distinction and award from the Colonial Dames Society of Alabama. The Ramist and eschatological issues touched upon here are being developed in a paper entitled "*Specularum maleficarum:* Early Modern Guides for the Identification of Witches."

[2] My dissertation, *The East Anglian Witch-Hunts*, constitutes the first full scholarly study of these events. Abstracted court records are in Cecil l'Estrange Ewen's *Witch Hunting and Witch Trials, The Indictments for Witchcraft from the Records of 1373 Assizes held for the Home Circuit A.D. 1559-1736* (London, 1929). Alan Macfarlane surveyed the onset of the hunts

in Essex in Chapter 9 of his *Witchcraft in Tudor and Stuart England: A Regional and Comparative Study* (London: Routledge, 1970), and also amplified Ewen's compilation, 254-309. Richard Deacon's book on Matthew Hopkins, *Matthew Hopkins: Witch-Finder General* (London: F. Muller, 1976) considers many of the relevant materials. Jim Sharpe's *Instruments of Darkness: Witchcraft in England 1550-1750* (Philadelphia: University of Pennsylvania Press, 1996) devotes a chapter to the subject; he reviews this and lists contemporaneous tractates in his essay, "The Devil in East Anglia: the Matthew Hopkins Trials Reconsidered," in *Witchcraft in Early Modern Europe: Studies in Culture and Belief*, ed. Jonathan Barry, Marianne Hester, and Gareth Roberts (Cambridge: Cambridge University Press, 1996). Gilbert Geis and Ivan Bunn include very creditable discussions of the influences of the trials in their *A Trial of Witches: A Seventeenth-Century Witchcraft Prosecution* (London: Routledge, 1997). Peter Elmer touches on the events in his essay, "Towards a Politics of Witchcraft in Early Modern England," in *Languages of Witchcraft: Narrative, Ideology and Meaning in Early Modern Culture* ed. Stuart Clark (Basingstoke: St. Martin's Press, 2000); Elmer's forthcoming study should provide a valuable analytical perspective on 16th- and 17th-century English witchcraft contexts and concerns as they were negotiated in contemporaneous publications. Finally, passing mention of the East Anglian events is found in nearly all 20th-century studies of early modern witchcraft, although the unfortunate inclination to abstract witchcraft from religion and politics is endemic.

[3] Terms are difficult here. Throughout this essay (except in one case) I used the contemporaneous term "godly" rather than another contemporaneous but now hotly-disputed one: "Puritans." The term "godly" captures a bit more of the resonance of the issues I am discussing, whereas the idea of the "Puritans"— especially in North America—has become quasi-mythological. I hope, of course, that the specific referent is always clear even if the terms *in vacuo* are not.

[4] The grounds for characterizing the godly as the "Saints" may be found in Anthony Woolrych, *The English Civil War and After*, ed. R. Parry (Berkeley: University of California Press, 1970), 59-77. William Hunt, *The Puritan Moment: The Coming of Revolution in an English County* (Cambridge: Harvard University Press, 1983) contains valuable commentary on the increasing tendency to associate national events with the conditions (and assumption) of a divine covenant between England and God. Notable also are essays by Bernard Capp, Michael Murrin, C. A. Patrides, Paul J. Korshin, and Stephen J. Stein in *The Apocalypse in English Renaissance Thought and Literature*, eds. C. A. Patrides and Joseph Wittreich (Manchester: Manchester University Press, 1984).

[5] Stephen Marshall, *Meroz Curse for not Helping the Lord against the Mightie* (London, 1641), 2. All italicization, capitalization patterns, spellings and punctuation are in the originals unless otherwise noted.

[6] Matthew Newcomen, *The Craft and Cruelty of the CHURCHES Adversaries: Discovered in A Sermon ... [and] published by Order of the House of Commons*, (London, 1643), 2.

[7] Perhaps 50 accusations were heard, and a *billa vera* returned against 36, of which 19 were hanged, 9 died in jail, 6 were held in jail for at least 6 years, and 2 met unknown fates. See next note for sources.

[8] I base specific trial and verdict information on two works by Cecil l'Estrange Ewen: *Witch Hunting and Witch Trials* (London, 1929) and *Witchcraft and Demonianism* (London, 1933). I incorporate, however, information in Wallace Notestein, *A History of Witchcraft in England from 1558 to 1715* (Washington, 1911) and follow the corrections to Ewen in Alan Macfarlane, *Witchcraft in Tudor and Stuart England* (London: Routeldge, 1970) and Jim Sharpe, *Instruments of Darkness*.

[9] Macfarlane, *Witchcraft in Tudor and Stuart England*, 135-37.

[10] The local ministers were George Eatoney, Joseph Longe, and John Edes (who would survive to sign the 27th Presbyterian classis). Cambridge divines Edmund Calamy, Sr., and Samuel Fairclough, along with Robert Rich, also served in the trials. Rich was a Justice of the Peace; Calamy and Fairclough ostensibly arrived as part of a special commission of *Oyer et Terminer*, although I have found no record of a Parliamentary Commission ordering this.

[11] Jonathan Stearne, *A Confirmation and Discovery of Witchcraft* (London, 1648), 8 and 57-58. In both cases, Stearne offered as the grounds for this assertion 5 Micah: "Now gather thyself in troops ... he hath laid siege against us: they shall smite the judge of Israel with a rod upon the cheek.... Thine hand shall be lifted up upon thine adversaries, and all thine enemies shall be cut off.... And I will cut off witchcrafts out of thine hand; and thou shalt have no more soothsayers."

[12] Stuart Clark aptly describes eschatological fears as "polarizing," a characterization now widely adopted. *Thinking with Demons* (London: Clarendon Press, 1996).

[13] Sharpe, *Instruments of Darkness*, 128.

[14] Notestein, *Witchcraft in England*, 201. Ewen identified these foreign ideas as the result of "Master Hopkins' reading of some continental authority" (*Witchcraft and Demonianism*, 52). Macfarlane echoed this idea,139).

[15] George Lyman Kittredge, *Witchcraft in Old and New England* (New York, 1929).

[16] Macfarlane, *Witchcraft in Tudor and Stuart England*, 6, 139.

[17] Keith Vivien Thomas, *Religion and the Decline of Magic* (New York: Penguin, 1971), 458. Thomas explicitly argued that "the Civil War was not followed by a Puritan crusade to harry sorcerers out of the land ... [and E]vidence of sectarian [*viz.*, "Puritan"] considerations in the trials is singularly lacking," 500-501.

[18] Sharpe notes that "something like effective governmental structures were in place" in East Anglia and that any sense to the contrary is misfounded, *Instruments of Darkness*, 140.

[19] For a similar intersection of context and response, see Wolfgang Behringer, *Hexenverfolgung in Bayern: Volksmagie, Glaubenseifer und Staaträson in dern Frühen Neuzeit* (Munich: Oldenbourg, 1987), 95.

[20] Hunt, *The Puritan Moment*, 238.

[21] Marshall, *Meroz Curse*, 3.

[22] Harbottle Grimstone, Kt., "Mr. Grimstons Speech in the High Court of Parliament," *The Thomason Tracts: The foure first volumes containes The Speeches made in Parliament from 3d of November 1640 untill 31 October 1642,* vol. 3, series E, no. 198 (London, 1641), 8, 14-15. The particular authors of the woes Grimston relates were a marvelous mish-mash of biblical and contemporaneous villains: "Achitophells, Hammans and Woosies, Empsons and Dudlies, Tricilian and Belknapp," 8.

[23] Thomas Temple, *Christ's Government In and Over His People* (London, 1642), 4f. The precise mechanisms of Christ's rule were contested within the ministry. Francis Woodcock, in his *Christs Warning-Piece* (London, 1644), 6, warned that "when Antichrist being reduced to last exigents, sends abroad warning spirits ... then is Christ a making ready for his second coming." By comparison, William Gouge—in his sermon, *The Progresse of Divine Providence* (London, 1645), 29—ridiculed "all conceits of our ... Millenaries ... who imagine that Christ shall personally come down from heaven ... and raign [*sic*] here a thousand years with his Saints." Nonetheless, the applications of doctrines based primarily on the New Testament (particularly the "Revelation" of S. John), the idea of the unity of the earthly and heavenly kingdoms, and the strengthening of distinctions between the godly and the ungodly inherent to the general contemporaneous acceptance of Christ as King transcended these internecine arguments.

[24] Newcomen, *Craft and Cruelty,* 2-5, 7, 9.

[25] Stearne, *Confirmation and Discovery,* 56-58.

[26] Wallace Notestein, *Witchcraft in England,* 165, 234-237, commented lucidly on Bernard's career and ideas, but inexplicably analyzed only Hopkins's tract in his section on the East Anglian hunts. He thus failed to identify Bernard's influence on the 1645-1647 events. Kittredge, *Witchcraft in Old and New England,* 273, correctly identified Bernard's expertise in "Continental lore" but immediately abandoned the subject, making only the trivial observation that the connection between the Jacobean minister and the Civil War witch-hunters was that all of them believed in the witches' sabbath.

[27] Bernard, *Guide to Grand-Jury Men,* 249, 253.

[28] See Kittredge.

[29] Geis and Bunn, *A Trial of Witches,* briefly surveyed the use of Bernard in the 1662 trial of Amy Denny and Rose Cullender, both of whom eminent jurist Matthew Hale—whose work still forms part of English case law—ordered executed in Bury St Edmunds. Geis and Bunn also argued for connections between the English witchcraft trials and those in Massachusetts. Their discussion of Bernard lacks, however, any substantive acknowledgement of the intellectual and theological doctrines implicit to these connections, concentrating instead on Bernard's explication of the "witches' marks" that was adopted in the trials.

[30] *The Sermon Notebook of Samuel Parris 1689-1694,* eds. James F. Cooper, Jr., and Kenneth P. Minkema, vol. 66 (Boston: Publications of the Colonial Society of Massachusetts, 1993).

[31] Sacrament Day sermons were those "preached at the gathering of the church ... prior to or in the afternoons following celebrations of the Lord's Supper." "Introduction," *Sermon Notebook*, 9.

[32] My analysis of the sermons led to the same ominous conclusions as those advanced by Cooper and Minkema in their "Introduction" to the *Sermon Notebook*, 12-21. I used their summary when writing this list.

[33] He based this on 48 Jeremiah 10. *Sermon Notebook*, 52-55.

[34] Ibid., 69.

[35] Ibid., 194-98.

[36] Boyer and Nissenbaum, op. cit., passim. Also, Larry Gragg, *The Quest for Security: The Life of Samuel Parris, 1653-1720* (New York: Greenwood Press, 1990), 10-12.

[37] *Sermon Notebook*, "Introduction," 8 fn17.

[38] At my request, Stephen Tabor, Curator of Early Printed Book at the Huntington Library, San Marino, California, kindly examined their copy of the *Thesaurus Biblicus*. After reviewing the work, Mr. Tabor concurred with the attribution of authorship I assert here. I should add that the universal failure to recognize that the same Richard Bernard who wrote the ministerial guides also wrote the guide to witchcraft prosecutions was fostered by cataloguing errors. Richard Bernard died in 1641, so the reasonable source for a list of his works is the *Short Title Catalogue of Books Printed in England, Scotland, and Ireland and of English Books Printed Abroad 1475-1640*, compiled by A. W. Pollard and G. R. Redgrave, 2nd ed. (Oxford: Oxford Univesrity Press, 1985). This listing, which notes both his *Abstract and Epitomie* and *Thesaurus Biblicus*, fails, however, to include the *Guide to Grand-Jury Men*. The *Guide* is found instead in Donald Wing's *Short Title Catalogue of Books Printed in England, Scotland, Ireland, Wales, and British America and of English Books Printed in Other Countries 1641-1700* (New York: MLA, 1945), which— *mirabile dictu*—omitted inclusion of the ministerial guides.

[39] Richard P. Gildrie's *The Profane, the Civil, & the Godly: The Reformation of Manners in Orthodox New England, 1679-1749* (State College: Pennsylvania State University Press, 1994) provides a good overview of this process, which he traces as of the Reforming Synod of 1689.

[40] Gragg, *Samuel Parris*, includes accessible discussions of these issues, the historiography accreted unto Parris due to his role in the witch-hunts and trials, and Parris's ministry itself. The "Introduction" to the *Sermon Notebook* addresses the ministerial *milieu* in which Parris existed as well as the structure and purpose of the sermons represented in the *Notebook*.

[41] *Sermon Notebook*, 178-185.

[42] Though Bernard was not the only Jacobean minister to make such assertions, he was the one being consulted by the principal actors in the witch-hunts.

[43] The standard explication of Ramist logic remains Walter J. Ong's *Ramus: Method, and the Decay of Dialogue* (Cambridge, MA, 1958). Perry Miller's *The New England Mind: The Seventeenth Century* (New York: Harvard University Press, 1939) gives famous attention to the influence of Ramism, although his *explanans* has suffered sustained and worthwhile attack. Michael P. Winship's *Seers of God: Puritan Providentialism in the Restoration and*

Early Enlightenment (Baltimore: Johns Hopkins University Press, 1996) and T. Dwight Bozeman's *To Live Ancient Lives* are excellent recent reconsiderations of the religious *mentalité* of England, Old and New.

[44] *Sermon Notebook*, 99-116. He drew the Beza quote from Trapp's *Commentary or Exposition Upon All of the Epistles and the Revelation of John the Divine*, 145. The Latin tag—"Possumus hinc Asseverare ex Latere Christi fluxisse nostra Sacramenta" ("We may safely say that our Sacraments issued out of God's side")—was lifted from Trapp's marginal note on Calvin's discussion of the purifying and sacramental aspects of the Crucifixion. Trapp, 136; *Sermon Notebook*, fns. 23 & 24.

[45] *Sermon Notebook*, 196-7; Hopkins, *Discovery*, 6; Stearne, *Confirmation and Discovery*, 38-9.

[46] Bernard, *Guide to Grand-Jury Men*, 258-266.

[47] Bernard, *Abstract and Epitomie*, 88-89, 90-91, 51-53.

[48] The *Thesaurus Biblicus* ended up being published posthumously. John Conant, in his biolgraphical introduction to the *Thesaurus Biblicus* entitled, "To the Christian Reader," commented that "we may find [Bernard] sometimes dissenting from the more received and common sense of Expositours." Bernard himself, in his prefatory "To the Studious Reader" (in which he discussed the structure and recommended use of the *Thesaurus*) had rather more mildly instructed that "if any place (through the Scribes negligence) be either omitted, or misquoted, then to supply what is wanting, and to right what is mistaken, look into Cottons *or* Newmans *Concordance* ... [to] find the text which thou seekest for."

[49] Stuart Clark, *Thinking with Demons*, 463-66.

[50] John Conant, "To the Christian Reader," *Thesaurus Biblicus*.

[51] Thomas Goddard Wright, *Literary Culture in Early New England*, 138. The full list is: "Bernard[;] Baxter and R. Burton, their Histories about Witches...[;] Finch: Common Law[;] St. Germans: Abridgement of Common Law[;] Wierus: De Præstigiis Demonum." Wright's notes on this page give full references for these works.

[52] This is the central tenet of T. Dwight Bozeman's *To Live Ancient Lives: The Primitivist Dimension in Puritanism*.

[53] Exodus 22: 18.

Part Two:
Racial Encounters in the Contact Zone

Chapter 4

Mulattos Accused of Witchcraft and Sorcery in Late Colonial New Spain

Lars Ivar Owesen-Lein Borge

The archives of the Inquisition contain some of the few available sources from which ordinary people—individuals from the lower classes of colonial Mexican society—address us directly and allow us to participate in their private social realities, their models of the world, and their everyday experiences. It is perhaps the only source that allows them to speak for themselves as individuals, although never directly.[1] Jean Pierre Dedieu argues that the archives of the Inquisition "let the humble, the poor, those outside history, talk and say what they believe ... to a superlative degree," and that these records allow us indeed to hear authentic voices of "humble individuals outside history."[2] The utterances must, however, always be properly and carefully contextualized and interpreted in light of the conditions under which they were created.[3] The Inquisition did not, after all, interrogate people in order to document their lives or collect ethnographic information on various topics. The sole purpose of the questioning was to determine whether or not the accused had committed "crimes against the Catholic faith" in thought and action. If this could be established, the next line of inquiry aimed at determining whether these crimes had been committed consciously or out of ignorance, in order to decide which punishment would be appropriate. Therefore, these records are necessarily heavily biased. Similar dilemmas confront all researchers who attempt to write the social history of groups and individuals who have not left any direct written testimonies of their own. However, the records of the Inquisition are in many ways even more problematical because they seemingly offer so much. The archives offer vivid descriptions and a rich variety of individual utterances made during the trials, in addition to abundant biographical and personal information on each individual. Many records can virtually be read as novels.

This chapter is based on the testimonies of a number of individuals who were accused of witchcraft or sorcery and investigated by the Inquisition in late colonial New Spain. The selected cases involve accusations directed against individuals who seemed to possess a distinct "otherness" from the persons who made the denunciation. All records contain information on the ethnic status of the interrogated individuals as well as that of all other people mentioned in their testimonies. The interrogated were always asked to classify themselves in ethnic terms, and their answers often reveal interesting information which hardly could have been extracted from other available sources— information that often calls into question our traditional interpretations of colonial Mexico's race consciousness. The processes of ethnic classification that are documented in the Inquisitorial records indicate the need for a more critical attitude to the actual meanings of such classifications in colonial New Spain.

To a large extent, the ethnic labels used during the interrogations reveal nothing but the stereotypes and highly subjective perceptions of the individual who made the classification. Nothing indicates that there existed any commonly accepted standards for racial classification in the daily discourse of the lower classes. Racial identification was primarily something that was required in encounters with the Spanish bureaucracy, but which had limited relevance for the people's daily lives. There are, however, certain patterns in the use of these labels which may reveal how each racial term was interpreted and used by different groups in the late colonial period. One group seems to have been disproportionately accused of harmful sorcery in New Spain, namely those individuals commonly classified as "mulattos."

New Spain never experienced a witch craze comparable to the prosecution of witches in early modern Northern and Western Europe. Only a relatively small percentage of the cases that were investigated by the Holy Office concerned witchcraft and sorcery.[4] The majority of the cases concerned "mistaken" moral beliefs and practices, blasphemy, bigamy, or swearing.[5] Suspects of witchcraft normally got away with a warning, and even in more serious cases the Inquisitors would often let the accused go if they showed sincere repentance and confessed. The Inquisition's attitude towards magic and superstition in general became even more lenient during the 18th century, as the institution seemingly lost interest in these more profane matters that mostly concerned the lower, "irrelevant" classes of society.[6] In late colonial New Spain, magical healers, soothsayers, fortune-tellers and the like were arrested if they caused commotion, but they were mostly judged by a secular court and in most cases treated as common criminals. The Inquisitorial records offer examples of transmutations, witches' sabbaths, and pacts and intercourse with the devil, in which the entire classical vocabulary of European demonology is applied (although always with a distinctly Mexican flair).[7] The muleteer Sebastián de Soso, for instance, who was classified as an "assimilated mulatto," was accused at Puebla de los Angeles in 1705 of having undertaken a voyage to the submarine world, where he signed a pact with the devil in order to become a good toreador.[8] However, it was commonly assumed that individuals from all social and ethnic groups regularly deployed magic and sorcery as effective and concrete tools to deal with their everyday struggles, problems, conflicts, domestic issues, poverty, and illness.

The testimonies are often very personal and the main issues are overwhelmingly domestic and intimate. A large number of the accusations of witchcraft seem to originate in personal quarrels and differences between neighbors and colleagues or even close relatives. This was probably the case when Juana Theresa Gómez, a Spanish woman from the small community Ayo el Chico, accused her own mother and an Indian woman of being witches and of having sealed a pact with the devil. The daughter took this step in order to save her mother's soul, and she emphasized that her mother had been misled by her Indian companion. The accusation was thus a strategy to remover her mother from "bad company".[9]

The traditional magical healers in the smaller communities used magic to make a living; but other individuals could also periodically earn a few *tomines* with their abilities. The free mulatto woman, María de Concepción, from Mexico City, was among other *maleficiados* accused of using witchcraft in order to find stolen animals in 1732.[10] Josepha de la Encarnazión y Ábrego, from San Juan del Río, who was brought before the Holy Office in 1719, was said to have performed rites in order to find out when a person would die, and to foretell the sex of a baby before it was born.[11] She could do the same with animals. The reward for such services seems to have been rather slim. Most practitioners were paid off with food, cloth, or other small gifts. The amounts of money mentioned are mostly very small. In general, the archives suggest that men were able to make a larger profit from their abilities than women were. Cristóbal de Argomedo from Mexico City, who was tried in 1712, used various spells in order to discover mines. He was in fact successful a few times, but was finally denounced by a discontented customer once his luck ran out.[12]

There are many fortune-tellers in the archival material. The *castiza*, María Theresa Robles, was accused of utilizing the herb *pippilinche* in order to foretell the future and for various other rites.[13] The most common varieties of magic in colonial New Spain, however, were related to sexuality and marriage, directly or indirectly. Love magic made up a significantly larger percentage of the cases in New Spain than in the European tribunals. It seems that a large repertoire of remedies and spells was current in colonial New Spain, combining elements from the different traditions.[14] Individuals who were known to possess the power to cure broken hearts, make people fall in love, or help them to eliminate competition, were highly esteemed. There are also many descriptions of magical practices aimed at preventing sexual abuse, pregnancies, and matrimonial violence. This is perhaps the area where the different traditions mixed and interacted the most, and where the official, theologically sanctioned magic of the Church had the least to offer.

On April 3, 1721, the humble mestizo woman, Maria de la Cruz, appeared in the chancery of Thias Suarez San Antonio, commissioner of the Holy Office in the Apostolico Collegio de Nuestra Señora de Guadelope in Zacatecas.[15] She had recently gone to confession with her regular priest. After having heard her confession, however, he had refused her absolution for her sins until she had informed the Inquisition about the matters. More than a year earlier—it had been a Wednesday, around 8 o'clock in the morning—Maria had been sitting outside her house, crying because her husband had been with a woman "de mal estado" and she had been very jealous. Sebastiana, an Indian woman, passed by, saw Maria crying, and asked her why. Maria told her about the causes of her grief, and Sebastiana reassured her that she need not cry, because she knew how to remedy the situation. The utensils she needed in order to do this were a candle, a small bowl of *aqua bendita*, and 5 grains of salt. Maria prepared these remedies and gave them to Sebastiana, who cut the candle into 5 pieces. She put a cross into the bowl of *aqua bendita*, together with the grains of salt, and instructed Maria to kneel and say three credos to each piece of the candle, which she also did. Maria did this once a day for a week. At the end of the week, Sebastiana visited Maria again and asked Maria if she wanted to have her husband's lover killed. This would require some hair from her husband, a piece of his shirt, and a *tostón*, a small coin, which Sebastiana intended to give to a mysterious man whose name she did not reveal. After this visit, Maria panicked and began to fear the possible results of Sebastiana's sorcery. She did not have anything more to do with Sebastiana or her mysterious male helper, and she stopped performing the rituals. According to the Inquisitor, Maria regretted her part sincerely and honestly, and she swore never again to indulge in superstitious actions nor have faith in them. He gave Maria a letter for her confessor, recommending that she now be given absolution. In many respects, this is a typical case. Maria's main reason for presenting her auto-denunciation to the Inquisition was to receive a letter from the commissioner of the Holy Office that she could present to her confessor in order to be granted absolution. We do not have any information concerning the outcome of Sebastiana's *brujerias*, but it seems that nothing at all was achieved. Maria's husband continued to see his mistress and Sebastiana was never punished for her deeds.

The newly converted Indians were declared spiritually immature and were formally removed from the jurisdiction of the Inquisition in 1571.[16] The Inquisition therefore became almost exclusively devoted to the Hispanic sector of the colonial society, in which *castas* greatly outnumbered Spaniards. Indians could evidently be tried by the Inquisition after 1571, but the majority of those accused appear to have been more or less uprooted or living on the fringes of Spanish society, where their status as Indians was rather unsure. Any individual who was not identified unequivocally as a *tributario* and subject to a *pueblo de indio* could be redefined as a *casta* and be tried as such. A large number of the accused *castas* seem to have belonged to this category. There are also some examples of Indians being consciously reclassified in order to make a trial possible.[17] These racial terms appear, however, to have been of little interest to the accused themselves. I have not been able to find any case where a *casta* shows any emotional attachment to the label he is given, or who protests because he is classified differently than expected. The only real objections came from a number of individuals whom the accuser had labeled as *castas* but who claimed status as Indians, which would relieve them from the hands of the Inquisition. A number of individuals who labeled themselves Spaniards, but apparently were not accepted as such by their community, presented some objections; but the overall impression is that *castas* did not really care about how they were labeled, and paid little or no respect to this aspect. Although numerous racial terms existed in the *sistema de castas*, only 4 terms were used in daily discourse in Central New Spain: *indio*, *español*, *mestizo*, and *mulatto*. When the mestizo woman, Maria de Cruz, was questioned about the identity of Sebastiana's male companion, she was not able to say whether he was "*indio, mulatto, mestizo ó español.*" Other terms were seldom used spontaneously by anyone, except in order to clarify a person's physical appearance. In a trial that took place in Durango in 1732, Clara de Almaguar was accused of having performed "certain acts of sorcery" against Matilda Josepha de Aldana. Clara was classified as "*coyota o española.*"[18] Maria Theresia Loya, who in 1720 was accused of sorcery in the city of Querétaro, was designated "*negra o mulatta.*"[19] In neither of these cases was the accused able to classify herself, and the Inquisitors had to use their own personal judgment in order to place them. In a case that took place in 1715, María Xaviera, the slave of Don Joseph de Luna, a *vecino* of San Luis Potosí, was accused of having invented a story where the Virgin appeared before her and performed many wonderful miracles.[20] She was classified with the puzzling term *negra amuletada*. It is important to remember that racial categories of this kind did not necessarily refer to actual racial or ethnic differences, but rather placed an individual in the social hierarchy as a member of a corporate organization or community of some kind. It is difficult to detect any kind of racial or ethnic solidarity or identification among any groups in late colonial New Spain, perhaps with the exception of the highest levels of the Spanish elite in their concern for *liempieza de sangre*. In most cases, we find a strong community solidarity and identification that always seems to have overshadowed ethnicity or class in determining an individual's identity. Similar conclusions have often been made with regard to the indigenous populations. It is however, often argued that the *casta* population in general was very race-conscious, that race must have determined their lives and limited their social options, and that they deployed a variety of strategies to free themselves from their racial stigma—for instance, by marrying into a higher social category. But when confronted with the utterances made by such individuals before the Inquisition, a completely different picture emerges. Ethnicity and, to some extent, class were apparently secondary factors in the construction of an individual's identity and loyalties. The community was always the most important, and members of all ethnic and social categories participated in every social context, linked together through various forms of personal bonds like *compradazgo* or varieties of the patron-client relationship. This is perhaps one of the most striking conclusions that can be drawn from the Inquisitorial records.

One often gets the impression that race was almost totally irrelevant in the daily lives of most individuals from the lower classes. Repeatedly, one sees in the Inquisitorial records that the interrogated are not even able to define themselves in ethnic terms, let alone putting an ethnic label on other individuals in their surroundings. Even close friends, colleagues, and relatives were difficult to classify. Nothing indicates that racial categories or racial identification was part of the daily discourse among these groups. The Spanish elite seems to have been obsessed with lineage and the maintenance of hierarchies and, at least rhetorically, hostile to social climbers; but the plebeian groups did not share the elite's notions.[21] It seems that people in general mostly were unaware of their own ethnic or racial status until they were forced to pick one when they married or if they were confronted with the Spanish bureaucracy for other reasons. If a person was hesitant or was unable to choose an ethnic label, the authorities would assist by making suggestions. The questioned person would be relatively free to choose any label that felt appropriate, and many individuals chose a new racial designation every time they were required to designate themselves. These self-chosen terms did not necessarily correspond with the terms that had been assigned by their community.

Catarina de la Cruz was labeled *india ladina* when she was questioned by the Inquisition in Real e Minas de San Gregorio in 1714. She was accused of *brujerias*, witchcraft. Among other things, she had transformed herself into a *cacalote*, a crow, together with an elderly woman called Juana de Santiago, and the women had flown around in the night and sucked blood from goats (a charge to which she also confessed in a detailed narrative to the Inquisitor). Although the two women must have developed a rather close relationship, Catarina had difficulties in labeling Juana: "To me she appeared to be a *coyota*," she confessed, and in the same sentence described her as relatively old and weak. Juana was definitely not a member of an indigenous cooperation, she spoke Spanish, and she probably had a relatively light complexion, which did not correspond with Catarina's ideas of how Negroes or mulattos looked. Her low social status prevented her, however, from being identified as a Spaniard. Therefore, *coyota* must have been the most logical designation that Catarina could think of under the circumstances. Phenotype or physical appearance was never sufficient to label an individual; other criteria such as occupation, social status, lifestyle, language, or dress were always mentioned, too, so that one easily gets the impression that each individual designated others according to very personal and subjective criteria.

In most cases, people identified others by referring to the community to which they belonged. Racial descriptions, when they were used, were applied to others they did not know well. Maria de la Conception, a *mulatta libre* from the town of Salvaterra who was accused of witchcraft, was known as La Salvetierreña after she had settled in another area. It was a typical naming pattern for individuals who moved to a new town or village. Sometimes, we also find designations like "Maria La India," but this was likely to mean that this particular Maria dressed like an "Indian" or cultivated distinct Indian features, such as long dark hair styled in an Indian fashion, but who lived in an area where the majority of the women styled themselves differently. Such designations often accompanied very common names like Maria, and may have been used as a way of distinguishing one Maria from all the others.

It appears that eccentric and potentially dangerous outsiders were most likely to be classified as mulattos after they had aroused suspicion. In most cases, it is impossible to determine the actual background and ancestry of any of these individuals. In order to find out how each term actually was understood by most people, it is necessary to see the process by which other individuals were designated with the same label a similar social context. What, in particular, made accusers most likely to choose the term "mulatto" in describing practitioners of harmful sorcery? The archives of the Holy Office of the Inquisition in Mexico are filled with cases in which people designated as mulattos are accused of performing practices of an undomesticated indigenous Mexican origin or those that are obviously inspired by unassimilated indigenous rites. Hallucinogenic herbs seem to have been used by many individuals, and they also had a central place in traditional indigenous medicine.

In Quimichtlan, on February 28, 1701, the mulattos Bartholomée Rodrígues and his wife, Maria López, were accused of "*maleficio en papel amate.*"[22] In the *congregacion* San Pedro Piedragorda, on June 3, 1729, the mulatto, Diego Barajas, was accused of practicing sorcery with candles and magical songs and using peyote.[23] In Puebla, around 1730, a number of accusations were raised against Joseph de Zepeda, a mulatto slave called "Tata Pepe," and his female companion, Madre Juana. On September 23, 1728, a *relacion* was written about these two individuals accusing them of "superstitious actions" designed to bring souls out from Purgatory.[24] A further *relacion* was submitted on December 20 about further "supernatural" actions committed by this couple.[25] On April 23, 1730, the commissioner of the Holy Office wrote down a *relacion* about the appearance of the ghost of the deceased husband of a woman of the city and attached it to Tata Pepe's file.[26] On May 18, Tata Pepe and Madre Juana were accused of having held conversations with the dead.[27] This couple appears to have organized something like a magical circle in Puebla with participants drawn from all of the town's ethnic and social groups. All these mulattos have in common their relatively peripheral, "outsider" status in their communities, and their attachment to unassimilated indigenous rituals.

The term "mulatto" appears to have been used to designate any individual of relatively dark complexion who did not belong to a corporate group or who was not known well. This might explain the disproportionately large number of individuals classified as mulattos and accused of witchcraft and sorcery in the late colonial period. Much indigenous magic was in some ways perceived as less threatening by the Hispanic community than mulatto magic, since indigenous magic had to a large degree been domesticated or assimilated. Many Spaniards had direct experiences with indigenous *curanderos* and magic, due to the scarcity of Spanish physicians. In 1617, a Spanish woman, Doña Mariana Lopez de Rivera, called for an Indian to come to her house in order to cure her sick son with psalms. Archival statements in this case document an intimacy between such Indian healers and their Spanish customers, which is mostly lacking in the descriptions of mulatto healers.[28] The church, especially local parish priests, often attacked *curanderos*, and repeatedly raised the suspicion of "heathen" remnants in their curing rites; but in general they were free to operate as long as they did not use hallucinogens or spells that too obviously were derived from non-Christian beliefs. The Spanish settlers tended to accept the local indigenous magical healers more or less as they did the local healers in Spain, who from time to time also had to struggle with the church and accusations of witchcraft.[29]

Most of the cases that I have analyzed took place in the areas of Central and Northern New Spain, among a comparatively small but important group of individuals of African ancestry, who often occupied an intermediate position between Indians and Spaniards. In areas like Vera Cruz, with a large African slave population, different meanings were attached to terms such as "mulatto" and "mestizo," and a large variety of other terms were also used. It is of course not surprising that a large group of individuals with part-African ancestry would be accused of witchcraft in areas like Vera Cruz or Mexico City, where mulattos made up the largest *casta* group. It *is* surprising, however, that more mulattos than mestizos or members of other *casta* categories were accused of harmful sorcery, even in rural areas of Central New Spain, during a period in which the previous Indian-African-European continuum was being rapidly replaced by an Indian-European one.

In contemporary discourse, we commonly speak of mulattos primarily as the products of mixture between Africans and Europeans. The term "mulatto" is also generally defined as such in most contemporary dictionaries in most European languages. Modern usage of terms like "mestizo" or "mulatto" does nothing but obscure the actual meanings these conceptions held in colonial New Spain. In a colonial Mexican context, the term "mulatto" normally refers to the mixture between Africans and indigenous Mexicans—often, but not necessarily with, a European component. It has also been suggested that "mulatto" referred to all mixed individuals who were not legally mestizo; and sometimes mestizos were referred to as mulattos. In reality, however, these terms had little to do with actual or even perceived ancestry.[30] The actual complexity is often overlooked, partly because *mestisaje* in Mexico traditionally has been regarded as the assimilation of indigenous individuals into Hispanic society. The importance of the African component in this process is largely ignored. At the same time, the importance of African-Indian interaction in colonial Mexico has never been systematically established. It is also mostly forgotten that the original slave populations did not just consist of Africans, but also of individuals from many other groups. A large percentage of the slave population was of Indian extraction in the formative years of the plantation economy, and Indians were still enslaved in areas in the Caribbean and South America in the 18th century and sold to Mexico. It should also be noted that a large number of the original slave population in the Americas did not consist of just black Africans or even local Indians, but also more or less "white" Caucasoid-looking individuals, especially from the Balkans and North Africa.[31] The slave populations were extremely mixed in origin and ethnic diversity, and almost everywhere Spanish evolved into the common language of the slaves, even in areas where the local indigenous population was enslaved in large numbers. Mostly, Indian slaves captured locally would be separated and sold to other regions in order to prevent alliances and loyalties between local free Indians and the slaves. Indians from Nicaragua, Florida, or Venezuela were as foreign to the local indigenous population in Mexico as direct imports from Africa were, and no need was felt to distinguish them from the Africans.

It is impossible to determine to what extent Indians were reclassified as mulattos (or to what extent the term "mulatto" was used to designate indigenous Mexicans in general), but it must have been significant. There were few direct imports of slaves directly from Africa to New Spain, and therefore we might assume that in physical appearance, the colonial mulatto population did not differ too strongly from the indigenous population. We might suppose that they often had a somewhat darker complexion than most Mexican Indians, but not necessarily. Their mixture with local Indians and *castas* would have further diminished the physical differences in succeeding generations. In light of such uncertainty, we are obliged to pay special attention to archival descriptions of cultural traits or beliefs among individuals designated as mulattos or Negroes. Nothing indicates that freed Indian slaves were treated differently from Africans, and no attempts were made to distinguish these two groups. Freed Indian slaves, mostly labeled "free Negroes" just as freed Africans were, were assimilated into the lower levels of Hispanic society. Their offspring from local Indian or *casta* women were also legally classified as mulattos, even if they themselves did not necessarily have any African ancestry at all. Freed foreign Indians would in any case have been in the same situation as freed Africans, uprooted and culturally and linguistically separated from the local indigenous population. Their only alternative after manumission would be to embrace Spanish culture and Spanish ways.

We can never know for certain whether a person classified as *negro* or *mulatto* in a colonial source actually was the descendant of slaves brought from Africa, or an indigenous American from (for example) Nicaragua or Venezuela, or of mixed blood. It seems, however, that slaves who had been brought directly from Africa were mostly classified according to their place of origin. In 1774, Juan Nepomuceno was held in captivity in the ecclesiastical jail of the archdiocese of Mexico City, accused of "*conculcador de imágenes, blasfemo y reb[aptizado].*"[32] He was explicitly classified as a "*Negro de Costa del Oro*," the Gold Coast of West Africa. The slave Maria Blanca, who was tried for blasphemy in 1610 in Mexico City, was identified as a *negra* from the Congo.[33] A person labeled *negro* without reference to place of origin would most likely have been born a slave in the Americas, so the term can in fact refer to any number of racial combinations.[34]

I have tried to show that when confronted with ethnic terminology in colonial Mexican documents, the terms should never be interpreted in a straightforward manner. Instead of using the ethnic labels as a means of identifying individuals as members of a distinct social category, it would be much more helpful to our understanding of the colonial reality to explore *why* an individual in a given context would choose a specific term to label another person. Many of the individuals accused as witches and sorcerers were marginalized, outsiders in the communities where they attempted to use their knowledge to make a living. If they, in addition, had a relatively dark complexion (but not dark enough to be classified as *negro*), they would easily be referred to by the local community as "mulatto." In this way, deracinated individuals of any ethnic origin, with or without African ancestry, could become mulattos overnight if they moved to a new community. The term "mulatto" thus mainly indicated "otherness" in the perception of the local community, the combination of strangeness and dark complexion making them easy targets for accusations of witchcraft and sorcery.

---

[1] Many works based on archival study in the Inquisitorial collections have appeared in the last decades. See Mary E. Giles, ed., *Women in the Inquisition: Spain and the New World* (Baltimore: John Hopkins University Press, 1998); M. E. Perry and Anne J. Cruz, eds., *Cultural Encounters: The Impact of the Inquisition in Spain and the New World* (Berkeley: University of California Press, 1991); Nicholas Griffiths and Fernando Cervantes., eds., *Spiritual Encounters: Interactions between Christianity and Native Religions in Colonial America* (Lincoln: University of Nebraska Press, 1999); Behar et al., "Sex and Sin: Witchcraft and the Devil in Late-Colonial Mexico," *American Ethnologist* 14 no 1 (1987); Joaquin Pérez Villenueva and Bartolomé Escandell Bonet, *Historia de la Inquisición en España y América: Conocimiento certífico y el proceso histórico de la Institución, 1478-1834* (Madrid: Centro de Estudios Inquisitoriales, 1984); Richard E. Greenleaf's *The Mexican Inquisition of the Sixteenth Century* (Albuquerque: University of New Mexico Press, 1969) A bibliographical overview of works on the history of the Mexican Inquisition is also offered by José Toribio Medina in *Historia del Santo Oficio de la Inquisición en Mexico* (Mexico City: Universidad Autónoma de México, 1987). Works like Martha Few, "Women, Religion, and Power: Gender and Resistance in Daily Life in Late-Seventeenth-Century Santiago de Guatemala," *Ethnohistory* 42 no 4 (1995), and Ana Luisa Izquierdo, "Un documento novohispano del siglo XVII, como fuente para el estudio de la religion Maya," *Estudios de Cultura Maya* XIX (Mexico: UNAM, 1992) present case studies involving Indians and castas. Alejandra B. Osorio, "El callejón de soledad: Vectors of Cultural Hybridity in Seventeenth-Century Lima," (Griffiths and Cervantes, 1999: 198-229) discusses cultural hybridity and magic in colonial Lima based on Inquisitorial records.

[2] Jean Pierre Dedieu, "The Archives of the Holy Office as a Source for Historical Anthropology," in Gustav Henningsen, John Tedeschi, and Charles Amiel, eds., *The Inquisition in Early Modern Europe: Studies on Sources and Methods* (De Kalb, IL: Northern Illinois University Press, 1986), 161.

[3] See Renato Rosaldo, "From the Door of His Tent: The Field Worker and the Inquisitor," in James Clifford and George Marcus, eds., *Writing Culture: The Poetics and Politics of Ethnography* (Berkeley: University of California Press, 1986). In his critique of the use of Inquisitorial materials as historical evidence, Rosaldo takes the extreme position that the use of Inquisitorial records to "give voice" to 14th century French peasants is nothing but an abuse of ethnographic authority, given the circumstances under which these statements were written down.

[4] The decades between 1560 and 1630 had been a period of vitality and high activity for the Inquisition. In this period, the Inquisition gave priority to bigamy, incest, adultery, and every form of sexual activity that took place

outside legitimate marriage, but the number of superstition and witchcraft trials also increased. The impact of these reforms on popular culture in 16th- and 17th-century Spain and the impact of Tridentine piety are discussed in Sara T. Nalle, *God in La Mancha: Religious Reform and the People of Cuenca, 1500-1650* (Baltimore: John Hopkins University Press, 1992). In the period 1560-1614, only 4% of the cases that were brought in for the Inquisition in Spain fell into the witchcraft category. In the period 1615-1700, the number increased to 17%. See Geoffrey Parker, "Some Recent Work on the Inquisition in Spain and Italy," *Journal of Modern History* 54, no. 3 (1982): 519-532, (529).

[5] As might be expected, the priorities of the Inquisition differed considerably between the American and the Spanish tribunals. In Mexico, 42% of the cases involved "religious crimes," 18% involved "sexual crimes," 13% involved heresies, and Only 0.7% of the cases involved idolatries. In Spain, however, 43% of the cases involved heresies, 40% involved religious crimes and only 7% involved sexual crimes.

[6] Behar argues that the Inquisition "increasingly abandoned the challenge of evangelising the lower classes" (45) as it evolved into an active agent in secular politics during the 18th century.

[7] See Fernando Cervantes, *The Devil in the New World: The Impact of Diabolism in New Spain* (New Haven: Yale University Press, 1994) for a thorough study of diabolism in colonial Mexico.

[8] Document from Archivo General de la Nación, tomo: Inquisición, Mexico City (hereafter AGN Inq.): Inquicision Vol. 729, exp. 11, fol(s). 391r-392v

[9] AGN Inq. Vol. 1175, exp.38, fol(s). 409v-410r

[10] AGN Inq. Vol. 844 (segunda parte), exp. Sin número, fol(s). 482r-485r

[11] AGN Inq. Vol. 533, exp. 47, fol(s). 242r-245r

[12] AGN Inq. Vol. 753, exp. Sin número, fol(s). 412r-412v

[13] AGN Inq. Vol. 753, exp. Sin número, fol(s). 386r-386v

[14] Behar, 37-38, mentions the use of the hummingbird and its sexual symbolism in late colonial love magic as one example of the extent to which "indigenous elements formed part of [the] multi-layered magical repertoire" of the sorcerers.

[15] AGN Inq. Vol 791 exp. 31 fol(s). 487r-488r

[16] Still, a large number of Indians continued to be accused of witchcraft and sorcery by other non-Indians, but most of these cases were dismissed by the Inquisition without trial after a preliminary investigation. However, as Greenleaf (1966: 75, 1969: 173) shows, the Inquisition continued to investigate instances of native idolatry and superstition even if these investigations did not lead to trial.

[17] See Quezada, 1991: 39-41.

[18] AGN Inq. (primera parte), exp. 2, fol(s). 99r-101v

[19] AGN Inq. Vol. 1151, exp. 15, fol(s) 312r-313v

[20] AGN Inq. Vol. 760, exp. 8, fol(s) 135r-136v

[21] See Cope, 106-124. Upwardly mobile *castas* first became receptive to Spanish elite notions on race when *castizos* or *mestizos* tried to move into the

Spanish category, but failed to make the transition despite relative wealth and a high social standing.

[22] AGN Inq. Vol. 544 Segunda parte, exp. 29, fol(s). 551r-552v

[23] AGN Inq. Vol. 826, exp. 8, fol(s). 206r-206v

[24] AGN Inq. Vol. 828, exp.1, fol(s). 12r-19v

[25] AGN Inq. Vol. 828, exp.1, fol(s). 231r-237v

[26] AGN Inq. Vol. 828, exp.1, fol(s). 170r-170v

[27] AGN Inq. Vol. 828 exp.1, fol(s). 2r-5v

[28] AGN Inq. Vol 304, exp. 28, f. 200-204 (letter from fray Ambrosio Corrilo dated 1617), AGN Inquisicion vol.317 exp. 19, f 2 (testimony against Gaspar de Solis and his wife Doña Mariana de Rivera).

[29] It was also accepted that the indigenous specialists possessed important knowledge about local medical plants and diseases, which were largely unknown to Spanish physicians. In the 16th century, works like *Codex Badianus* (1552) appeared, in which indigenous medical knowledge about local herbs and medicinal plants was presented for Spanish physicians.

[30] See Jack D. Forbes, *Africans and Native Americans: The Language of Race and the Evolution of Red-Black Peoples* (Urbana: University of Illinois Press, 1993).

[31] Only a few studies deal with European or "white" slavery in Spanish America. See Juan F. Maura, "Esclavas Españolas en el Nuevo Mundo: Una Nota Histórica," *Colonial Latin American Historical Review* 2, no. 2 (Spring 1993), for a recent study of female Christian Spanish slaves in the New World.

[32] AGN Inq. vol. 1165 exp. 1 fol(s). 123r

[33] The Document is kept in Hispanic Document Collection, no 20, Gilcrease Museum, Tulsa, Oklahoma.

[34] Even the Indian category is problematical. A person classified as *indio*, or even *indio tributario*, could in many instances be an individual with African or European forefathers whose ancestors had been assimilated into Indian society. See Bernardo García Martinez, *Los Pueblos de la Sierra. El poder y el espacio entre los indios del norte de Puebla hasta 1700* (Mexico City, 1987) and "Pueblos de Indios, Pueblos de Castas: New Settlements and traditional Corporate Organization in Eighteenth-Century New Spain," in Arij Ouweneel and Simon Miller, eds., *The Indian Community of Colonial Mexico* (Amsterdam: CEDLA, 1990).

Chapter 5

A Taste for Flesh: British Slavery, Sentiment, and the Epistemology of Race and Domination[1]

Richard Milton Juang

Toward the end of a course on British slavery, an undergraduate of mine mused that she found it surprising that the humanitarian effort to end slavery should have failed to alleviate the racisms shaped in the crucible of the transatlantic slave trade. By 1834, I suggested, the philosophical foundations for what would later be known as scientific racism had been laid with a degree of independence equal to that of biology, anthropology, and medicine. Yet in retrospect, my answer was insufficient, for the philosophies of scientific racism were never so much a part of English *popular* parlance as were the images born of England's substantial role in the slave trade and made visible in the racial typologies of 18th- and 19th-century literature. What remains to be more fully accounted for are the ways in which racial hierarchies were diffused through beliefs about human nature—at what Antonio Gramsci calls the "common-sense" level of ideology—and embedded in "popular system[s] of ideas and practices" for making sense of subjectivities and bodies.[2]

Following upon Edward Said's seminal *Orientalism*, recent studies have recognized racialized colonialism as historically integral to the project of constructing the ideal of the European bourgeois subject. At the height of imperialism, that ideal governed the metropolitan discourse of interiority and subjectivity through and against the backdrop of highly regulated and intensely analyzed "marginal" subjectivities. As Ann Laura Stoler has argued, the discourse of subjectivity was not securely centered in Europe, but located in a circulation between imperial peripheries and metropolitan centers, wherein the process of colonialism "was not only about the importation of middle-class sensibilities to the colonies, but about the *making* of them."[3] Within the context of transatlantic colonialism and the slave trade, the imagining of European interiorities and European bodies— including the formation of a discrete concept of whiteness—cannot be separated from the discursive "shaping" of slave bodies and the imagining of slave interiorities across the 18th century. I hope to trace here one of the pivotal transformations in what I would call the epistemology of slavery and race, and its role in the persistence of racism after British emancipation.

In 1774, the Jamaican justice, Edward Long, asserted that "the White and the Negroe are two distinct species," and that Africans were biologically closer to "ourang-outangs" than to Europeans.[4] Both statements are all too familiar to us as entrenched parts of the idiom of biological racism; our familiarity has tended to occlude the fact that, as Roxann Wheeler notes, Long's view was a minority one at the time and a "radical departure from centuries of assumptions about the shared nature and capabilities of humans."[5] Long's biologism is meant to act in the service of aligning claims about physiology with his overarching belief in the superiority of the inner nature of white Europeans over that of black Africans—a belief patently visible throughout the 3 volumes of his *History of Jamaica*. As George Mosse observes, the interest in human classification of 18th-century naturalists was "fused" with classical aesthetic ideals so that "human nature came to be defined in aesthetic terms, with significant stress on the outward physical signs of inner rationality and harmony."[6] What is at stake for Long is the creation of a structure of knowledge in which the nature of the body fits the nature of the mind—premised, of course, upon the inferiority of both black bodies and minds.

A significant dimension of the slavery debates was the struggle not only over competing claims about the racial character of "inner" natures and bodies, but also about the particular epistemological framework that would shape and define those claims. In the late 17th and early 18th centuries, prior to the emergence of organized abolitionism, the rationalism and materialism of the early Enlightenment did not stand substantially in the way of slavery, even though the seeds of a challenge to its legitimacy were certainly present. It is worth recalling that Locke's famous opening declaration in his first

Treatise of Government—that slavery was "so vile and miserable an Estate of Man" as to be antithetical to the English national character—was followed in the *Second Treatise* by a justification of slavery as a private war between master and slave. Critical to the early Enlightenment's orchestration of knowledge and power was a framework in which, as Paul Gilroy argues, "racial terror [was] not merely compatible with occidental rationality, but cheerfully complicit with it."[7] The articulation of reason as a locus of power relations gives us a way of rereading the Enlightenment's relationship to the simultaneously ancient practice of slavery, and the modernity of its organization and articulation on the West Indian plantation.[8]

The Domination of Reason

In the course of his Barbadan travelogue, the 17th-century planter, Richard Ligon, observes that slaves

> believe in a Resurrection, and that they shall go into their own Countrey again, and have their youth renewed. And lodging this opinion in their hearts, they make it an ordinary practice, upon any great fright, or threatening of their Masters, to hang themselves.
> But Collonel *Walrond* having lost three or four of his best *Negroes* this way ... caused one of their heads to be cut off, and set upon a pole a dozen foot high; and having done that, caused all his *Negroes* to come forth, and march round about this head, and bid them look on it, whether this were not the head of such a one that hang'd himself. Which they acknowledging, he told them, That they were in a main errour, in thinking they went into their own Countreys, after they were dead; for, this mans head was here, as they all were witnesses of; and how was it possible, the body could go without a head. Being convinc'd by this sad, yet lively spectacle, they changed their opinions; and after that, no more hanged themselves.[9]

While perhaps most well known as an early source of the tale of Yarico and Inkle, Ligon's *True and Exact History of the Island of Barbados* is also a report on the mechanics of the sugar industry and a travel narrative that becomes a significant reference point for later histories of the West Indies.[10] It is important to recognize here that suicide, along with sabotage, work stoppages, and outright rebellion, was often a mode of resistance, a kind of rebellion of last resort. Insofar as suicide here stands within the framework of a return to "their own Countrey again," it represents a refusal of the severing of familial and community identities and the "social death" that form the sociological foundations of enslavement.[11] Within a context of struggle, then, the account of Colonel Walrond's response operates as a fantasy of reasserted domination. The dimension of fantasy in Ligon's account lies not so much in the sense that this is more fiction than fact, but in the dramatic staging of this plantation scene; the orderly march of the slaves around the head, Colonel Walrond's speech, the deliberation of the slaves and their submission to reason are all moments in a kind of pedagogical high drama, one pervaded by a strong element of wish-fulfillment.

At the heart of Ligon's account is the orchestration of power and the claim, not only of greater knowledge, but of superior rationality. Ligon imagines the severed head, the classic motif of domination through terror, transformed into a demonstration of the power of reason. The head ceases to be a synecdoche for violence and subordination; rather, its coercive power is imagined as being in harmony with the power of Enlightenment reason. More specifically, Colonel Walrond's slaves become positioned within the domain of what David Brion Davis calls the Enlightenment's "rational theology"; the supposed "errour" of Walrond's slaves lies not only their adherence to an African religion, but in that religion's errors of reasoning. The desired effect is not only to convince the slaves of a "main errour, in thinking" but to interpellate them as subjects who can be mastered by the presumed superiority of European reason and materialism.

Such pedagogical dramas and their blending of the fantasy of domination by reason with the materiality of violent coercion are not uncommon in the early 18th century. Indeed, they are central to narratives of social disorder concerning slaves and slave rebellion. In 1704, the slave trader, William Snelgrave, quelled an uprising aboard his ship and his 1734 recollection of it imagines the terrain of struggle as not only material but discursive. His slaves not only resist their bondage but challenge its legitimacy in a manner that both compels and allows Snelgrave to respond in kind:

> After we had secured these People, I called the Linguists, and ordered them to bid the Men-Negroes between Decks be quiet; (for there was a great noise amongst them.) On their being silent, I asked, What had induced them to mutiny? They answered, I was a great Rogue to buy them, in order to carry them away from their own Country; and that they were resolved to regain their Liberty if possible. I replied That they had forfeited their Freedom before I bought them, either by Crimes, or by being taken in War, according to the Custom of their Country; and they being now my Property, I was resolved to let them feel my Resentment, if they abused my Kindness: asking at the same time, Whether they had been ill used by the by the white Men, or had wanted for any thing the Ship afforded? To this they replied, They had nothing to complain of. Then I observed to them, That if they should gain their Point and escape to the Shore, it would be no Advantage to them, because their Countrymen would catch them, and sell them to other Ships. This served my purpose, and they seemed to be convinced

of their Fault, begging, I would forgive them, and promising for the future to be obedient, and never mutiny again, if I would not punish them this time. This I readily granted, and so they went to sleep.[12]

Like Ligon, Snelgrave offers a vision of the efficacy of a convergence between coercion and the discourse of reason in the maintenance of domination. The starkness of the transformation from active rebellion to active submission in Snelgrave's narrative imagines slaves reshaped through a pedagogical imposition of the languages of market rationality and social contract that are the equivalent of overwhelming force. Both Ligon and Snelgrave ask their readers to recognize the presumed virtues of a certain calculus of reason and direct domination in assuring social order. Indeed, both men express a kind of perverse Enlightenment optimism about the power of empirical observation and deliberation. Where persuasion is structured as power, the concept of "reason" operates as an external force imposed upon the mind of slaves, complementing the violence that coercion inflicted upon the body. There is little interest in either slave interiorities or in the immanent logic of African culture and theology. Ligon and Snelgrave claim to provide an understanding of the nature of the slaves only to the extent that their knowledge is a means of imaging how best to render them tractable instruments of a slave economy. Within such an economy of knowledge, slaves' minds and bodies are imagined largely as objects within a field of power and simple surfaces to be written upon and molded to assure social order. Indeed, for Snelgrave, the pedagogical fantasy becomes exchanged with the practice of violent subordination: the slave revolt resumes the next day and is subdued only by the raw terror of a man "hoisted up to the Yard-arm" and executed.[13]

The Culture of Sentiment

From the mid-18th century onwards, the representation of slave bodies, minds, and imaginations undergoes a sea-change, and the question of slave interiorities and inner natures becomes central to the slavery debates. The shift is prompted to some extent by the failure of what might be termed simple objectification and domination; Snelgrave's inability to "persuade" his slaves to willingly remain enslaved is a telling case in point. However, the representational shift was not solely an event at the cultural periphery; rather, there is a transculturation that takes place around the discourse of subjectivity in both colony and metropole.[14] The broader cultural logic I want to attend to here is the emergence of a culture of sentiment in which the civilized and cultivated man or woman of the 18th century is defined by the capacity for empathy, for recognizing and echoing the pains and pleasures of others, and conversely, experiencing revulsion towards suffering and immorality. David Hume in *An Enquiry Concerning the Principles of Morals*, observes that

> no qualities are more entitled to the general good-will and approbation of mankind than beneficence and humanity, friendship and gratitude, natural affection and public spirit, or whatever proceeds from a tender sympathy with others, and a generous concern for our kind and species. These whenever they appear, seem to transfuse themselves, in a manner, into each beholder, and to call forth, in their own behalf, the same favourable and affectionate sentiments which they exert on all around.[15]

Sentiment was a vocabulary for conceiving of interiority, and the 18th century's "man of feeling" was constructed as one of its ideals. The debates over slavery and the representations of slave bodies by both pro- and anti-slavery forces are caught up in the development of this culture of sentiment, with both sides appealing to what David Brion Davis aptly calls "the posture of the sensitive spectator."[16] As Mary Louise Pratt observes:

> In part through the rise of the abolitionist movement, and in part through the rise of travel literature as a profitable print industry, sentimentality consolidated itself quite suddenly in the 1780's and 1790's as a powerful mode for representing colonial relations and the imperial frontier. In both travel writing and imaginative literature, the domestic subject of empire found itself enjoined to share new passion, to identify with expansion in a new way, through empathy with individual victim-heroes and heroines.[17]

The defenders of slavery also take up the language of sentiment and interiority and commence an ideological struggle that centers, in no small part, around the "domestic subject" and the imagining of white and black bodies.[18] To be sure, slave bodies in the late 18th century remained a site for demonstrating social relations, just as they had earlier done for Ligon and Snelgrave. However, with the emergence of organized abolitionism, the defenders of slavery also drew upon the idiom of sentiment and sensibility with the hope of reclaiming their eroding moral ground. Indeed, Edward Long presents Snelgrave as an example of the "benevolent" slaver whose actions are those of an 18th-century man of feeling. Snelgrave becomes, in Long's recounting, an upholder of domestic affections, when, during a voyage to Africa, he saves a child from human sacrifice and reunites him with his mother:

> Snelgrave redeemed the child at the king's own price, and carrying his bargain on board ship, found that this infant's mother had been sold to him the very day before; whose joy on thus meeting again with her son,

so unexpectedly rescued from the brink of slaughter, he pathetically describes; adding, that the story coming to be known among all the Blacks on board, it dispelled their fears, and impressed them with so favourable an opinion of the white men, that although he had three hundred in all, they gave him not the least disturbance during the voyage. When their prejudices were dissipated by so striking an example of humanity shewn to a Negroe, they perceived the Whites were not such bugbears as they had been induced to believe, and grew happy and peaceable, on finding that a white master was more likely to be more merciful toward them than a black one.[19]

Snelgrave is rewritten by Long, not as the master of superior force, but as the man-of-feeling able to both "impress" and draw out good feeling among others. That both mother and child will be sold as chattel is of little consequence to Long; instead, the "pathos" of domesticity becomes the avenue for social order. The affirmation of racial subordination is achieved here, not by greater reason or force, but by the imagined acknowledgement by the slaves of a racialized hierarchy of compassion, wherein "a white master was more likely to be more merciful toward them than a black one."

In short, *both* abolitionist and pro-slavery arguments contained a host of knowledge claims about slave interiorities attached to speculations about the relationship between black interiorities and black bodies. In 1789, the historian Bryan Edwards, an influential voice of the West Indian plantocracy, a contemporary of Edward Long and an admirer of his *History of Jamaica*, offered up a narrative of a slave rebellion to show the dangers of emancipation:

The rebels took the opportunity of their owner's absence to surround the dwelling house, and seize the person, of their unhappy mistress. She was a young lady of great beauty, meek modest and unoffending; had been married about two years, and was in bed with a lovely infant, when the bloody savages surrounded the house and demanded her person. Resistance and prayers were equally fruitless. The female Slaves who attended her, dared not to express their pity, if pity they felt, but having hastily thrown a loose robe over her, delivered the miserable victim into their hands, and she heard the savages calmly deliberate on the means of putting her to death, by the most lingering torments, without uttering a single groan; so entirely were her faculties absorbed in astonishment and horror. It happened, however, that her person and appearance (for the moon shone bright) excited the appetites of the ringleader of the savages, who declared that he would carry her into the woods, and preserve her to be his mistress. The others, dreading his resentment, reluctantly consented, and the next object of their cruelty was the child, which they devoted to instant destruction.—Nature now resumed her seat in the bosom of the unfortunate mother. She screamed aloud, and clasping the knees of him

who had spared her life, implored him to save her infant. She implored
in vain. The savages derived a luxury from her cries, and holding up the
poor babe by the feet, in the mother's sight, they cleft it in twain with a
hatchet.[20]

Edwards's audience is asked not only to champion but also to identify
with the terrorized mother: her astonishment is supposedly our
astonishment; her horror, our horror. It is not by chance that a figure of
female domesticity is chosen here; as Nancy Armstrong has argued,
novels that centered around domesticity and female sensibility were
cornerstones for the construction of bourgeois self-imagining and
subjectivity.[21] At the simplest level, Edwards asks us to comprehend
these rebellious slaves as implacable embodiments of gothic terror.
What is more crucial here, however, is that our gaze moves through a
thick matrix of affects, sentiments, and identifications. The "plot" of
Edwards's narrative is driven less by a struggle over superior claims to
reason (as in Snelgrave's account) than by the workings of affects and
sentiments—the forces of "pity," "appetites," "dread," and
"resentment"—emerging, apparently, from within the slaves
themselves. Not least of all, the narrative calls for its audience to
recognize and recoil from an intrinsic sexual sadism carried within the
implacable black body, and the vulnerability of white flesh against its
force and desire. These incommensurable forms of embodied
subjectivity allow for the concept of an absolute racial division—one
that is perilous to cross—cast in the language and ethics of sentiment,
and articulated as a "natural," intrinsic part of subjectivity and moral
agency. Social order, according to Edwards, rests on the domination
and regulation of this complex web of racialized inner natures,
sentiments and passions.

Of course, portraits of African and black savagery have a lengthy
history; early Barbadian slave laws placed slaves outside the social
realm, figuring them as personifications of the Hobbesian state of
nature—a state "of Barbarous, Wild, and Savage Natures, and such as
renders them wholly unqualified to be governed by the Laws, Customs,
and Practices of our Nations."[22] Within the slave laws, an intricate
system of tortures and regulations was thus provided as the means to
master the ungovernable. What is novel in Edwards's account is his
attempt to bring the problem of governance into the interior world of
slaves and racial identity. Within Edwards's use of the discourse of
sentiment, it become possible to imagine a transformation of slaves
from dangerous savages to grateful servants, not through the imposition
of an external force but through an appeal to an interior logic of natural
sentiments and sensibility. If savage appetites are unleashed when
slaves are unbound, then the same slaves can be made gratefully

submissive when enslaved, as in this example of an ill slave who appears dejected: "*Massa* said the Negro (in a tone of self-reproach and conscious degeneracy) *since me come to White man's country me lub* (love) *life too much!*"[23]

Overall, Edwards defends the morality of subordination and enslavement not by reference to an external logic, such as the legitimacy of purchase, but by the inner tendency of slaves to make immoral choices on one hand, and their gratitude for subordination on the other. Edwards imagines slaves as simultaneously and somewhat paradoxically driven by innate racial characteristics—a mixture of craveness and brutality—and a moral agency with the capacity for "self-reproach" and "conscious degeneracy." The capacity for reason present in Ligon's and Snelgrave's accounts is not lost; rather, in Edwards's imagination, it is turned inwards as a kind of rudimentary self-awareness and individuation. This is, to some degree, a concession of agency and individual consciousness forced upon slavery's advocates by the work of slave resistance, slave narratives, and abolitionists. However, as with modern racializing thought, Edwards imagines an individuation of slaves into moral agents who, in turn, represent a generalized racial nature and hierarchy.

What is at stake in Edwards's writings is the construction of whiteness as it takes place against the backdrop of claims about and over black interiorities and bodies. In Ligon and Snelgrave, we see a racialization of the figure of reason and the power of reason, through the slave master. In the early Enlightenment, whiteness exists in a relationship of zero-sum domination, reason and legitimacy against black rebellion. By the early 19th century, confrontations between white and black take on a different tenor, centered around the ability of white authority to elicit willing subordination. Nowhere is this more strikingly played out than in one of the stranger moments in the representation of slave rebellion; R. C. Dallas's 1803 *History of the Maroons* provides a portrait of the famous Maroon leader Cudjoe who, at the cusp of the signing of a treaty, suddenly takes on, according to Dallas, a posture of craven submission:

> As the gentlemen approached Cudjoe, he appeared to be in great trepidation, but whether caused by joy or fear was doubtful; though he was certainly under the protecting fire of his own men, and the negotiators were unarmed. Colonel Guthrie advanced to him holding out his hand which Cudjoe seized and kissed. He then threw himself on the ground, embracing Guthrie's legs, kissing his feet, and asking his pardon. He seemed to have lost all of his ferocity, and to have become humble, penitent and abject. The rest of the Maroons, followed the example of their chief, prostrated themselves, and expressed the most unbounded joy at the sincerity show on the side of the white people.[24]

Cudjoe's actions seem, at best, improbable; Thomas Thistlewood, a Jamaican slave driver, records Cudjoe traveling fearlessly afterwards around the island in 1753.[25] Dallas seems unaware of the mockery and parody that were most likely part of Cudjoe's actions. Instead, his causal account of such a stark transformation lies within the language and ethics of sentiment—from ferocity and fearfulness to joy to gratitude—and is linked to elaborate physical postures of submission. An inherent cravenness, according to Dallas, is at once embedded in and expressed through a body whose postures are "humble, penitent and abject." In this drama of white authority confronting black rebellion, the inner world and outer physical performance of blackness become harmoniously aligned (in Dallas's view) within a framework of subordination. As with the ideological system exemplified by Edwards's writings, a natural ferocity and a natural subservience stand side by side, waiting to be shaped by the ascendance or failure of white authority.

For Edwards and others, a crucial component of "knowing slaves" is the self-assumed capacity of whiteness not only to oppose and dominate black bodies but to enter into black interiority. Some years after the abolition of the slave trade, George Pinckard provides a revealing transformation of Ligon's narrative of the impaled head:

> The faith of these poor ignorant slaves, regarding a happy transmigration, after death, might seem calculated to lead them to the crime of suicide; and this effect of their superstition is said not to have been unfrequent among them. A tale is told of a singular remedy having been practiced against this fatal proceeding of the negroes. Several individuals of a gang having hanged themselves in order to escape from a cruel master; and others being about to avoid his severities by similar means, he prevented them, by the happy expedient of threatening to hang himself also, and to transmigrate, with them, carrying the whip in his hand, into their own country; where he would punish them ten times more severely than he had hitherto done. The stratagem is said to have succeeded. Finding they could not, thus, escape from the tyrranic lash, they resolved, rather than receive disgraceful stripes, among their African friends, to continue their existence under all the hardships of slavery.[26]

Unlike Ligon's Colonel Walrond, the tale offered up here does not oppose black reason to superior white reason. Rather, white reason is claimed to able to enter into the logic of black beliefs and work from within it. In a sense this is the fantasy of slave owners in the early 19th century who, in the context of growing abolitionist and emancipationist feeling, imagine possessing a capacity to pursue slaves into those realms of spirituality, interiority and identity that have persistently eluded them.

Voiceless Bodies

I have suggested thus far that by the end of the 18th century, slavery's advocates, in response to abolitionism, sought to condemn slaves to slavery, and Africans and blacks more generally to subservience, by recasting the concept of racial hierarchy within the language of sentiment and interiority. Having themselves already begun by working within the framework of sentiment, abolitionists and emancipationists could not, in turn, fully extricate themselves from the terms of what would be an increasingly invasive epistemology imposed upon black bodies and subjectivities.

In 1823, an emancipationist pamphlet portrayed the horrors of the illegal traffic in slaves by turning the reader's gaze upon the condition of black bodies on board the slave ship: "[T]hey were chained to each other by the arms and legs.... From their confinements and sufferings, they often injured themselves by beating; and vented their grief upon such as were next to them, by biting and tearing their flesh."[27] The pamphlet goes on to appeal to the reader not only to identify with the feelings of the slave, but with the slave encased, first in the ship, then in his tormented body and, finally, in a crush of black flesh:

> Reader! look at the Plate, and dwell for a few moments on those emotions which thou must feel. Think of the miseries to which these wretched, harmless sufferers are subjected. Picture to thyself a scene, in which, in this narrow space, one is bemoaning the loss of his nearest connexions in life, and brooding, in melancholy sadness, over the cruelties and sufferings under which he is to spend the remainder of his days. See another pining with sickness, languid from loss of appetite, and from the noxious air which he must breathe, treated in this wretched condition with indifference, and even with unkindness by those who lie next to him. Look at a third, subjected to the torture of the thumb-screw, or some other instrument of pain, because he refuses to partake of food which, in his mournful state, he cannot relish. Think of others who are biting each other's flesh, and thus, in the bitterness of their grief, attempting to vent the anguish of their hearts.
>
> ... [W]ilt thou any longer hesitate to raise thy voice on behalf of enslaved Africans; to do thy utmost to make known to others the continuance of scenes of agony and cruelty; and boldly assert that, although their colour is different from thine, and their rulers may sell them into cruel bondage, they are equally with thyself entitled to the blessings of liberty?[28]

It is important to note that what is rhetorically central in this text is the silencing of the slaves themselves by an equation of black slaves with voiceless bodies. Within the pamphlet's rhetoric, such silence is necessary in order to create a space that may then be filled with the voices of emancipation. It is the emancipationist who must "vent the anguish of [the slaves'] hearts." Despite the circulation of slave narratives and the presence of black servants and workers in Liverpool, Bristol, and London, anti-slavery writings tended to favor an appeal to the empathic abilities of emancipationists by imagining scenes of abjection. In making this brief critical note of emancipationist writings, I do not mean to undermine the value of the anti-slavery movement or to underplay the venality and viciousness of slavery's advocates. However, as Saidiya Hartman argues, often present in anti-slavery representations is a "precariousness of empathy and the thin line between witness and spectator," by which "the effort to counteract the commonplace callousness to black suffering requires that the white body be positioned in the place of the black body in order make this suffering visible and intelligible...." Hartman further argues "that empathy is doubled-edged, for in making the other's suffering one's own this suffering is occluded by the other's obliteration."[29] What becomes visible in the representation of slavery generally is a struggle centered around claims about the nature of slave interiorities within which the authority of white readers take center stage, and black bodies and subjectivities become a backdrop to the cultivation and calibration of white European sensibilities.

The articulation of reason as an instrument of domination in West Indian slavery was inseparable from the new economic and sociological realities being formed by transatlantic mercantile interests and the emerging bourgeois plantocracy. Robin Blackburn notes that "the British Caribbean was the setting for a prodigious new reality, a plantation system at a new pitch of intensive organization and commercialization.... By comparison with Brazilian methods, the new plantation required a more intensive, and a more closely invigilated, work regime."[30] The mid-century transformation of the epistemology of domination thus mirrors a general shift in the "disciplining" of subjects and bodies, whereby, as Michel Foucault describes it,

> an art of the human body was born, which was directed not only at the growth of its skills, nor at the intensification of its subjection, but at the formation of a relation that in the mechanism itself makes it more obedient as it becomes more useful, and conversely ... [t]he human body was entering a machinery of power that explores it, breaks it down and rearranges it.[31]

Where the 17th century saw the black body as a slate to be forcibly written upon by European claims of knowledge and domination, the late 18th century brings to bear an excavation of the body, and the claims to know slave subjectivities from within. It is an excavation of knowledge that takes place within a highly physicalized register that, in its worst manifestations, imagines black bodies as marionette-like extensions of European sensibilities.

By the end of the 18th century, enslaved black bodies were no longer epistemologically outside the social. They were subject to the same disciplinary structures of knowledge that created other "docile bodies," to use Foucault's vocabulary. This did not erase the legacies and ideologies of racial domination so central to the slave trade. On the contrary, racial hierarchies were incorporated into and diffused throughout the emerging vocabularies for making sense of individual subjectivities and bodies, so that by the end of the 19th century they would be part of Gramsci's "common-sense" level of ideology, so necessary for the hegemony of race-thinking.

Finally, it is crucial to end by distinguishing between the projection in these narratives of an agency that imposes the authority of whiteness and one that implicitly asserts a counteracting critical consciousness. What remains latent in these particular texts are the violent discursive conflicts and negotiations between masters and slaves that are always present in the narratives of slavery. I noted earlier that Cudjoe's actions in Dallas's narrative might be read as mocking and parodic. In similar fashion, the invocation of "Liberty" by the rebelling slaves aboard Snelgrave's ship implies the presence of a kind of reverse-discourse, or a contestation over legitimacy. Domination is not absolute, not even in the most venal of the pro-slavery texts, and the thread of resistance that runs through these texts traces nothing less than an anti-racist counter-history.

---

[1] This paper was supported generously by the staff of the Cornell Rare Book and Manuscript Collection and by grants from the Cornell Graduate School and the Mario Einaudi Center for International Studies.

[2] Michael Omi and Howard Winant, *Racial Formation in the United States* (New York: Routledge, 1994), 67. The turn to Gramsci's work on ideology, particularly the concept of hegemony, has been fruitful for grappling with race as a discourse that appears at once highly fragmented and systemically all-pervasive. See also Stuart Hall, "Gramsci's Relevance for the Study of Race and Ethnicity," in *Stuart Hall: Critical Dialogues in Cultural Studies*, ed. David Morley and Kuan-Hsing Chen (London: Routledge, 1996).

[3] Ann Laura Stoler, *Race and the Education of Desire: Foucault's* History of Sexuality *and the Colonial Order of Things* (Durham: Duke University Press, 1995), 99.

[4] Edward Long, *The History of Jamaica*, 3 vols. (London, 1774), 2: 336.

[5] Roxann Wheeler, *The Complexion of Race: Categories of Difference in Eighteenth-Century British Culture* (Philadelphia: University of Pennsylvania Press, 2000), 37.

[6] George L. Mosse, *Toward the Final Solution: A History of European Racism* (New York: Howard Fertig, 1978), 2.

[7] Paul Gilroy, *The Black Atlantic: Modernity and Double Consciousness* (Cambridge: Harvard University Press, 1993), 56.

[8] Particularly productive and recent attempts to account for the concept of race, the specific contours of racism, and the uses of racial hierarchies and subordination have emphasized race not only as a social construction, but, as Ira Berlin insists, a "historical construction" wherein "race, no less than class, is the product of history, and it only exists on the contested social terrain in which men and women struggle to control their destinies." See also Ann Laura Stoler, "Racial Histories and Their Regimes of Truth," *Political Power and Social Theory* 11 (1997): 190-91.

[9] Richard Ligon, *A True and Exact History of the Island of Barbados* (London, 1673), 50-51.

[10] Ligon's anecdote about the belief in resurrection and its correction is particularly valuable in the fact of its circulation. In his 1707, 3-volume compendium of the flora and human fauna of the West Indies, the physician Hans Sloane refers to the belief, citing Ligon as his source.

[11] See Orlando Patterson, *Slavery and Social Death* (Cambridge: Harvard University Press, 1985). Patterson proposes a 3-part mutually-reinforcing structure of domination consisting of natal alienation (the severing of kinship ties), the stripping of honor and power, and social death.

[12] William Snelgrave, *A New Account of Guinea and the Slave Trade* (London, 1734), 170-71.

[13] Ibid., 183.

[14] See Fernando Ortiz, *Cuban Counterpoint*, trans. Harriet de Onis (Durham: Duke University Press, 1995). Transculturation "better expresses the different phases of the process of transition from one culture to another because this does not consist merely in acquiring another culture, which is what the English word *acculturation* really implies, but the process also necessarily involves the loss or uprooting of a previous culture, which could be defined as a deculturation. In addition it carries the idea of the consequent creation of new cultural phenomena, which could be called neoculturation .... the result of every union of cultures is similar to that of the reproductive process between individuals: the offspring always has something of both parents but is always different from each of them." Ortiz, 102-103.

[15] David Hume, *An Enquiry Concerning the Principles of Morals* (1777) (Oxford: Oxford University Press, 1975), 178.

[16] David Brion Davis, *The Problem of Slavery in Western Culture* (Oxford: Oxford University Press, 1966), 356.

[17] Mary Louise Pratt, *Imperial Eyes: Travel Writing and Transculturation* (New York: Routledge, 1992), 87.

[18] Indeed, Hume's famous footnote in "Of National Character," dismissively comparing the black Jamaican poet Francis Williams to a parrot, suggests that

the articulation of physiological *dis*-identification was no less part of the discourse of race within a culture of sentiment.

[19] Long, 2: 398.

[20] Bryan Edwards, "A Speech Delivered at a Free Conference between the Honourable the Council and Assembly of Jamaica Held the 19th November, 1789 on the Subject of Mr. Wilberforce's Propositions in the House of Commons concerning the Slave-Trade" (Kingston, 1789), 69-70.

[21] Nancy Armstrong, *Desire and Domestic Fiction: A Political History of the Novel* (London: Oxford University Press, 1987).

[22] "An Act for the Governing of Negroes" (Barbados, 1688), from the Cornell University Rare Book and Manuscript Collection.

[23] Bryan Edwards, *The History, Civil and Commercial of the British Colonies in the West Indies* (London, 1794), 1: 68-70.

[24] R. C. Dallas, *The History of the Maroons*, 2 vols. (London, 1803): 55-56.

[25] Thomas Thistlewood, *In Miserable Slavery*, ed. Douglass Hall (London: Macmillan, 1989), 57.

[26] George Pinckard, *Notes on the West Indies*, 2 vols. (London, 1816), 1: 133-34.

[27] Committee of the Religious Society of Friends, *Case of the Vigilante, a Ship Employed in the Slave Trade; with Some Reflections on that Traffic* (London, 1823), 10.

[28] Ibid., 12.

[29] Saidiya Hartman, *Scenes of Subjection: Terror, Slavery and Self-Making in Nineteenth-Century America* (New York: Oxford University Press, 1997), 19.

[30] Robin Blackburn, *The Making of New World Slavery: From the Baroque to the Modern, 1492-1800* (London: Verso, 1997), 260.

[31] Michel Foucault, *Discipline and Punish*, trans. Alan Sheridan (New York: Vintage, 1979), 138.

Chapter 6

Spirits of Earth and Sky: The Dynamics of European Encounters with Great Plains Aboriginal Groups

Michael C. Wilson

The northern Plains area of Canada and the United States is a land of earth and sky, where the horizon circle appears to be complete and unbroken. For its aboriginal groups, this land is unified by the four cardinal directions, radiating from center and touching the horizon. The circle is the symbol of perfection, the cosmogram. The dome of the sky meets the disc of the land in an eternal duality, suffused with the powers of spirits. The balance of the cosmos is a dominating concern, too easily mistaken by people of the Western cultural tradition for an obsession with the "balance of nature."

To all people—lengthy occupants or new arrivals—the land has meanings, both inherent and ascribed. Each group has claimed important places by naming and sometimes modifying them, creating a palimpsest of cultural landscapes that reflect their diverse, deeply held ideologies and values.[1] The reality that one cultural group assigns to the world may be, to another group, a distortion. Across cultures, difficulties in communication arise from both ambiguity of delivery and true differences in values, leading to misunderstandings, distrust, and even open conflict. Resolution can take generations of intercultural accommodation. Even in cases of perceived cultural hegemony, the oppressor can hardly fail to be influenced by the oppressed. However, there can be asymmetry to the flow, and the influences may or may not be directly acknowledged as such by the recipient.

Two Worlds Meet

Only 200 years ago, the northern Great Plains were the domain of such peoples as the Blackfoot, Atsina, Crow, and Assiniboin. They were largely nomadic, fitting their lives to seasonally-available resources such as the migratory buffalo (or bison) and elk (or wapiti). They had their profound differences and conflicts, but also lived in a fickle environment that favored flexible residence, interdependence, and intercultural negotiation. Their languages were varied and seldom mutually intelligible, from Athapaskan tonal languages to non-tonal Algonkian, Siouan, Salishan, and other stocks. Yet linguistically distinct groups were often co-resident; individuals were bilingual or even multilingual. Intercultural communication was further facilitated by a highly developed sign language that was rich in use of metaphors because of its limited vocabulary. Thus they had a long history of accommodation, negotiation and shared values, belying the stereotype of Plains Indians as tribes engaged in constant warfare with neighbors. Warfare was linked to prestige and involved an emphasis on raiding rather than battle; it was balanced by ritualized trading systems. Groups who were sworn enemies would still trade, using the calumet (pipe) ceremony to mark the seriousness and sanctity of the relationship.[2] Economic systems could therefore be maintained despite shifting political winds, a vital survival mechanism in the face of an equally fickle environment. Transient alliances and co-residence responded to changes in the land as well as to outside threats that overrode other, inherent sources of conflict. The most dramatic outside influence that they experienced was the arrival of Europeans.

European explorers and traders made forays into the area in the 1700s, but the Blackfoot in particular remained largely in control of their territory until the 1870s. Encounters between these groups from the Old and New Worlds underwent an evolutionary progression as each learned more about the other. By "evolution" I imply simply *change*, for the trajectory is only visible in retrospect; yet the history of these changes is one of intercultural accommodation as well as conflict. Basic world views of New and Old differed dramatically, for example, in terms of disposal of the dead and of the acceptance (or not) of exclusive and individual ownership of land, a European perspective profoundly different from the collective domain exercised by the aboriginal groups. These differences reflected equally profound differences in cosmology and in the relationships between people and nature, people and landscape.

The Canadian and United States Plains differed in that only in the latter were there "Indian Wars" of conquest; in Canada, treaties were achieved through negotiation facilitated by economic coercion in the face of the disappearance of the buffalo as a natural resource. Yet despite these differences, congratulations are not in order: incoming Europeans in both countries went to comparable lengths to edit out the presence of native peoples. Sir Cecil Denny, leading a military excursion for the North West Mounted Police in 1875, said this about Blackfoot territory:

> The view from the hill on the north side of the Bow [at Calgary], ... amazed us. ... of man we saw at first no sign. Indeed, toward the south no human dwelling existed nearer than Fort Macleod, though at Morley to the west the Rev. George McDougall had established a small mission among the Stony Indians. In fact, except for roving bands of Indians, all this vast country, for a thousand miles to the east at Winnipeg and two hundred miles to Edmonton in the north, at that time was utterly uninhabited.[3]

Apparently the portable tipis occupied by the Indians were not "human dwellings." Simon Schama commented that North American native peoples "were carefully and forcibly edited out" of documents and images produced by incoming Europeans, who developed a nonsensical concept of "wilderness" as empty of the very people who for millennia had structured it.[4]

As varied and successful as native adaptations had been, these people could not indefinitely withstand the European onslaught. Europeans possessed superior armaments, but native groups were also decimated by another means—introduced epidemic diseases. In some regions, 90% or more of the population was wiped out due to smallpox, whooping cough, tetanus, influenza, tuberculosis, measles, and other ailments: the bow wave of the oncoming European colonial vessel. Europeans took over the land. Some lands were willingly given by means of treaties, but to native peoples it was as if on loan, and they did not understand the treaties they were signing. Possessing a relationship of mutualism with the land, they did not conceive of the possibility that individuals could take ownership of specific tracts; they that they were entering into joint-use or loan agreements. A group of Blackfoot in Montana asked George Grinnell in the early 1900s "when they were to receive back the land which they had lent to the white people nearly forty years before."[5]

Landscapes Superimposed

The aboriginal landscape of circle and axis, held collectively by ethnic groups who occupied overlapping territories, was overprinted by a surveyed rectangular grid of fields and roadways imposed upon the Plains with little reference to landscape features. European settlers came with the ideal of a "productive landscape" and the idea that one must "improve" the land to produce "useful" commodities, most of which were introduced exotics like their producers. The Western ideal was for a family to lay claim to a circumscribed block of land, and Christian teachings gave the view that resources were put there for the use of people. A landscape of circles could not be adapted to the parceling of owned land: thus the square became the symbol of perfection and order.

Incoming Europeans brought their own values and constructed their own cultural landscapes, reorganizing and renaming landscapes that had been highly valued by native groups. Places that were once loaded with spirit power fell to secular use, while elsewhere churches were built and new sacred lands designated and named. Native peoples were relocated to reserves, separated from their places of memory. The newcomers either did not realize or did not care that the native groups, who did not possess writing, had developed powerful mnemonic systems that linked ceremonial activities and collective history to specific landscape features and in some cases to constructed monuments. In the landscape lay devices of collective memory, "places of memory" or *lieux de mémoire*—history remembered by association.[6] When native people were displaced and resettled to other lands, the loss of these memory devices made it difficult if not impossible for ceremonial cycles to be maintained. In some cases, the destruction of structures and of entire symbolic landscapes by Europeans resulted from insensitivity or lack of understanding. In other cases, however, the destruction was intentional, to disrupt native practices and weaken opposition to colonization, linked to the oft-repeated slogan, "A good Indian is a dead Indian." Some symbols that resided within the landscape were eradicated because they were taken to be claims of specific territorial "ownership," claims interpreted in a European way that was strangely inconsistent with native ideology. As the land was made empty both of people and of symbols of their presence, it could now be reinterpreted as a pristine "wilderness" awaiting productive colonization:

[The Indians] were a part of nature like the animals and left no mark "or scar" upon the land. ... In 1876, the few starved remnants signed Treaty No. 6 which surrendered the Battle River watershed to the Crown. The buffalo were gone; the Indians were gone. Our land lay empty "awaiting its new inhabitants."[7]

There was great variety in the structures of the aboriginal cultural landscape, which were indeed marks upon the land; yet many disparate forms could be related back to the underlying symbols of circle and vertical axis. These were the fundamental expressions of the unity of the cosmos: the circle of this plane of existence and the vertical axis that linked (unified) it with the above and below worlds. Medicine wheels, cairns, and antler piles were typical iterations of these ideas.

Hilltops were important places because they could be seen to embody both concepts, and reached up toward the above world. True, the earth was inseparable from the cosmos, and spirit powers of the other world pervaded this existence. But power was much greater in some areas than in others, facilitating communication with the spirit world. Not all structures were on hilltops but their settings had meaning. Monuments derived their power *from* a place rather than giving power *to* it, so each monument was the essence of its locality. Among these structures were burials in a variety of forms but dominantly, on the Northwestern Plains, in the form of scaffold structures.

Another linkage of the structures was with animal ceremonialism, for the killing of animals, while necessary, was a threat to the continued harmony of the cosmos. What is often portrayed as "hunting magic" to ensure the killing of game animals was actually the opposite: an effort to encourage the rebirth of animals and to placate the feelings of spirit animals who had been offended by the hunt, and thereby to restore cosmic harmony. Preoccupation with cosmic harmony was a richer, deeper concept than its frequent portrayals as "primitive conservation," "primal environmentalism," or "earth wisdom" as figured by modern non-aboriginals. Ironically, a belief in the fundamental balance of the cosmos embodied a desire to control the ever-dangerous variability of the Plains environment. This preoccupation with harmony and the spirits extended to the human burials as well.

Burials: Bones of Contention

The record of Euro-Canadian and Euro-American treatment of native burials is a telling example of cosmological differences as well as an expression of political dominance and the reactions to it. Most northern Plains groups at the time of white contact buried their dead on platforms called scaffolds—either constructed with poles or fastened to the branches of trees—or placed them in death lodges that were abandoned tipis. The dead were typically wrapped in buffalo robes and accompanied by possessions that they would need in the above-world. The Blackfoot, like many of their neighbors, believed that burial in the ground would trap the spirit there, making it unable to escape to the other world and possibly posing a continuing threat to passersby. This was of more than local significance; any such disruption of order could threaten the balance of the cosmos, bringing problems elsewhere. Burial, then, was not simply for the dead, but also for the living, who would benefit from the maintenance of order.

Incoming missionaries, traders, and then settlers expressed distaste or disgust for the practice of above-ground burial and soon imposed a preference for interment, posing an immediate ideological dilemma for aboriginal groups. The scaffold and death lodge burials were rapidly cleared or destroyed by the newcomers for a variety of stated and unstated reasons, even as new ones were still being erected. It is striking that few incoming Europeans viewed the burials as in any way sacred, an attitude that was reinforced by church declarations that these individuals had not been given "proper burials."[8]

Some early travelers, more than a few of them outcasts or misfits from their own groups of origin, attacked the burials and their associated artifacts as sources of curios for collections or for trade. Some simply picked apart the burials out of curiosity to see what was there, but most appropriated the grave goods and left the remainder in disarray. The bones themselves became raw material for crude jokes; one author in 1880 described an evening meal at a "festive board ... graced with a bottle adorned with an old scalp and skulls for candlesticks."[9]

The skulls were duly noted by museum collectors and, among a host of others, artists George Catlin and John James Audubon supplemented their painting and sketching activities with clandestine visits to burial grounds to grab prized skulls, even of known and recently buried individuals, for display in the east.[10] Such was the extent of this kind of collecting that a Dakota (Sioux) widow in 1874 was offered a large sum of money for the corpse of her unusually tall husband. Refusing the offer, she placed his bones in a box that she carried with her constantly on her horse travois, more than 150 kilometers per year, out of fear that the Army surgeon at Fort Totten, Dakota Territory, would steal it.[11]

There were many other stated motivations for destruction of the above-ground burials by whites, as the author has summarized elsewhere. Human bones were shipped east along with buffalo bones to be made into charcoal for sugar refining, and later to be made into fertilizer and even explosives. Fears about the spread of disease were used to whip up public sentiment in newly established settler communities against the burials. Simple aesthetic disgust was often used to rationalize destruction.[12] Underlying it all was the desire to edit native people out of the landscape.

The native groups were far from passive recipients, however, and their reactions make it clear that what was involved was a lengthy process of intercultural negotiation over values. A key consideration was to allow the soul to escape. Native groups were willing to accommodate the use of coffins or burial boxes, but chose to place them in trees or on the surface of the ground, often on hilltops or other powerful landscape settings as with the scaffold burials. But so powerful was the resistance to interment that well into the 1920s in Alberta tree scaffolds were still being used regularly for infants and burial boxes were being placed on the ground surface for others, along with possessions as before.[13] In that decade the burials were collected up by the Department of Indian Affairs and given "proper" treatment.

Enforced interment prompted a degree of negotiation; compromises were reached and, for example, the renowned Blackfoot leader, Crowfoot, was placed in a coffin in the ground but near the surface, with earth mounded over but the corner of the coffin exposed to allow the soul to escape. Such mounded burials are still used on occasion. Other people who accepted the idea of interment undertook the practice in more clandestine fashion without use of coffins and in extremely shallow graves. While this has been attributed simply to the difficulty of digging in the prairie sod, shallow burial also most closely maintained the ideology of exposure. Among the Blackfoot a pattern of "burial houses" or "ghost-houses" was also adopted in the 19th century; in this case, structures were built over surface burials to hide them from view and protect them. Large, cabin-like ghost-houses averaged 2 meters in width and 3 to 4 meters in length and within them were placed burial boxes, coffins, or wrapped corpses. They were sometimes placed on isolated hills but in other cases were simply in the vicinity of clusters of houses along streams, and one possibility is that they represented an updated version of the tipi-style death lodge.[14] Smaller versions were built in reserve cemeteries, a practice more widespread among the neighboring Cree and more prevalent in the boreal forest to the north and east. Alas, these did not "pass muster" either, and when Conservative party politician R. B. Bennett (later Prime Minister) visited the Blackfoot Reserve in 1927, agent G. H. Gooderham "cleaned things up":

> It was the RC cemetery, and to clean it up it was necessary to tear down a number of little death houses and remove all the bones and skeletons so that it would be clean and nice. The Indians wouldn't do it, so I had a white man clean up.[15]

By removing the remains, Gooderham was in effect reinventing the concept of the town park.

The complex of changes in burial practices is to a degree observable archaeologically. The Late Prehistoric period on the Canadian Plains is represented by very few human remains, often secondary interments of bundled bones from scaffold burials. With the Historic period one sees a "transitional burial horizon" of mixed and variable practices from flexed to extended interments with or without coffins.[16] At present most native people have accepted the imposition of the standard Christian interment, though it is ironic that more and more white people in Canada and the United States are being buried with grave goods to accompany them to the other world. Evidently there has been a two-way flow of ideas, though it remains to be seen whether the New Age infatuation with spirits in the landscape will lead to further changes in burial ideology.

Transatlantic Boomerang

Far from being a one-way assimilation of European values by Plains groups, the overall intercultural relationship has included a lesser, yet significant diffusion of aboriginal ideas to Europeans. Writings by European visitors about Plains groups certainly fed a demand in Europe, but there was also a notable degree of visitation by aboriginal people to Europe as well as a number of cases of emigration, particularly from Canada to Great Britain. Many traders and support personnel (farmers, blacksmiths, hunters, etc.), either from eastern North America or from Great Britain and France, took native wives "in the fashion of the country," a practice that was at first discouraged but ultimately tolerated by the Hudson's Bay Company (HBC) and other fur companies. These wives often served as crucial links with the community, increasing the chance of business success; but the result was a growing underclass of children of mixed parentage. HBC offspring had to be "placed," for example, and the question was whether or not to send them to England for schooling. Of those many who did go to England or Scotland, some stayed on; most were fostered with "home" families. In addition, though many HBC men abandoned their wives (out of "compassion" lest they miss their own people) upon retirement, others took their wives to Great Britain where in some cases they could partake of middle class society befitting their husbands. The influence of these women and their offspring upon British culture has been under-studied.

By 1832, James Vincent, half-blood son of Chief Factor Thomas Vincent, was running a school at Hackney, near London, teaching practical clerking and related skills. The two sons of Chief Trader Alexander McTavish in the 1830s "returned" to the Highlands of Scotland to be educated; one became a clerk in Inverness and the other, at first a cabinet-maker, apparently moved to New South Wales to keep livestock. Many company daughters returned to England and Scotland, married, and raised families. Depending upon their appearance, many such children could be accepted into British society, but others found no such acceptance and returned to the New World.

Alexander Kennedy Isbister was grandson of Chief Factor Alexander Kennedy and his Indian wife and therefore was one-quarter Ojibwa. The young man was educated in the Orkneys and returned to the Red River of Manitoba to work with the HBC as postmaster. He left this service to travel and published papers in the *Journal of the Royal Geographical Society* and through the British Association for the Advancement of Science. In the 1840s he was a student at King's College, Aberdeen. In 1858 he received an M.A. from Edinburgh and in 1864 an LL.B. from the University of London. At London he had already become a teacher and headmaster. He published some 21 textbooks, covering practically all basic school subjects of the time, and enjoyed both middle-class status and a high reputation as an educator. Yet he kept, throughout, a lively interest in the development and well-being of the mixed-blood community at Red River and sponsored petitions to the British government, becoming a noteworthy advocate on their behalf.[17]

Many of the HBC men came to the New World from Scotland, particularly from the Orkneys in the north and such an island as Colonsay in the west, their actions contributing to their characterization as "a national culture of mobility."[18] Given that most maintained ties with home, it is no surprise to find that people of North American aboriginal ancestry live there today. Nor, given the degree of taunting that some forebears evidently suffered at the hands of fellow schoolmates, is it a surprise that such ancestry has been hidden by some families, new generations of whom are only now learning of their truly transatlantic heritage.[19]

The meeting of people from the Old and New Worlds was a meeting of cultures and a meeting of landscapes, since the land itself carries different meanings for different people. Northern Plains groups such as the Blackfoot were nomadic but still strongly tied to a landscape, just as strongly tied as would be a Scottish trader to his ancestral homeland. When two cultures collide in the same natural landscape, they apply different meanings to its features. Depending upon the dynamics of the contact, there can be devastating losses for one group, the other, or both, even as cultural elements are being exchanged. Some groups are strongly tied not to owned pieces of land, but to places of memory; history is remembered by association, and if such a group loses its land, it can lose its collective history. Placelessness is one of the factors resulting in dysfunction among displaced aboriginal groups anywhere such contact has occurred. If one is tempted to see such people as without direction or without ambition, one must accept that such views are ethnocentric, out of context, and ahistorical.

In subtle ways, cultures of western Europe have been influenced by the First Nations people of Canada and the United States. Many of the influences are not recognized as such; the English words "chipmunk" and "toboggan" pass almost unnoticed today as borrowings. But how many other cultural traits are similarly borrowed? Certainly it is acknowledged that corn (maize), pumpkins, and turkeys, the symbols of American Thanksgiving, are all North American domesticates that have graced palates in the Old World as well. The tobacco that Walter Raleigh triumphantly introduced to European *haute couture* is now denounced as an exotic scourge.

Much to the dismay of early Missouri River explorers such as James MacKay and John Evans, the Mandan people of North Dakota turned out (despite rumors of light skin and white hair) *not* to be itinerant Welshmen after all. But today, how can physiologists reliably contrast the genetic codes of the English or Scottish with those of North American native peoples when for more than two centuries there *has* been admixture? How many people in Western Europe have North American ancestry? Evidence begins to suggest that there is a richer two-way transatlantic heritage than has been suggested, a heritage of reciprocal ties begging for further study.

[1.] The concepts have been discussed in my 1995 paper, "The Household as a Portable Mnemonic Landscape: Archaeological Implications for Plains Stone Circle Sites" in *Beyond Subsistence: Plains Archaeology and the Postprocessual Critique*, eds. Philip Duke and Michael C. Wilson

(Tuscaloosa, AL: University of Alabama Press, 1995), 170-179, and form the basis of a book now under review.

2. Donald J. Blakeslee, "Assessing the Central Plains Tradition in Eastern Nebraska: Content and Outcome," in *The Central Plains Tradition: Internal Development and External Relationships*, ed. D. J. Blakeslee (State Archaeologist, University of Iowa, Report 11, 1978), 141-142.

3 Sir Cecil E. Denny, *The Law Marches West*, 2nd ed. (Toronto: J. M. Dent and Sons, 1972): 83.

4. Simon Schama, *Landscape and Memory* (New York: A. A. Knopf, 1995), 7-8.

5. George B. Grinnell, "Tenure of Land Among the Indians," *American Anthropologist* 9, no. 1 (1907): 1-2.

6. Pierre Nora, "Mémoire Collective," in *La Nouvelle Histoire*, ed. J. LeGoff et al. (Paris: CEPL, 1978); Joseph R. Llobera, "Halbwachs, Nora and 'History' Versus 'Collective Memory': a Research Note," *Durkheimian Studies/Études Durkheimiennes* 1 (1995): 37; Schama, 7-8.

7. Donna Orr, ed., *As the Wheels Turn: A History of Rosalind, Kelsey and Districts* (Rosalind, AB: Rosalind and District Senior Citizens Society, 1982), 1, 2.

8. Michael C. Wilson, "Symbols Under Siege: Canadian Native Ceremonial Landscapes and the Impact of White Settlement," *Gakuen Ronshu, Journal of Hokkai-Gakuen University* (Sapporo, Japan) 72 (1992): 1-18; Michael C. Wilson, "Bones of Contention: Treatment by Whites of Native Burials on the Canadian Plains," in *Kunaitupii: Coming Together on Native Sacred Sites*, ed. B. O. K. Reeves and M. A. Kennedy (Calgary: Archaeological Society of Alberta, 1993), 65-85.

9. Charles Schafft, "A Visit to 'Whoop Up' in the Days Gone By," *The Benton Weekly Record*, 16 January 1880.

10. See, for example, Maria K. Audubon, *Audubon and His Journals* 2 vols. (1897; reprint New York: Dover, 1960), 72-73.

11. P. Beckwith, "Notes on the customs of the Dacotahs," *Annual Report for 1886 of the Board of Regents of the Smithsonian Institution* (Washington, D.C., 1886), 253-254.

12. Michael C. Wilson, "Symbols Under Siege" 1-18.

13. V. E. Williams, "Indian 'Graveyards' on Prairie Recalled: Exposed Coffins a Thing of Past," *The Calgary Herald*, 11 August 1954.

14. Sue Nuttall, "The Ghost-house: Acculturation in Blackfoot Burial Patterns," *Philadelphia Anthropological Society Bulletin* 13, no. 2 (1960): 24-25.

15. G. H. Gooderham, *Collected Papers* (undated; compiled 1978), unpublished; Glenbow Archives, Calgary, File R2693.

16. Michael C. Wilson, "The Scarboro Burials, Calgary, Alberta, and the Transitional Burial Horizon," *Alberta Archaeological Review* 18 (1989): 7-10.

17. These individual vignettes are after Jennifer S. H. Brown, *Strangers in Blood: Fur Trade Company Families in Indian Country* (Vancouver: University of British Columbia Press, 1980), 178-186.

18. John W. Sheets, "'National Culture of Mobility': the Colonsay-Canada

Connection," in *Transatlantic Studies*, ed. Will Kaufman and Heidi Slettedahl Macpherson (Lanham, MD: University Press of America, 2000).

[19.] Bruce Thorson, "The Bay Connection: Orkney Islanders Discover Their Métis Heritage," *Canadian Geographic* 120, no. 7 (2000): 102-104.

Part Three:
Transatlantic Artistic Exchanges

Chapter 7

Transatlantic Romanticism: The Case of the Painter-Poet, Thomas Cole (1801-1848)

Philippe Mahoux-Pauzin

Transatlantic literary relationships, especially those between America and England, are particularly significant in the study of poetry. Such relationships are, however, a site of great paradox. Consider the nominally "home-grown" tradition of sacramental verse developed in 17th-century New England by ministers and divines of the Congregational faith, when North America—both culturally and politically—was still in the firm colonial grip of England. Michael Wigglesworth and Edward Taylor obviously looked to *Paradise Lost* and to some of the Metaphysical poets of the Jacobean era for inspiration, and it is questionable as to whether the versified spiritual diary of Taylor may be considered a genuinely "American" form, as it is conventionally argued. Nor does the advent of independence and then nationhood seem to have given rise to a specifically vernacular brand of poetic inspiration, form, or subject matter. Philip Freneau indeed wrote political and polemical poems related to his involvement in the Revolutionary War; but some of his other texts bespeak a taste for the supernatural reminiscent of the English Graveyard School of

Robert Blair and Edward Young. Joel Barlow and Timothy Dwight used traditional English poetic forms already outdated in England—such as the mock epic—to sing the new nation. American reviewers and editors were mostly Federalists who looked to the norms of 18th-century English poetics as standards by which to assess contemporary works (and to reject the modernity) of such English poets as Wordsworth, Coleridge, and Southey. The first three decades of the 19th century are therefore seemingly as barren poetically in America as they are teeming with new ideas, forms, and theories in England. In this period, William Cullen Bryant appears as the only nature poet remotely reminiscent of Wordsworth.

This chapter explores the manner in which a specific brand of British Romanticism expresses itself in America through the encounter between an English painter-poet, Thomas Cole, and the American landscape. It further examines the course of this Romantic strain through the American 19th century, when—with the admittedly major exceptions of Walt Whitman and Emily Dickinson—American poetry kept itself within the bounds of this more or less foreign aesthetic. From Longfellow to Whittier, from James Russell Lowell to Sidney Lanier, poets shied away from adapting to the challenge of modernity, in spite of Emerson's encouragement. However, in focusing on the work of Thomas Cole, one might still identify a fertile imaginative role in what is undoubtedly a problematic link between the British and American romantic modes.

Ironically, it fell to an Englishman from the smoked-palled industrial belt of Lancashire to inaugurate the first national school of painting in the young United States. The Hudson River School glorified the American landscape of the East Coast—the mountains of New Hampshire, the Catskills, the Hudson Valley, the Adirondacks—before branching out into the wild West and the Rockies. Even though Cole was already a young man of 17 when he settled in America with his parents—first on the East Coast and then in Ohio—to his friends and patrons he soon grew to epitomize American art, the spirit of American landscape, and even American nationhood itself. Indeed, one can scarcely overrate the importance of Cole and the Hudson River School in the America of the 1820s, and subsequently. William Cullen Bryant, in his 1829 sonnet, "To Cole, the Painter, Departing for Europe," wrote of his lifelong friend, who was leaving to study the Old Masters:

> Thine eyes shall see the light of distant skies;
> Yet, COLE! Thy heart shall bear to Europe's strand
> A living image of thy native land

Such as on thy own glorious canvas lies....[1]

There were, of course, American-born landscapists older than Cole who were already active when he started sketching and painting the outdoors in about 1823; Thomas Doughty and Asher B. Durand were among the most renowned. But as Cole's biographer, Louis Le Grand Noble remarked in 1853, his was a peculiar case because he seemed to have a particularly literary perception of landscape, of its meaning, and more significantly, of himself as a Christian artist: "[He was always the poet, when he was the painter—which of course, is to say almost more than can be said of any landscape painter that has appeared."[2] Not only did Cole write poems, but also long and detailed accounts of his extensive rambles in the mountains, valleys, and woods, which he came properly to worship, so that virtually each of his many paintings is accompanied by a written account, often a poem. These accounts provide an insight into a fundamental Romantic notion: through nature one contemplates art, and art reveals the Beautiful, so that the student of art is necessarily also a student of nature, and vice versa. This vision of landscape as divine handiwork and therefore as art, and the consciousness of one's spiritual and aesthetic mission as an artist, may be seen as a primary feature of European and especially English influence. Cole is explicit in his own Romantic associations in his essays: "Poetry and painting sublime and purify thought, by grasping the past, the present, and the future—they give the mind a foretaste of its immortality."[3]

Such associations are a staple of 18th-century English Romanticism, in which nature (either for its own sake or, later, as a repository of the divine soul) may be frequently visualized through so-called "hill poems" or "topological poems": James Ward's "Phoenix Park" (1717), or John Dyer's more famous "Grongar Hill" (1726). In the latter, the author, like Cole both a poet and a painter, describes an ascent of a hill overlooking the Towy Valley in Camarthenshire, focusing on the various *visual* changes that occur. And as the 18th century drew to a close, the idea of looking at landscapes as masterworks of art led to the common use by travelers of the so-called "Claude glasses"—named after the great, early landscape painter—which were dark or silver-lined. Landscapes almost literally became paintings of sorts. English readers had already encountered Burke's *Philosophical Enquiry into the Ideas of the Sublime and the Beautiful* (1752) and William Gilpin's *Three Essays: On Picturesque Beauty; On Picturesque Travel; On Sketching Landscape* (1794). Even earlier than these highly influential treatises, the work of the French Abbé Dubos had been available in translation across the Channel. His 1784 *Critical Reflections on Poetry, Painting, and Music* dwelled upon the Horatian tag, "*Ut Pictura Poesis*," and argued that painting was more likely to move the passions than poetry.

In any event, it was Thomas Cole who became the Anglo-American interpreter *par excellence* of three English aesthetic theorists: Burke, on the sublime, and, respectively, Gilpin and Uvedale Price on the picturesque. Burke had explored the awestruck human's contemplation of gloomy, deep, or elevated scenery that could arouse feelings of terror; Gilpin wrestled with the distinction between balanced composition and the wildness of scenery, while Price studied the variations and alternations between smoothness and roughness, or dimness and brightness. Cole was especially keen in applying such problems to various landscapes, comparing the respective qualities of Scottish, Welsh, Italian, or Swiss mountains, lakes, and hills to their American counterparts. The outcome was almost always that the primeval forests and mountain ranges—on the whole, what could still be called the American wilderness—carried the day because they reflected the important characteristics of these three English aesthetic categories. Page after page of Cole's landscape descriptions and topographical analyses drift into purple patches of pure lyricism. In his *Essay on American Scenery*, he writes:

> [I]n the mountains of New Hampshire there is a union of the picturesque, the sublime, and the magnificent; there the bare peaks of granite, broken and desolate, cradle the clouds while the valleys and broad bases of the mountains rest under the shadow of noble and varied forests; and the traveler who passes the Sandwich Range on his way to the White Mountains, of which it is a spur, cannot but acknowledge, that although in some regions of the globe nature has wrought on a more stupendous scale, yet she has nowhere so completely married together grandeur and loveliness—there he sees the sublime melting into the beautiful, the savage tempered by the magnificent.[4]

Cole tended to write at great length, both in prose and poetry; he produced over 100 poems that earned him a place in the early nationalist canon equal, possibly, to that of Bryant. But it is in his epic reading of the American landscape where his identity as an Anglo-American artist comes into play, making the issue of his place in American Romanticism rather complex. Like Bryant, Cooper, Irving, and Emerson, he lavished praise on the American landscape and celebrated its alleged "superiority" over that of Europe, which had been tamed or too often tampered with. His vision thus dovetailed with the nationalist conception of scenery as primal wilderness, garden of the world, and original paradise, albeit threatened by the railway, cities, and industry. However, unlike such painters as Washington, Doughty, or Durand, or even the poet Bryant, Cole entertained an artistic and poetic vision of the American landscape informed by an apocalyptic hermeneutic that rang more of Milton than of Emerson, his exact contemporary. His vision, however, was to some extent tempered by his voluntary and necessary conformity to the requirements of the age: the spirit of Jacksonian democracy, perhaps; certainly the advice of his various patrons, such as Luman Reed; and obviously the demand of the American public, who gloried in its nation, both primeval and on the move.

It is questionable whether, in the aggregate, the American public—who indeed wanted to see their nation represented visually—cared much for Cole's allegorical sequences, such as *The Voyage of Life*, which represents the "Four Ages of Man," or *The Way of Empire*, an indictment of, and warning against, national vanity. Yet no matter how hard he tried to steer his tendencies toward the spectacular and the sublime in the service of some allegorical object lesson, the nature that Cole read as an open book went beyond being the "moral teacher" of the highly Protestant Bryant: it became a set of inspirational forms bound, in the Romantic fashion, to trigger the imagination to extreme heights or depths. Thus, in his undated poem, "Lines Suggested by a Voyage up the Hudson on a Moonlit Night," Cole pens his landscape in images and epithets that are obviously more akin to Coleridge than to Emerson:

> From out thy depths the mountains rise
> And lift their shadows to the skies—
> In silent awfulness they tower
> Like spectres that by magic power
> Are call'd from some vast black abyss
> Cav'd in earth's bosom bottomless,
> Whilst round and round each huge brow rough and sear
> The moonlight trembles as in fear.[5]

If this extract is plainly indebted to the then current taste for the sublime, especially in its evocation of vertical lines, this continuum between height and depth is a very English brand of sublime, one which may well hark all the way back to *Paradise Lost*, but which surely finds its way into Coleridge's "Kubla Khan."[6]

One scarcely ever encounters such evocations in the poetry of William Cullen Bryant, however comparable the two writers' inspiration may be in other respects. Consider in comparison two "forest" poems, one by Cole and the other by Bryant. Cole's "The Lament of the Forest" is made up of a lengthy introduction and of a final section appropriately entitled "Lament," in which the trees themselves are meant to express their sorrow at the axe that has started decimating them, voicing it in epic fashion as they are framed by a long evocation of the damage wrought on the earth by human civilization. The following passage, in which the trees themselves are speaking, is typically cast in elegiac terms of sentimental bathos:

> ... And thus comes rushing on
> This human hurricane, boundless as swift
> Our sanctuary this secluded spot,
> Which the stern rocks have guarded until now,
> Our enemy has marked. This gentle lake
> Shall lose our presence in it limpid breast,
> And from the mountains we shall melt away,
> Like wreaths of mist upon the winds of heaven.
> Our doom is near: behold from east to west
> The skies are darkened by ascending smoke.[7]

The conclusion is eminently pessimistic, but the lines glory in the privileged *rapport* that they formalize between the poet and the garrulous trees that rhetorically address him; he is "a mortal, whose love for our umbrageous realms/ exceeds the love of all the race of man."[8] On the other hand, Bryant's "A Forest Hymn" is indeed a celebration of the grandeur of God, half a dithyramb and half a prayer offered up by humble poet who stands beside the tall trees that are living witnesses to the Deity. Significantly, whereas Cole's trees are made to voice their own ruefulness, the brook in Bryant's poem can "tell no tale of all the good it does." As for the trees, they are solely the forthright emanations of God's power and benevolence:

> ... Grandeur, strength and grace
> Are here to speak of thee. This mighty oak—
> By whose immovable stem I stand and seem
> Almost annihilated—not a prince,
> In all that proud old world beyond the deep,
> E'er wore the green coronal of leaves with which
> Thy hand has graced him. Nestled at is root
> Is beauty, such as blooms not in the glare
> Of the broad sun....[9]

Bryan's 1825 poem is almost as sacramental as Cole's is dialogic: the poet lets his mind be filled with the living prayer of thanksgiving that these oaks embody, and in turn utters it forth in poetic form. Not so with Cole who, though deeply religious as well, receives the trees' confidence and simultaneously manages to speak from the trees' own consciousness, as it were. This clear illustration of what Coleridge calls the "primary imagination"—the prime agent of all human perceptions—necessarily foregrounds the poet's *human* ego, even if only as a recipient of the trees' lament.[10] We may thus wonder whether it is in fact the invocation of the imagination that provides the link between British and American Romantic expression, especially as evinced by Cole.

The Romantic elevation of the imagination seems as European as the Cole's trees and mountains are American. However, such conclusions cannot be so simple. In his study, *That Wilder Image*, titled after the famous line from Bryant's sonnet to Cole, James Thomas Flexner argues that

> Cole was balanced on the final, continental divide between aristocratic and democratic thinking. Down one slope, philosophy flowed backward to the tragedy of Eden, (which Cole was to paint). Down the other, it flowed ahead to a confidently foreseen Utopia. The Old Conception saw nature infected with original sin. The new believed that whatever was natural was good.[11]

This remark reminds the reader that if Cole's inspiration is indeed spatial both in his poetry and painting, it also has a temporal dimension that, again, links him with a specifically English tradition initiated by Wordsworth. In this regard memory is fully as central to the poetic endeavor as imagination was declared to be by Coleridge. Concomitantly, loss—the elegiac impulse—and thus introspection as well as retrospection are essential to the poet's work. Through such considerations, one realizes how ambiguous Cole's case is. Not unlike that of Wordsworth, the poet Cole most admired, his art is also drawn from "emotions recollected in tranquility." Cole himself declared that he never was able to paint scenes directly after seeing them on the course of his long walks, but always had to wait for time "to throw a veil over the common details."[12] For him, "the poetic mind clothes the dim and shadowy forces of the past with a drapery of its own."[13] In Cole's "The Song of the Spirit of the Mountains," "Shroon Mountain," and "Lines on Lake George," the subject matter is as much the poet himself as the mountain, the dawn, the twilight, or the lake. More pointedly, it is the woeful impossibility of a common eternity, an eternal physical bond between the lake or the mountain and the artist himself. In other words, because, for all his cherishing of the breadth and minutest details of American scenery, and all his topographical fidelity, both in painting and poetry, for all his very fervid Christian faith, which caused him to revere nature as the work of God, it is predominantly the *poet* that is the central figure in most of the poems. This departure from 18th-century poetics, which may be seen as some sort of inchoate kinship with the Wordsworth of *The Prelude*, could very well tip the scales in favor of describing Cole's poetics as a product of British Romanticism, and, beyond, of what Julian Powell Ward calls the "English Line of Poetry: a poetic involvement with the self in a world that can never fully accommodate it. Hence the sense of loss or of the failure to achieve.[14]

According to Paul de Man, *The Prelude* marks a shift in Wordsworth's work, whereby nature acquires a new value as an entity that enables the poet to discover his own mind, therefore leading beyond itself and teaching the poet to transcend it.[15] *The Prelude* reverberates with the elation Wordsworth experiences upon discovering that the new faculty revealed by nature during his trip across the Alps is indeed "Imagination! Lifting up itself." Wordsworth's retrospective discovery of the power of his imagination suggests a much more sophisticated process than Cole ever uses in his poetry, and the Hegelian solipsism whereby the perception of nature leads ultimately back to the perceiver's mind is conditioned by Wordsworth's Christian faith, as opposed to the pantheism prevalent among the English Romantics. Herein one may probably speak of Cole as a mediator between a European tradition which gestures toward the allegorical—whether nature shadows forth man's mind or God's spirit, or both—and the nascent American one, the Transcendentalism postulating an identity between nature and God, and therefore advocating a virtual withdrawal of the subject-as-artist. In fact, Cole's poetry is pervaded by this tension—or rather, this indecision: either ego-suffused or holding its subject matter at arms' length, it seems to be concerned with the thorny assumption and management of emotion in a way that Emerson's poems are not. Sometimes the two modes are present in the same poem, which creates a dialectic, as in "Lines on Lake George":

> The eastern mountain's summit lingers there
> Enamoured: no earthly wave besides
> Returns her silver brightness to the skies,
> Unmingled with its own dark turbidness;
> The stars are pictured here so faithfully,
> That the lone wanderer on its pebbly shore
> Doubts his own vision and with caution treads—

Upon the margin of the lower sky.[16]

These lines are already more Transcendental than Romantic in the European sense of the word. A nondescript wanderer has replaced the privileged poet himself and marvels at the perfect reflection of the stars in the lake, without claiming (as does the poet elsewhere) any special intercourse or dialogue with nature. To the contrary, he does not trust his own senses, let alone engage in a lyrical representation of the landscape, brought up as he is against phenomena that are beyond him, no matter how natural and ordinary. Mute contemplation and elementary physical action are enough. This links to a telling passage from Emerson's "Nature" in which the thinker implicitly warns his reader against the meretriciousness of eager literary imitation, in a way that sharply contrasts with Cole's declarations in his notebooks and essays: "The shows of day, the dewy morning, the rainbows, mountains, orchards in blossom, stars, moonlight, shadows in still water, and the like, if too eagerly hunted, become shows merely and mock us with their unreality. Go out of the house to see the moon, and 'tis mere tinsel...."[17]

When, a few lines further, Emerson goes on to mention "[t]he high and divine beauty which can be loved without effeminacy" when it "is found in combination with the human will," he suggests (here as in his other essays) how far the tenets of American Transcendentalism drift from the European-inspired Romanticism represented by Thomas Cole. As expressed in the last lines of Emerson's poem, "Each and All," this act of will consists essentially in letting oneself become immersed in the whole divine scheme of nature ("Beauty through my senses stole;/ I yielded myself to the perfect whole").[18] Characteristically, Cole frequently substitutes for this centrifugal tendency a reflexive attitude that necessarily polarizes the self as distinct from nature, since the latter enables the artist to probe into it more deeply. Hence these lines from the poem, "Evening Thoughts," written in 1835, just one year before Emerson drafted his essay, "Nature":

> But whence the shade of sadness o'er us thrown
> When thoughts are purest in the quiet hour?
> From sense of sin arises that sad tone?
> Knowing that we alone feel passion's power,
> That touches not the mountain far and lone?[19]

What seems most to signal Cole's indebtedness to European Romanticism, and thus his potential rather than actual anachronism in the very inchoate American poetic output, is his pessimism. In the same way as he bemoaned the inexorable transformation of the landscape at the hand of what he called "dollar-godded millionaires" and "copper-hearted barbarians," he was also painfully aware of a double sense of estrangement—from his subject matter, as exemplified by the lines just cited, as well as from his own audience, unreceptive as they were to the pathetic fallacy, emotionalism, and most of all to the grandiose allegories of his most ambitious narrative paintings.[20] Again, like the Wordsworth of *The Prelude* or "The Solitary Reaper," Cole's very technique of note taking and painting was bound to lead him to a poetry of nature as one of possession and loss, absence and presence. To the Transcendentalists, this dialectic was less of a threat, since for them the structure of the universe duplicated that of the individual self: the two were, so to speak, on a par, once the thinking mind could conceive the principle. Becoming one with nature was thus the natural outcome of such an approach, and once it had been achieved, it entailed much fewer misgivings than the ego-enhancing effect of the British absorption with nature. But then, one could add, this dialectic also considerably interfered with poetic writing, or rather with the poetic impulse, since it bypassed contradiction. In the end, American Transcendentalism was perhaps less concerned with the imagination, and thus tended to avoid this ego-related dilemma of presence-absence, the impossible quest, and the irreducible inequality between nature and the self that makes up the dynamic core of Cole's poetry.

In conclusion, it is worthwhile to turn to Emerson's celebrated essay, "The Poet" (1844). In it he sets forth the functions and main idiosyncrasies of the poet, in a possibly less didactic but more philosophical fashion than does Wordsworth in his preface to *The Lyrical Ballads* of 1802. Although Emerson makes much the same points regarding the nature of language, insight, vision, inwardness, the love of beauty, and the prophesying gift of the poet, the seeds of a fundamental difference are planted in his ambiguous declaration that imagination, which he calls "a very high sort of seeing," results from the "intellect being where and what he sees."[21] He dwells upon the poet's necessity to unlock "at all risks, his human doors, and suffer ... the ethereal tides to roll and circulate through him," affirming that "then he is caught up into the life of the Universe, his speech is thunder, his thought is law, and his words are universally intelligible as the plants and animals." Indeed, the English Romantics, especially Coleridge, had evolved a very similar, if more elaborate, theory some 30 years earlier. Once the "primary imagination" has mediated between sensation and perception (or the so-called raw materials of sense existence), the secondary imagination reworks its product through a double process of deconstruction and reconstruction: as Coleridge argues, "it dissolves, diffuses, dissipates, in order to recreate...."[22] In other words, it very consciously lays down the exhilarating experience in symbolic terms, a highly intellectual operation, and one therefore that apotheosizes the poet's mind, the poet's ego. Perhaps Emerson's yearning for a "Liberating God"—an American poet capable of verbalizing that part of him that lives in the wind, the flower, and the mountain—gestures toward what Harold Bloom in *The Anxiety of Influence* calls *askesis*: a movement of self-purgation or curtailment whereby the later poet separates himself from his precursors (here perhaps Wordsworth and Coleridge) by yielding up part of his own imaginative endowment. (Bloom himself doubts it because of the Emersonian reliance on sight and vision at all costs.)[23] Emerson concluded, famously, that America was a poem in its own right, but one that had not yet found its meters.[24] Perhaps his ignorance of Cole's poetry was due to his failure to consider that an English-born and bred Romantic could turn the American landscape into a poem in paint as well as in verse.

---

[1] George McMichael, et al., eds., *Anthology of American Literature* (New York: Macmillan, 1967), 1: 907.

[2] Louis Le Grand Noble, *The Course of Empire, Voyage of Life and Other Pictures of Thomas Cole* (New York: Cornish, Lamport and Co., 1853), 80.

[3] Thomas Cole, "Essay on American Scenery," in *The Collected Essays and Prose Sketches* [1836] ed. Marshall Tymn (St. Paul, MN: John Colet Press, 1980), 3.

[4] Ibid., 9

[5] Marshall Tymn, ed., *Thomas Cole's Poetry* (New York: Liberty Cap Books, 1972), 176.

[6] This vertical continuum was, according to Burke, one of the causes and the characteristics of the sublime. See Edmund Burke, *A Philosophical Enquiry into the Origin of Our Ideas of the Sublime and Beautiful* (Oxford: Oxford University Press, 1957), 66.

[7] Tymn, *Thomas Cole's Poetry*, 113.

[8] Ibid., 109.

[9] McMichael, 904.

[10] Notably in part XIII of his *Biographia Literaria*.

[11] James Thomas Flexner, *That Wilder Image* (Boston: Little, Brown and Co., 1962), 40.

[12] Ibid., 42.

[13] Ibid, 51.

[14] See Ward's enlightening work of the same name, *The English Line* (London: Macmillan, 1991).

[15] Paul de Man, "Intentional Structure of the Romantic Image," in M. H. Abrams, ed., *Wordsworth: A Collection of Critical Essays* (Englewood Cliffs, NJ: Prentice Hall, 1989), 142-144.

[16] Tymn, *Thomas Cole's Poetry*, 46.

[17] Ralph Waldo Emerson, "Nature," in *Selected Essays, Lectures, and Poems* (New York: Bantam, 1990), 23.

[18] Ibid., 366.

[19] Tymn, *Thomas Cole's Poetry*: 80.

[20] Flexner, 40.

[21] Ralph Waldo Emerson, "The Poet," *Selected Essays, Lectures, and Poems*, 215.

[22] Samuel Taylor Coleridge, *Biographia Literaria*, Chapter XIII, in M. H. Abrams, ed., *The Norton Anthology of English Literature* (New York: W. W. Norton, 1981), 351.

[23] Harold Bloom, *The Anxiety of Influence* (Oxford: Oxford University Press, 1973), 132-133.

[24] Emerson, "The Poet," *Selected Essays*, 221.

Chapter 8

European Modernity-Awareness and Transatlantic Intertextuality: Poe's Significance for Baudelaire, Benjamin, and Foucault

Steve Brewer and Martin Jesinghausen

The First Triangle: Europe, Poe, Baudelaire

The development of European modernity-awareness receives a major boost from an exchange of cultural substance between Europe and North America around the middle of the 19th century. The exchange in question takes the shape of a triangle: the European literary tradition forms one side of it, with the other two sides represented by the exchange of literary matter across the Atlantic, involving the writers Edgar Allan Poe and Charles Baudelaire. With the intellectual contact between Baudelaire and Poe, Europe met Europe squared. Through American mediation, contemporary European literary culture had an encounter with itself.

The intercontinental shuttle of literary matter works something like this: Poe receives European culture in North America; he synthesizes American, French, German and English literary impulses and translates them into a poetic language of his own. From America, Poe transmits the recycled European substance back to Europe, enthusiastically received in Paris by Baudelaire. The latter, a writer deeply rooted in French and European cultural traditions, synchronizes his writings with Poe's by translating and adopting them and by propagating the American's "philosophy" as a role model of European modernity-awareness. Thus Baudelaire instigates the French Poe-inspired Symbolist/Modernist tradition spearheaded by Mallarmé and Valéry.[1] And from this initial transatlantic intersection of literary matter, as has recently been comprehensively shown,[2] springs a vast European network of Modernist and postmodern writing.[3]

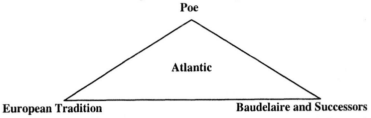

Poe

Atlantic

European Tradition   Baudelaire and Successors

This encounter substantially contributed to the development of 20th century European modernity-awareness by laying the foundations of a new style and methodology for many later writers. Thus, for example, through Baudelaire's translations, Poe's tales reached Dostoyevsky and made a substantial impact on the writings of Thomas Mann and Kafka.[4] Their influence can be traced in Expressionism in literature, music and film. Poe's poetry and "Philosophy of Composition" form a key inspiration for European Symbolism, from Mallarmé, Valéry and Wilde, to Maeterlinck (and Debussy) Hofmannsthal, the early Schoenberg and Stefan George. Poe's "cultural philosophy" inspired numerous Modernist and postmodern cultural theorists, from Benjamin to Foucault, Barthes, Lacan and Derrida. Poe's influence can also be detected in Modernist painting: a good example would be Gauguin's Fauvist painting *The Raven*. Traces of Poe's urban representation are also perceptible in postmodern film (*Taxi Driver*, for example).

In this chapter, we look at 3 triangles of intertextual transatlantic exchange. First, we explore the detail of the Poe/Baudelaire exchange. Secondly, we investigate the impact of the transatlantic meeting on European modernity-awareness, highlighted in Benjamin's and Foucault's position on modernity. Thirdly, we will briefly consider what can be deduced from this process of transatlantic exchange and the impact it has made on the development of modern cultural processes in general.

Poe as American Transmitter of European Tradition

The Poe/Baudelaire event was one of the most influential of all Euro-American cultural exchanges up to that time. What was it in Poe's writings that attracted Baudelaire, and, through him, other French and European writers? Poe's tales are imbued with "Europeanness" because as a prolific linguist and critic, he read, translated and critiqued European texts. He looked to the literature and philosophy of Europe for inspiration and incorporated the European spirit of the age into his own writing. Europe is the physical backdrop of many of his tales. The 3 genre-founding detective stories are set in Paris. "The Man of the Crowd" is set in London. In Poe's writings, regarded by Europeans as a paradigm of modernity, Europe recognized its own heritage as if in a mirror.

For the French, Poe embodied the quintessential spirit of Frenchness perhaps more than French writers themselves. Much is made here of Poe's "lucid intelligence," his Cartesian frame of mind, comparable to that of Pascal and the "Encyclopaedists."[5] Critics refer to the clarity embodied in Poe's work, reflecting qualities long associated with the French language and thought: "Ce qui n'est pas clair n'est pas français." Paul Valéry highlights lucidity as one of the major characteristics that attracted Baudelaire (and Valéry himself) to Poe. But in *The French Face of Edgar Allan Poe*, Patrick F. Quinn argues that lucidity is only half the story; equally telling is the combination in Poe's writing of lucidity and the threat of incoherence, the struggle between order and disorder, the conscious versus the unconscious, the normal versus the horror.[6] There is in Baudelaire the same existential angst dissected with forensic precision found in Poe's tales and which points forward to the insecure and neurotic side of Modernism, to the works of Kafka and the Absurdists.

Poe synthesizes the European tradition. He puts Europe in touch with itself, or rather, different European national cultures in touch with one another.[7] Poe's writings are well received in France because they show a French predisposition of mind; but they also enable the French to interact with German culture in a circuitous—and at this time of post-Napoleonic nationalist strife—politically and culturally acceptable way. To quote Quinn, Poe

> combined ... a sense of form and a respect for the intellect, with the very thing Nerval, for one, had gone to Germany to find, the ability to move as in dreams through the depths of the mind and to illuminate the kind of verities the reason knows not of.[8]

E. T. A. Hoffmann entered the French cultural space via Poe in this way.[9]

Paradoxically, it is perhaps also the Americanness of Poe's writing which attracts his European audience.[10] To start with, Poe re-locates European culture by viewing it from an American perspective, thus defamiliarizing it, in an almost Brechtian sense. Furthermore, the intertextual basis of his innovative synthetic style might be regarded as a new, specifically American quality of modern writing. Poe absorbed European literary role models and constructed the texture of his own "original" style through them.

This interdiscursivity shades into concrete intertextuality, and sometimes outright plagiarism: Poe's tales are sometimes partial or even extensive "translations" of European literary sources. The same can be claimed for some of his aesthetic texts.[11] First, Walter Benjamin perceives correspondences between "The Man of the Crowd" and the last of Hoffmann's stories, "The Cousin's Corner Window" (to which we will return later). The second example is a case of plagiarism rather than intertextuality: Arno Schmidt has shown that "The Fall of the House of Usher" is almost completely plagiarized from a little known short story, "*Das Raubschloss*," published 1812 by the obscure German writer Clauren. Schmidt reconciles himself to Poe's "intellectual theft" by interpreting it as "an incomparably improved second creation."[12] The third example is a case of almost academic source research: Régis Messac has identified as a possible source for *The Narrative of Arthur Gordon Pym* an anonymous 1723 French manuscript, *Relation d'un voyage du pôle arctique au pôle antarctique par le centre du monde.*[13] It is clear from this that Poe and—as we shall see shortly—Baudelaire developed their own creative voices as modern writers via the appropriation and transformation of other textual sources. The author is dying: to a certain extent, texts are beginning to write themselves, leading to a deconstructing of the fiction of absolute authorial control over the composition process. As Valéry says: "The Lion is made of assimilated sheep."[14] That is, the power of originality is constituted through a synthesis of sources. Valéry aphoristically turns Poe's method of intertextual composition into a positive principle of modern writing, one which he adheres to in his own writings.[15]

The significance of Poe's writing for Europe can also be seen by the fact that it advances the European debate on modernity through its critique of Enlightenment optimism and its doctrine of progress. Poe's "philosophy" is a skeptical one. Mario Praz has compared Poe (and Baudelaire) to de Sade.[16] Like de Sade, Poe aims at a disinterested record of extreme human situations, physical and mental atrocities. Poe is the chronicler of post-Enlightenment, post-revolutionary humanity in pain, an encyclopedist of the decline of modern civilization. There is a visionary, even prophetic element in Poe's diagnosis that modernity is rotten to the core and will soon end in general neurasthenia and neurosis.

Baudelaire as European Transmitter of Poe

Baudelaire emphasised the shock of recognition when he first encountered Poe: here was a kindred spirit whose uncanny similarity caused him to invest huge energy into the translation of his works, probably to the detriment of his own writing:

> In 1846 or '47 I came across a few fragments by Edgar Poe. I experienced a singular shock. His complete works were not assembled into a single edition until after his death, so I had the patience to make contact with Americans living in Paris to borrow from them collections of newspapers edited by Poe. And then —believe me if you will—I found poems and short stories that I had thought of but in a vague, confused, and disorderly way and that Poe had been able to bring together to perfection. It was that that lay behind my enthusiasm and my long years of patience.[17]

And indeed, similarities between works by Poe and Baudelaire are apparent in 3 main areas: aesthetic theory, literary subject matter and methodology of literary composition.[18] In the area of aesthetics, Baudelaire, in his essay "Edgar Allan Poe: His Life and Works," identifies a number of characteristics of Poe's writing which are arguably consonant with his own aesthetic preoccupations: he refers to Poe's "indefinable accent of melancholy,"[19] highlights his "love of Beauty," describes him as a "writer of the nerves,"[20] and claims he "hurls himself into the grotesque for love of the grotesque and the horrible for love of the horrible."[21] In "Further Notes on Edgar Poe," Baudelaire writes that "from the midst of a world avid and starving for materialities, Poe has soared up into the element of dreams."[22] For Poe, he argues, "the imagination is the Queen of the Faculties" and continues: "The Imagination is an almost divine faculty which perceives at once, quite without resort to philosophic methods, the intimate and secret connections between things, *correspondences* and analogies."[23] Poe has "clearly seen and dispassionately asserted the natural Wickedness of Man"[24] (no truck with Enlightenment optimism and American belief in progress here). Any one of these pronouncements of Baudelaire could be enlisted in support of the argument that he was deeply influenced by Poe because of similarities of disposition and interest.[25]

Regarding subject matter, Baudelaire was not above plagiarizing the American's work; his 1857 edition of Poe's tales contains an introduction written by himself which is for all intents and purposes an unacknowledged translation of Poe's "The Poetic Principle." Baudelaire also drew inspiration from Poe as a poet, as Lois Vines has noted. She makes a persuasive case for Baudelaire's literary magpie activities by comparing Poe's poem "To Helen" with Baudelaire's "Le Flambeau vivant," highlighting correspondences in language, tone and form. Baudelaire asserted that the similarities between the two works were a fortuitous coincidence of material, a rather thin claim in view of the evidence.[26]

Not only do Baudelaire and Poe converge on principles of aesthetic theory and literary subject matter, but there is also a deep-rooted affinity between them in the area of literary temper, style, and a modern methodology of writing. A curious process of duplication manifests itself here: Baudelaire was drawn to Poe because he shared with him the methodology of intertextual composition itself. Baudelaire utilizes Poe as source material in exactly the same way as Poe borrows from his European sources. In both writers we can see the elevation of a generally despised practice into a positive methodology of composition. This revolutionary approach to textual (re-)creation anticipates methods of postmodern writing: pastiche, bricolage, text as world-creation.

Baudelaire's "The Painter of Modern Life" features as a seminal text in the modernity debate. In it, Baudelaire enthusiastically reveals his intellectual debt to Poe's "The Man of the Crowd":

> Do you remember a picture ..., painted—or rather written—by the most powerful pen of our age, and entitled *The Man of the Crowd*? In the window of a coffee house there sits a convalescent, pleasurably absorbed in gazing at the crowd, and mingling, through the medium of thought, in the turmoil of thought that surrounds him. But lately returned from the valley of the shadow of death, he is rapturously breathing in all the odours and essences of life; as he has been on the brink of total oblivion, he remembers, and fervently desires to remember, everything. Finally he hurls himself headlong into the midst of the throng, in pursuit of an unknown, half-glimpsed countenance that has, on an instant, bewitched him. Curiosity had become a fatal, irresistible passion![27]

Poe's "The Man of the Crowd" exemplifies for Baudelaire the principles of his own contemporary aesthetic. "The Painter of Modern Life" points forward to Benjamin and Foucault, to Modernism and postmodernism, because it defines and sets parameters for the notion of "modernity." "The Man of the Crowd" epitomizes literary modernity, the definition of which emerges from Baudelaire's discussion of the concept of beauty and its historicity. "Beauty," Baudelaire says, "is made up of an eternal, invariable element, whose quantity it is excessively difficult to determine, and of a relative, circumstantial element, which will be, if you like, whether severally or all at once, the age, its fashions, its morals, its emotions."[28] He continues: "By 'modernity' I mean the ephemeral, the fugitive, the contingent, the half of art whose other half is the eternal and the immutable."[29] Thus what is vital for Baudelaire is the importance of the contemporary in Poe's writing: there is no need to return to the Ancients to authenticate artistic creation. Like Poe, Baudelaire did not look backward to the museum of poetic tradition to justify his art, but forward to the modern world and its aesthetic experience. The eternal principles of beauty and validity are inherent in the historically contingent and the contemporary; the modern writer observes the manifestations of the perennial substance of humanity in his everyday environment. This tension between, on the one hand, the absolute values of the classical and the supra-historical, and on the other, the relative phenomena of contemporary historical reality in Baudelaire's theoreticizing of Poe's writing is at the heart of a tradition which points forward to Modernism and beyond. The modernity of Baudelaire's *Les Fleurs du mal* springs from the dialectic between classical form within which recurrent human themes are imbedded and the observation of the contemporary state of the human condition. The collection of poetry thus forms the aesthetic incarnation of Baudelaire/Poe's theory of modernity.

As we have seen, Baudelaire assimilates Poe's writings but he also to a certain extent dilutes their initial radicalism, a view shared, as we shall see, by Walter Benjamin. Baudelaire's reading of "The Man of the Crowd" reveals different preoccupations from those of the original text. Whereas "The Man of the Crowd" centers on the "decrepit old man" observed, Baudelaire's "The Painter of Modern Life" focuses on the figure of the observer himself, of whom he says:

> The crowd is his element, as the air is that of birds and water of fishes. His passion and his profession are to become one flesh with the crowd. For the perfect *flâneur*, for the passionate spectator, it is an immense joy to set up house in the heart of the multitude, amid the ebb and flow of movement, in the midst of the fugitive and the infinite.[30]

There is a real sense here of the fascination, the thrill and the elation of modern urban life. By contrast, Poe's original text expresses the fascination, but it is more a horrific fascination with the anomie of collective urban existence than thrill or elation. The narrator concludes:

"The worst heart of the world is a grosser book than the 'Hortulus Animae,'[31] and perhaps it is one of the great mercies of God than *es lasst* [sic] *sich nicht lesen.*"[32] This pessimistic conclusion is not shared by Baudelaire's observer of the modern world: "he delights in universal life."[33] The narrator of Poe's tale inhabits the heart of darkness rather than the transfigured, created world of Baudelaire's painter of modern life, described as follows: "And the external world is reborn upon his paper, natural and more than natural, beautiful and more than beautiful, strange and endowed with an impulsive life like the soul of its creator."[34] Baudelaire admires *Les fleurs du mal*. He is decadently susceptible to the strange beauty of the bad and the grotesque. Poe, in contrast, is drawn with fear and loathing to the things that disgust and terrify him.

There are differences in emphasis, then, between "The Man of the Crowd" and Baudelaire's response to it in "The Painter of Modern Life." We should also acknowledge that the evident enthusiasm for the modern world demonstrated in "The Painter of Modern Life" is moderated by Baudelaire's diatribe against progress (what he terms "that great heresy of decline") in "Further Notes on Edgar Poe."[35] But of Baudelaire's fascination with the manifestations of modern life in the city there can be no doubt: the *Petits Poèmes en prose* testify to it. Baudelaire recognised in Poe's work, and especially in "The Man of the Crowd," a defining and innovative approach to the conceptualization and aestheticization of modern urban life, an aspect which was in turn to stimulate Walter Benjamin and Michel Foucault and other post-structuralists.

The Second Triangle: Benjamin, Baudelaire and Poe

The case of Walter Benjamin is a significant example of the impact of the Poe/Baudelaire tandem on 20th century high Modernism beyond French borders. His critical analysis presents Baudelaire as representative of Parisian Modernism. It is through his studies of Baudelaire[36] that he laid the foundations of what was to be the fulfillment of his cultural-philosophical work, the unfinished Arcades Project.[37] For Benjamin, Baudelaire was the ideal critical object by means of which he could position his own mature theory of culture, one in which literature takes on the function of a symbolic social form.[38] By interpreting the work of the lyrical poet as symbolic cultural utterance, Benjamin laid bare the archaeology of his contemporary culture. From within the socio-cultural web around Baudelaire's writings, modernity as an attitude towards contemporary history and Modernism as a literary style can be reconstructed: the *flâneur* is the paradigmatic representative of modernity, *Les Fleurs du mal* and *Le Spleen de Paris* are stages on the way to literary Modernism.

Paradoxically, Benjamin regards Poe rather than Baudelaire as the true modern literary protagonist, lending aesthetic expression to the volcanic eruptions of modernity in the era of high capitalism. By contrast, Baudelaire is portrayed as a passive seismograph, picking up the central influences of the age that flow together in his work (a major one of these being Poe). Perhaps it is precisely this passive nature of Baudelaire's synthetic genius—the fact that he is fully exposed to the tremors of the age—that made Baudelaire, not Poe, the true representative of modernity for Benjamin. Passivity, vulnerability, being exposed—this is the leading leitmotif throughout Benjamin's career as cultural critic—are more authentic states of modern experience, and in this, Baudelaire and Benjamin are *frères semblables*. For Benjamin, a major part of Baudelaire's attractiveness as a representative is therefore that his achievements are, to a significant extent, dependent on Poe's. He singles out the three detective stories and "The Man of the Crowd" as pioneering works of modernity-awareness. Central elements of Poe's detective stories, so he argues, can be found fragmented in various poems in Baudelaire's *Les Fleurs du mal*: "the victim and the scene of the crime ('Une Martyre'), the murderer ('Le Vin de l'assassin'), the masses ('Le Crépuscule du soir')."[39]

According to Benjamin, Poe's significance for Baudelaire derives not just from issues of subject matter and form; Poe also provides him with an innovative blueprint for the expression of modern literary subjectivity: Poe and Baudelaire share a perspective from which to view modern life, that of the *flâneur*. For Benjamin, "The Man of the Crowd" represents the epicenter of the Baudelaire/Poe transatlantic exchange. It emerges from Benjamin's essay as one of the great pieces of 19th century writing. In fact, large proportions of it are devoted to this story. For Benjamin this famous tale

is something like the X-ray picture of a detective story. In it, the drapery represented by crime has disappeared. The mere armature has remained: the pursuer, the crowd, an unknown man who arranges his walk through London in such a way that he always remains in the middle of the crowd. This unknown man is the *flâneur*.[40]

Benjamin brings Hoffmann's story "The Cousin's Corner Window" into the debate by suggesting that this tale, though not exactly a direct precursor of Poe's *flâneur* narrative, is nevertheless linked to it by correspondences between similar urban aesthetic experiences.[41]

According to Benjamin, Hoffmann's protagonist remains a detached observer. He "is installed in his household, views the crowd with great constraint," whereas Poe's observer "who stares through the window-panes of a coffee house has penetrating eyes," indicative of emotional involvement.[42] Essentially, therefore, Benjamin interprets the observer figure differently from Baudelaire (and Foucault, as we shall see, for whom the heroism of observing is more positive than for Benjamin). For Baudelaire, Poe's observer experiences the ecstasy of mingling with the crowd. For Benjamin, Poe's observer is a cipher of neurotic suffering: this man is compulsively drawn to the crowd; he is in the grip of hysteria.

Benjamin compares 19th century urban experience in different European capitals: Hoffmann's preview of the *flâneur* was

> an attempt which was then due to be made. But it is obvious that the conditions under which it was made in Berlin prevented it from being a complete success. If Hoffmann had ever set foot in Paris or London, or if he had been intent on depicting the masses as such, he would not have focused on a market place; he would not have portrayed the scene as being dominated by women; he would perhaps have seized on the motifs that Poe derives from the swarming crowds under the gas lamps.[43]

"In the difference between the two observation posts [in Hoffmann's and Poe's tales] lies the difference between Berlin and London,"[44] Benjamin adds. Nor does the Paris of Baudelaire fully live up to the high standards of advanced urban modernity-experience available to Poe in London and cities of the US, because compared to them, Paris is still a provincial backwater:

> Ferries were still crossing the Seine at points where later there would be bridges. In the year of Baudelaire's death it was still possible for an entrepreneur to cater to the comfort of the well-to-do with a fleet of five hundred sedan chairs circulating about the city. Arcades where the *flâneur* would not be exposed to the sight of the carriages that did not recognise pedestrians as rivals were enjoying undiminished popularity. ... Around 1840 it was briefly fashionable to take turtles for a walk in the arcades. The *flâneurs* liked to have the turtles set the pace for them. If they had had their way, progress would have been obliged to accommodate itself to this pace.[45]

The predominant position Benjamin allocates to Poe's writings, and particularly to "The Man of the Crowd," is that of a symptomatic expression of modernity-awareness, tinged with prophetic insight:

The people in his story behave as if they could no longer express themselves through anything but a reflex action. These goings-on seem even more dehumanised because Poe talks only about people. If the crowd is jammed up, it is not because it is being impeded by vehicular traffic—there is no mention of it anywhere—but because it is being blocked by other crowds. In a mass of this nature the art of strolling could not flourish.[46]

The most valuable dimension of Poe's text is its prophetic vision: "It is a magnificent touch in Poe's story that it includes along with the earliest description of the *flâneur* the figuration of his end."[47] Benjamin holds "The Man of the Crowd" in such high regard as a central modern text because of its sociological and psychological diagnostic qualities: it links crowd behavior with revolutionized public transport, with hysteria and the weakening of individuation. Neither Hoffmann nor Baudelaire could have expressed the experience of modernity with the same intensity as Poe, because these writers had little awareness of alienation as the key ingredient of the modern experience. The restricted social environment of Poe's narrative scenario does not permit the leisurely attitude of Baudelaire's *flâneur*. Poe introduced the dimension of alienation into the concept of the *flâneur* very early on in the history of ideas. Through the key category of alienation, Benjamin established a link between 19th century writing and Marxist social theory. And the literary critic in Benjamin triumphed over the Marxist historian by concluding that Poe intuitively goes beyond what Marx's social theory was capable of diagnosing at the time when Poe was writing. Thus, for example, in the description of the bazaar episode[48] in the story—not unlike the experience of a department store of today—Poe anticipates the phenomenon of consumerism as part of crowd behavior under late capitalism. Marx himself only homed in on capitalist self-regeneration through consumerism (the maintenance of the capitalist cycle via the reconciliation of the consumer to alienated production through consumption) decades later (1865-66) in "The Fetishism of Commodities" in the first volume of *Capital*.[49]

The Third Triangle: Foucault, Baudelaire and Poe

The ripples of Poe's influence, via Baudelaire, have continued to spread out through European thinking. For example, the Poe-Baudelaire nexus resurfaces in Michel Foucault's essay "What is Enlightenment?" Baudelaire's definition of modernity in "The Painter of Modern Life" plays an important role in the development of Foucault's argument. For Foucault, the French poet is a figure of great importance in the development of a modern conception of human ontology. Baudelaire's example, he says is "almost indispensable" because his "consciousness of modernity is widely recognised as one of the most acute in the nineteenth century."[50] Foucault argues that Baudelaire's views on modernity represent an ontology which, like that of Kant in his essay of the same name, interrogates the positioning of human beings to their time and era. As will be recalled, Baudelaire—following Poe— identifies the two dimensions of beauty as the ephemeral and the eternal. Foucault picks up this dialectic. For him, what is particularly important about Baudelaire's description of modern subjects is not only that they observe the ephemeral and the contingent, and attempt to extract the eternal from it, but more crucially, that they re-create the world in a more potent form: "this deliberate, difficult attitude consists in recapturing something eternal that is not beyond the present instant, nor behind it, but within it. ... [M]odernity is the attitude that makes it possible to grasp the 'heroic' aspect of the present moment."[51] The painter of modern life (and the artist in general) performs an act of creation. As Baudelaire writes, and Foucault echoes, "And the external world is reborn upon his paper, natural and more than natural, beautiful, and more than beautiful, strange and endowed with an impulsive life like the soul of its creator."[52] Foucault regards Baudelaire's definition of modernity as a key moment in the history of ideas because it contributes to completing the Enlightenment project: "Baudelairean modernity is an exercise in which extreme attention to what is real is confronted with the practice of a liberty that simultaneously respects this reality and violates it."[53] For Foucault, Baudelaire's thinking on modernity is indicative of a paradigm shift which he identifies with the advent of the Enlightenment, namely the development of a "philosophical interrogation ... that simultaneously problematises man's relation to the present, man's historical mode of being, and the constitution of the self as an autonomous subject."[54] These are concepts which are central to Foucault's influential theorization of the human situation, and in his exposition of them he is clearly indebted to the Poe-Baudelaire tradition. They are notions which feed directly into the post-structuralist concern with the creative nature of language and symbolic creation of cultural reality.

When considering Poe's immense impact on the formation of modernity-awareness in Europe, what emerges is the particular significance of the transatlantic textual networking around the middle of the 19th century. This event was an important episode on the threshold of a fully-fledged globalization of culture which, from then on, increased in speed and intensity. Transatlantic cultural exchange now formed part of a more complex and multifaceted network of international cultural relationships. The actual manifestation of this process of intertextual connectivity as a generative force in global cultural change roughly coincides with new theories of historical development. Marx and Nietzsche (and in their wake Foucault and the post-structuralists) revolutionized historiology through what Nietzsche termed "genealogy." The transatlantic oscillation in question is one of the best examples of the genealogical form of development of literary and philosophical practices. It demonstrates that cultural development is driven by an interactive process rather than emanating from a fixed point of absolute beginning. Cultural evolution is thus based on what Deleuze and Guattari describe as rhizomatic forms of correspondence, on transmutations and affiliations; it has many roots and cannot be traced back to one definite origin. Greek civilization, as Nietzsche made his contemporaries painfully aware, is not a cultural degree zero. At the historical moment of transatlantic exchange under investigation here, where globalization makes a quantum leap forward, the genealogical approach comes into its own as a key modern historiological paradigm.

---

[1] See Lois Davis Vines, *Valéry and Poe. A Literary Legacy* (New York: New York University Press, 1992), particularly Chapter One, 11-42.

[2] In a collection of essays surveying Poe's impact worldwide, Lois Davis Vines, ed., *Poe Abroad. Influence, Reputation, Affinities* (Iowa City: University of Iowa Press, 1999).

[3] "There is no question," writes, for example, Eloise M. Boyle, "that Poe came to Russia via the French Symbolists, especially through Baudelaire." Quoted in Vines, *Poe Abroad*, 19.

[4] Note, for instance, the remarkable similarities between central ideas in "The House of Usher" and *Buddenbrooks* and "The Pit and The Pendulum" and *In the Penal Colony*.

[5] Many stories display a scientific or quasi-scientific plot, for example "A Descent into the Maelström" and "The Gold Bug." In "The Pit and the Pendulum," the life-saving idea is an analysis of what is mechanically possible at the brief moment before the pendulum kills. A moment of most extreme danger and the opportunity analytically to engage the mind to act and avert it coincide.

[6] Patrick F. Quinn, *The French Face of Edgar Allen Poe* (Carbondale: Southern Illinois University Press, 1971), 18.

[7] See Vines, *Poe Abroad*, passim.

[8] Quinn, *The French Face of Edgar Poe*, 44-45.

[9] Hoffmann played a crucial role in the Second Empire, as Siegfried Kracauer demonstrates in his seminal monograph *Jaques Offenbach und das Paris seiner Zeit* (Frankfurt/Main: Suhrkamp, 1976). One of Offenbach's most influential compositions is his only opera in the strict genre sense of the word, *Contes d'Hoffmann*.

[10] See Quinn, *The French Face of Edgar Poe*, 49-52, 61-65, where he discusses Poe's stature as an American writer.

[11] Quinn emphasizes that "Poe's literary theory ... derived chiefly from the thought of Coleridge and in this way may be tied up to antecedent ideas in Germany, those of A. W. von Schlegel especially," *The French Face of Edgar Poe*, 36.

[12] Arno Schmidt, "Der Fall Ascher," *Der Triton mit dem Sonnenschirm. Großbritannische Gemütsergetzungen* (Karlsruhe: Stahlberg, 1969), 423. Our translation.

[13] Pierre Messac, *Influences françaises dans l'oeuvre d'Edgar Poe* (Paris, 1929), 74-78, cited in Quinn, *The French Face of Edgar Poe*, 32. It may also be possible to read this story as a re-rendition of Coleridge's *Ancient Mariner*.

[14] Paul Valéry, *The Collected Works of Paul Valéry*, 15 vols. Ed. Claude Pichois (Paris: Gallimard, 1976), 14: 10.

[15] From as early on as *La Soirée avec M. Teste* (1896).

[16] *Liebe, Tod und Teufel. Die Schwarze Romantik* (Munich: Hanser, 1970), 147-155.

[17] Rosemary Lloyd, *Selected Letters of Baudelaire. The Conquest of Solitude* (Chicago: University of Chicago Press, 1986), 148.

[18] Regarding aesthetic theory, Lois Vines makes much of Poe's influence on Baudelaire. She argues that Baudelaire was particularly affected by Poe's analytical approach to the process of composition (as famously demonstrated in "The Philosophy of Composition" where he retraces the genesis of his poem "The Raven") and his principle that certain subjects—for example, history, science and morality—were properly the domain of prose and should be excluded from poetry. See Vines, *Poe Abroad*, 165-170.

[19] Charles Baudelaire, "Edgar Allan Poe: His Life and Works," in *The Painter of Modern Life and Other Essays*, ed. and trans. Jonathan Mayne (London: Phaidon, 1995), 83.

[20] Ibid., 90.

[21] Ibid., 90-91.

[22] Charles Baudelaire, "Further Notes on Edgar Poe," in *The Painter of Modern Life and Other Essays*, ed. and trans. Jonathan Mayne (London: Phaidon, 1995), 95.

[23] Ibid., 102.

[24] Ibid., 97.

[25] René Wellek, *A History of Modern Criticism 1750-1950. Vol.4: The Later Nineteenth Century* (Cambridge: Cambridge University Press, 1983), 435-452. This gives a good account of the points of contact between Poe and Baudelaire in the area of their aesthetic theory (see particularly 434-39).

[26] See Lois Vines, *Valéry and Poe: A Literary Legacy* (New York: New York University Press, 1992), 21.

[27] Baudelaire, "The Painter of Modern Life," 7.

[28] Ibid., 3.

[29] Ibid.,12.

[30] Ibid., 9.

[31] A probable reference to Isaac D'Israeli's *Curiosities of Literature* where Grüninger's Renaissance book *Hortulus Animae* is mentioned, containing religious meditations accompanied by inappropriately vulgar and trivial illustrations.

[32] Edgar Allan Poe, "The Man of the Crowd," in *Edgar Allan Poe: Poetry and Tales* (New York: Literary Classics of the United States, 1984), 396.

[33] Baudelaire, "The Painter of Modern Life," 10.

[34] Ibid., 11.

[35] Ibid., 98.

[36] The volume *Charles Baudelaire*, subtitled *A Lyric Poet in the Era of High Capitalism* (London: Verso, 1997) consists of the following sections: "The Paris of the Second Empire in Baudelaire"; "Some Motifs in Baudelaire"; "Paris—The Capital of the Nineteenth Century."

[37] Susan Buck-Morss, *The Dialectics of Seeing. Walter Benjamin and the Arcades Project* (Cambridge, MA: MIT Press, 1991).

[38] Benjamin worked in the Warburg Library in Hamburg and became a fairly close associate of the circle of scholars active around the founder member, Aby Warburg. Benjamin adopted the theory of symbolic form as put forward for philosophy put forward by Ernst Cassirer and for art history by Erwin Panofsky and applied it to literary criticism.

[39] Benjamin, "The Paris of the Second Empire in Baudelaire," 43.

[40] Ibid., 48.

[41] Poe was familiar with Hoffmann's work, to the extent that he adopted the Hoffmannian nomenclature of the "tale" for his own works.

[42] Benjamin, "The Paris of the Second Empire in Baudelaire," 49

[43] Benjamin, "Some Motifs in Baudelaire," 130-131.

[44] Benjamin, "The Paris of the Second Empire in Baudelaire," 49.

[45] Ibid., 53-54.

[46] Ibid., 53.

[47] Ibid, 54.

[48] See Benjamin, "The Paris of the Second Empire in Baudelaire," 54.

[49] See *Karl Marx. Selected Writings*, ed. David McLellan (Oxford: Oxford University Press, 1977), 435-442.

[50] Michel Foucault, "What is Enlightenment," in *The Foucault Reader*, ed. Paul Rabinow (London: Penguin, 1984), 39.

[51] Ibid., 39-40.

[52] Baudelaire, "The Painter of Modern Life," 11.

[53] Foucault, "What is Enlightenment," 41.

[54] Ibid., 42.

Chapter 9

Nineteenth-Century American Women Writers' European Connections: The Case of Elizabeth Stuart Phelps

María Dolores Narbona Carrión

Elizabeth Stuart Phelps (1844-1911) represents one of the many women writers of the 19th century whose great success among her contemporary readers was diminished by the biased comments of male literary critics—frequently colleagues and friends. They have provoked diverse derogatory comments, among which Hawthorne's "scribbling women" is one of the best known. The literature produced by these women has also received "labels" such as "sentimental fiction," "fiction of sensibility," "domestic fiction," and "domestic sentimentalism." According to Nina Baym, these designations not only restrict the content of women's fiction in the 19th century, but they also add to it a kind of adverse judgement instead of a description.[1] Indeed, much of 19th century women's writing is still presented and studied under stereotypical paradigms. Jane Tompkins argues that 20th-century criticism associates "popularity with debasement, emotionality with ineffectiveness, religiosity with fakery, domesticity with triviality, and all of these, implicitly, with womanly inferiority."[2] What this biased view does not recognize is that 19th century women writers showed great interest in producing literary and artistic work, which is particularly apparent in

> their literary expertise and business skills, in their deep commitment to their career, in their expectation of self-determination as a writer, in their acceptance of moral and interpretative roles for their own work, and in their understanding of the professional behaviors expected between authors and publishers.[3]

These women considered their profession very seriously, at a time when it was extremely hard for them to put into practice their literary ideals, since Victorian society placed so many obstacles in the path of the woman who dared aspire to culture; moreover, it was seen as improper for women to "abandon" parental homes in order to study as their male friends did. This denial of access to public life also exerted a very negative influence on literary women, because, according to some literary critics, it prevented them from having vital experiences to enrich their writings. In this period, there existed the paradox that the very society which propitiated that restriction on women, at the same time undervalued their literary works because they lacked the vividness and verisimilitude that an authentic outdoor life permits. Elizabeth Stuart Phelps felt such restrictions acutely, as she notes in her autobiography: being a girl, she was not allowed to see the factory accident at Pemberton Mills, whereas her brother was: "My brother [Stuart], being of the privileged sex, was sent over to see the scene; but I was not allowed to go."[4] Nevertheless, she managed to get enough information about it so as to write one of the first American social stories, "The Tenth of January" (1868).

Susan Coultrap-McQuin points out other virtues of these female professionals, among which their purpose "to say something worthwhile to their culture that would elevate their work above the commercial, material realm" stands out.[5] This opinion is supported by Tompkins, who contributes to a fairer evaluation of 19th century women's fiction by declaring that "this body of work is remarkable for its intellectual complexity, ambition, and resourcefulness.[6]" Many of these women were self-taught, devouring books that belonged to the male family members or friends. The libraries of middle-class 19th century families proved invaluable to the Victorian woman writer, enabling her to engage with a variety of texts from a number of different national origins, with a resultant high level of cultural awareness.[7] Elizabeth Stuart Phelps is a case in point.

Phelps was a professional writer whose literary works—which show a vast culture that transcends American frontiers—have almost been forgotten, despite being bestsellers in the 19th century.[8] Phelps was lucky to be "born into a family of writers and into a household where writing was an integral part of daily activities."[9] Nevertheless, she was denied entrance to the local seminary and she had to go instead to Mrs. Edwards School for Young Ladies, a female academy at Andover, New England. There, she received a "proper" education which never reached the heights of that offered to her male colleagues; certain subjects, such as Greek and trigonometry were "thought, in those days, to be beyond the scope of the feminine intellect." Phelps did note, however, that, with the exception of the subjects mentioned above, "we pursued the same curriculum that our brothers did at college."[10]

During the years of her education, Phelps managed to increase her cultural knowledge to the point of surprising the reader of her writings with direct references or echoes of a wide range of famous writers from all over the world. As an adult, she established contacts—and solid friendships—with some of the most outstanding personalities of the American literary sphere.[11] A thorough summary of her relationship with them can be found in her autobiography, where she dedicates chapters to eminent writers such as Harriet Beecher Stowe, Henry Wadsworth Longfellow, John Greenleaf Whittier, Oliver Wendell Holmes, Celia Thaxter, Lucy Larcom, Lydia Maria Child, Phillip Brooks and Edward Rowland Sill.

Among her European colleagues, George Eliot stands out. Phelps's letters show that she trusted Eliot not only with the events of her life—as her description of the atmosphere of Gloucester indicates—but also with her inner conflicts and sufferings during her various ailments. Phelps would tell Eliot about her future literary projects, expecting in return wise counsels, but they did also change their roles, as can be inferred from the letter that Phelps wrote on February 26, 1873. As Carol Kessler notes, this letter contains Phelps's

> evaluation of Eliot's *Middlemarch* (1872) that suggests a major theme of her own *Avis*—namely, the rejection of "wifehood as a métier" and the exploration of "woman's personal identity," with which Phelps believed "Society had yet to acquaint itself" and was "yet to be revolutionized;" she thought it would "require a *great novel* to proclaim the royal lineage of the Coming Woman to the average mind." But only Eliot could write the great novel: her own would be "a small one."[12]

A few years later, Phelps did indeed write such a novel—*The Story of Avis* (1877); it was not, however, in any way "a small one." This novel reveals the courage of a Victorian woman—Phelps—who dared to defend overtly some of the revolutionary ideas which she both mentioned to and shared with Eliot. To introduce Chapter 7, Phelps quotes from George Eliot's verse drama *Armgart* (1871), in order to convey some of the main points of Phelps's philosophy: that women should try new possibilities out of the safety that the model of the "True Woman" offered them, and that those "New Women" required a new type of man:

> *ARMGART:*
> *"I accept the peril;*
> *I choose to walk high with*
> *sublimer dread*
> *Rather than crawl in safety."*
> *GRAF:*
> *"Armgart, I would with all my heart I knew*
> *The man so rare, that he could make your life*
> *As woman sweet to you,*
> *as artist safe."*[13]

As Kessler suggests, Phelps and Eliot also exchanged a series of letters on this subject. They both seemed to coincide in the opinion that it was easier to find an egalitarian relationship in marriage by choosing younger husbands. In fact, 4 years before marrying Herbert Dickinson Ward—who was17 years her junior—Phelps publicly expressed her approval of the marriages to younger men of Germaine de Staël, Margaret Fuller, Charlotte Brontë, and George Eliot, in the *Independent*.[14]

George Eliot influenced Phelps's life in various ways, both small and large. For example, Phelps called her dog Daniel Deronda, but she also imitated the other woman's customs. In *Chapters from a Life* Phelps suggests that took Eliot's cue in refusing to read notices of her own work; she "felt reinforced in the management of [her] little affairs by this great example."[15] We could also deduce their interconnection from the fact that *The Story of Avis*, which clearly reflects Eliot's influence, was a pseudo-autobiographical novel. And, what is most important, Phelps's literary style showed Eliot's traces, too, to the point of being sometimes compared with hers. One of Phelps's short stories, "Jack the Fisherman," was, according to the *Nation*, "on a level with the realism of George Eliot or Tolstoy."[16] Coultrap-McQuin likewise notes, "Critics compared her [Phelps] favorably to Nathaniel Hawthorne, Harriet Beecher Stowe, and George Eliot."[17] Moreover, Phelps—who was the first woman to lecture to undergraduate students at Boston University —discussed George Eliot in a series of 4 lectures on "Representative Modern Fiction" in 1876.[18] She was later requested to repeat the talks at Abbot Academy and in local Boston parlors.

Coultrap-McQuin acknowledges the important support that George Eliot had represented for Phelps, arguing that her death, together with the deaths of other important literary friends (James T. Fields, Henry Wadsworth Longfellow, Edward R. Sill, Mary Clemer, and Helen Hunt Jackson) meant the beginning of the end of "the literary and social world that had supported her in the past."[19] Phelps and Eliot's close relationship led Phelps to dedicate a poem to the English writer. It can be found in one of her collections of verse, *Songs of the Silent World* (1884), where she also memorialized some of the other aforementioned poets.

Before commenting on other influences on Phelps, I would like to point out that she was convinced that one should not write unless this activity was required by God. Her conception of literature was based on a premise that she defines in these terms: "The province of the artist is to portray life as it is; and life *is* moral responsibility .... An artist can no more fling off the moral sense from his work than he can oust it from his private life"[20] This quotation—as well as the contents of Phelps's writings—reveals the importance that she concedes to the didactic function of literature. Always concerned to improve women's situation, Phelps puts into practice in her fiction the theories of some female reformers of her time. Thus, she facilitated their understanding and promoted the diffusion of their ideas, which were also present in the many essays that she wrote for some of the most relevant periodicals of her time.[21] A detailed reading of Phelps's writings brings to mind the reform proposals of such famous leaders of the women's movement as Margaret Fuller and Mary Wollstonecraft. Despite the fact that Phelps does not make overt reference to the influence that the main books written by these two women exerted on her philosophy— Fuller's *Women in the Nineteenth Century* (1845) and Wollstonecraft's *Vindication of the Rights of Women* (1792)—it is easy to detect such influences in her attitudes. Like Fuller, Phelps argues that "woman possessed the same intellect as man, the same will, and therefore might have similar hopes of self-culture and achievement," and she shares with Woolstonecraft "the arguments of natural law and the divine right of women to claim their due as children of God and nature."[22] *The Story of Avis* (1877) is Phelps's best elaboration of those statements. Avis, instead of adjusting herself to the strict Victorian conventions for women, puts all her efforts to discovering God's will for her, which she is convinced will be revealed by Nature:

> Avis climbed down from the apple-tree .... It had come to her now—it
> had all come to her very plainly—why she was alive; what God meant
> by making her; what he meant by her being Avis Dobell, ... –Avis
> Dobell, who had rather take her painting-lesson than go to the senior
> party,—just Avis, not Coy, nor Barbara.[23]

Together with traces like this one of Wollstonecraft's dictates, *The Story of Avis* is full of other European writers' footprints from all epochs, including Chaucer, Plato, Goethe, Shakespeare, Wordsworth, Alfred Lord Tennyson, Kant, Victor Hugo, and Robert Browning, to name just some. The most evident ones can be found in the quotations which introduce each of the 25 chapters that constitute the novel. The cornerstone of *The Story of Avis* was, however, Elizabeth Barrett Browning. Her verse novel, *Aurora Leigh* (1856), was in the minds of many 19th-century women writers, despite the fact that literary critics—considering the text pernicious for young ladies—did their best to silence it.[24] Showalter suggests that Browning's success was due, in part, to the need of American women poets "to search for precursors who could define the shape of a serious woman poet career as she matured in artistry, range, and technique .... Many of them turned to the English poets Elizabeth Barrett Browning and Christina Rossetti."[25] Browning attempted a new approach to poetry, which conveyed the portrait of her society, something that responded to the popular taste, but would not diminish its quality. Thus, this poet declared in 1844 that "a true poetical novel—modern and on the level of the manners of the day—might be as good a poem as any other, and much more popular besides."[26] Phelps became one of her most devoted admirers, and discovered her vocation in *Aurora Leigh*, as she notes in her autobiography:

> I was sixteen, and I read "Aurora Leigh." ... and what Shakespeare or
> the Latin Fathers might have done for some other impressionable girl,
> Mrs. Browning—forever bless her strong and gentle name!—did for
> me. I owe to her, distinctly, the first visible aspiration (ambition is too
> low a word) to do some honest, hard work of my own in the World
> Beautiful, and for it.[27]

This quotation highlights the autobiographical character of *The Story of Avis*, as its protagonist read the same book when she was 16, even in the same month, June, which the writer seems to associate with the awakening of women to their authentic vocations. Here is the paragraph which contains the protagonist's first contact with *Aurora Leigh*:

She had taken her blue-and-gold girls' copy of "Aurora Leigh," and rushed out fiercely with it into the wide June weather ... here they were, she and Aurora together, tossing like feathers in the apple-bough, high, still, safe from all the whole round, rasping world.[28]

Phelps reinforces her devotion for this book by declaring that she had learnt by heart large portions of it, something that Avis also did in order to avoid the domestic tasks that Aurora hated too, as the novel shows: "She had told aunt Chloe hotly, to that good lady's extreme perplexity, that *'carpet-dusting, though a pretty trade, was not the imperative labor after all,'* and so had run up to get the poem, and see in secret if she had her quotation right."[29] It is important to consider that *Aurora Leigh*'s shadow is not only present in concrete quotations throughout the novel,but that its content also conforms in a way the whole argument of *The Story of Avis*. Through Browning's work, *The Story of Avis* became indirectly influenced by the European writers who inspired *Aurora Leigh,* many of whom are also the authors of the quotations that introduce the chapters of Phelps's novel. Among them, we must mention Tennyson—especially his views about women shown in *The Princess*; Wordsworth's *Prelude* (1850) shares with *Aurora Leigh* the telling of the growing assurance of poetic vocation; Madame de Staël's *Corinne* (1870) shows the development of a woman's artistic vocation; from George Sand's *Consuelo*, Browning took the insistence on the right to liberty as a condition of art. To summarize, Browning recognized the presence of her "literary fathers and mothers" in her work, including as well Charlotte Brontë, Honoré de Balzac, Eugène Sue, and Edward Bulwer Lytton.[30] All the features that these writers and their novels "lent" to *Aurora Leigh* also appear and entwine the main theme of *The Story of Avis*. Both novels depict the struggles of a strong woman character who pursues her ambition outside the domestic sphere. Thus, they challenged the conservative "Cult of True Womanhood," which, according to Barbara Welter, was defined by 4 cardinal virtues: piety, purity, submissiveness and domesticity.[31]

One almost feels tempted to consider *The Story of Avis* the American version of the English *Aurora Leigh* due to the many similarities that these works share: they both depict the growth of a female artist whose vocation is revealed through Nature and who has to overcome societal constrictions; both protagonists are orphaned and educated by surrogate mothers who do not support their artistic purposes and try instead to impose Victorian female conventions on them; Aurora's and Avis's femininity is called into question because they attempt tasks which are traditionally associated with men. The first chooses to write epic poetry—long a man's province—and the second proposes to become a professional—not an amateur—painter, something unusual for her time.[32]

However, both works differ in their protagonists' reaction to their respective love proposals. Although both show the influence of Charlotte Bronte's *Jane Eyre* in the female characters' surrendering to the love of damaged men, *Aurora Leigh* follows literally the 19th-century conviction that suffering humanizes.[33] Thus, this poetic novel portrays its male protagonist overcoming sexist ideas and broadening his understanding of Aurora as his human equal. But Phelps goes a step further in her revision of Browning's fairy tale ending: Avis's suitor pretends to support her professional aspirations after receiving his war injuries, but, once married, he manages to ruin her artistic career. This argument brings to mind the experience of many Victorian professional women, but especially that of Rebecca Harding Davis, one of the women writers whom Phelps most admired. Despite the fact that Davis shared her life with a man who recognized her artistic gifts, her marriage to him hindered her career as a serious writer. Thus, Phelps—faithful to her conception of literature, "to portray life as it is"—tried once again to depict the difficulties that a "dual career"(a profession and marriage) might represent for a woman.[34]

This subject acquired enormous importance in Phelps's life and fiction, as can be quite logically expected from a woman who was convinced—as her own words in *Chapters from a Life* show—that her mother's death had been occasioned by the continuous conflict of her vocations of mother/wife and writer: "The struggle killed her, but she fought till she fell."[35] After that fall, Elizabeth Stuart Phelps junior took the baton of her mother's struggle and demonstrated it symbolically by changing her original name, Mary Gray Phelps, for her mother's. Coultrap-McQuin argues that this was "an act that seemed to destine her to her own literary career as well as to her own struggles with a dual nature."[36] From that moment, one of the main purposes of her life was to ameliorate the social conditions of women, so that no more women should have to face her mother's sad end. Her autobiography reveals her conviction that professional women should not have to renounce motherhood, as it might become part of their vocation and it would even increase their worth: "I learned that a mother can be strong and still be sweet, and sweet although she is strong; and that she whom the world and her children both have need of, is of more value to each, for this very reason."[37] The problem was how to make this possible in a society which did not favor "dual natures" at all. In *The Story of Avis*, the search for a solution to that "riddle" which might also lead women to a self of their own definition—the gist of the matter of many other Phelps's writings—is wisely identified with the Arthurian quest for the Grail, when the protagonist's daughter begs Avis to read her this story "till there is no more to read."[38] This association confirms once again our author's familiarity with European culture. However, Phelps, applying her technique of inversion to the Arthurian legend, eliminates its male protagonists and puts in their places women: by the end of the novel, Avis—instead of Sir Lancelot—delegates to her daughter—not to Sir Galahad—the task of discovering and developing her inner vocation, since she has not been able to do so.

Similarly, in her poem "Guinevere," Phelps makes the point that, no matter how often we may read the story of this queen and her husband, there is always something new to be discovered, especially from a female perspective. She acknowledges that the well-known tale

> was written in the story we have learned,
> between the ashen lines, invisible,
> in hieroglyphs that blazed and leaped like light
> unto the eyes. A thousand times we read;
> a thousand turn the page and understand,
> and think we know the record of a life,
> when lo! If we will open once again
> the awful volume, hid, mysterious,
> intent, there lies the unseen alphabet —
> re-reads the tale from breath to death, and spells
> a living language that we never knew.[39]

Phelps seems to have set herself up as a female re-interpreter of those Arthurian texts known in America in the versions of many eminent European authors. In fact, despite the fact that Arthurian literature is traditionally considered the domain of men, Phelps was not alone in her attempt to offer the female side of this legend. Many other 19th-century women writers, such as Letitia Elizabeth Landon, Dinah Maria Mulock Craick, and Lucy Larcom, among others, helped to create a tradition in America which "incorporates a broad spectrum of Arthurian works, some of which are remarkably prescient in their attitudes towards social problems, religion, philosophy, and feminism."[40] Indeed, according to Alan and Barbara Lupack:

> From the historical retellings of the legendary stories to the original reworkings of them, from the versions set in Arthur's day to those set in modern times, from fantasy and science fiction to mystery and children's literature, contemporary Arthurian novels by women have garnered critical attention and gained popular acclaim.[41]

As the Lupacks indicate, women, "by virtue of being outside the mainstream of Arthurian tradition," usually present radical reinterpretations and innovative reworkings of it.[42] Indeed, in Phelps's case, she tends to highlight female characters, who become the absolute protagonists of the stories she rewrites. Among the 6 Arthurian works written by Phelps, 4 include female characters in their very titles: "The Lady of Shalott," "The True Story of Guenever," "Elaine and Elaine," and "Guinevere." This responds to the more general tendency to recognize nobility in characters who were not male descendants of legendary figures (as was the custom) but who earned high status with their own virtues, which American women writers frequently show in their Arthurian literature. Phelps's writings based on the Arthurian legend reveal that, although she turned to literary Europe in order to find inspiration, she also distilled those cultural sources and imprinted on them her own particular style and way of thought. The result of this process, which many other Victorian women writers also adapted, conveys the form and basic content of cultural productions from one side of the Atlantic to the other, while reflecting contextual peculiarities.

Self-consciously professional, Phelps stands as an example of those many other 19th-century women writers of fiction who worked hard in order to reach a high level of cultural literacy—something that Victorian society did not facilitate. Phelps was multiply influenced by and an influencer of European cultural traditions; in this way, she was truly a transatlantic writer of acclaim.

---

[1] Nina Baym, *Woman's Fiction: A Guide to Novels by and about Women in America, 1820-1870* (Ithaca: Cornell University Press, 1978), 24. Some of Baym's objections to the denominations that this kind of literature has traditionally received include the following: "The term 'sentimental'... means that ... the author's depiction of real life is heavily slanted toward the pretty and tender and hence is not a comment on reality but an evasion of it" (24). Baym argues that "domesticity" is very commonly equated with entrapment. She also snotes that the "cult of domesticity" "assumes that men as well as women find greatest happiness and fulfilment in domestic relations, by which are meant not simply spouse and parent, but the whole network of human attachments based on love, support, and mutual responsibility. Domesticity is set forth as a value scheme for ordering all of life, in competition with the ethos of money and exploitation that is perceived to prevail in American society" (27).

[2] Jane Tompkins, *Sensational Designs: The Cultural Work of American Fiction 1790-1860* (New York: Oxford University Press, 1985), 123. Harris proposes another reason: "Devaluation of nineteenth-century women's novels is ... attributable to the devaluation of piety and sentiment, values that twenty-

century critics assigned exclusively to women but that nineteenth-century writers and readers did not." Susan K. Harris, *Nineteenth Century American Women's Novels* (Cambridge: Cambridge University Press, 1990), 79.

[3] Susan Coultrap-McQuin, *Doing Literary Business: American Women Writers in the Nineteenth Century* (Chapel Hill: The University of Carolina Press, 1990), 195.

[4] Elizabeth Stuart Phelps, *Chapters From a Life* (Boston: Houghton, Mifflin and Company, 1896), 91.

[5] Coultrap-McQuin, 197.

[6] Tompkins, 124.

[7] Although this essay focuses on Elizabeth Stuart Phelps, it is appropriate to illustrate how well-read 19th-century women writers were. For this purpose, I have chosen Louisa May Alcott because she shares with Phelps most of her favorite writers: "The young Louisa read widely in American, English, and European women's literature: Madame de Staël, Mary Wollstonecraft, Maria Edgeworth, Fanny Burney, George Sand, George Eliot, Elizabeth Barrett Browning, Charlotte Yonge, Fredrika Bremer, Lydia Maria Child, Harriet Beecher Stowe, Susan Warner, Gail Hamilton, Margaret Fuller, and Harriet Prescot Spofford." Elaine Showalter, *Sister's Choice: Tradition and Change in American Women's Writing* (Oxford: Clarendon, 1991), 47.

[8] Henry C. Vedder, to give an example of Phelps's popularity, declares that *The Gates Ajar* (1868), one of the more than 50 books she wrote, could be found "almost on every table." Henry C. Vedder, *American Writers of To-day* (New York: Silver, Burdett and Company, 1894), 187. Other authors give more concrete details: E. F. Harkins says that almost 100,000 copies of this book where published. E. F. Harkins, *Famous Authors (Women)*, (Boston: Colonial Press, 1906), 12. Carol Farley Kessler adds that *The Gates Ajar* had reached slightly over 100,000 copies in print in England by 1900 Carol Farley Kessler, *Elizabeth Stuart Phelps* (Boston: G. K. Hall, 1982), 30. Phelps herself explains that it had been translated into German, French, Dutch, and Italian. The book surpassed the American frontiers and entered England, as Phelps's complaints about its pirating in that country confirms. Elizabeth Stuart Phelps, *Chapters* 111-12.

[9] Lori Duin Kelly, *The Life and Works of Elizabeth Stuart Phelps: Victorian Feminist Writer* (Troy, NY: The Whitston Publishing Company, 1983), 1. Both of her grandfathers, Moses Stuart and Eliakim Phelps, were ministers and writers. Phelps's mother—also Elizabeth Stuart Phelps—wrote several books and short stories for children. Phelps's father, Austin Phelps, taught writing at Andover and published several books. All of these writers had in common their conception that the purpose of literature was to teach.

[10] Phelps, *Chapters* 60-61.

[11] To validate this statement, it seems appropriate to add this quotation from Phelps's own words: "Of our great pentarchy of poets, one—Lowell—I never met; and of another—Emerson—my personal knowledge, as I have said, was but of the slightest. With the remaining three [Henry Wadsworth Longfellow, John Greenleaf Whittier, James T. Fields] I had different degrees of friendship;

and to speak of them is still a privilege full of affectionate sadness." *Chapters*, 15.

[12] Kessler, 86. Kessler cites the letter written by Phelps to Eliot on December 1, 1876, and May 27, 1877, located in the Beinecke Rare Book and Manuscript Library, Yale University.

[13] Elizabeth Stuart Phelps, *The Story of Avis*, ed. Carol Farley Kessler (New Brunswick: Rutgers University Press, 1992), 66.

[14] "The Empty Column," *The Independent*, 4 September 1884, 36.

[15] Phelps, *Chapters*, 121.

[16] Kessler, 125.

[17] Coultrap-McQuin, 176.

[18] Phelps makes reference to this fact in *Chapters*, 254-55.

[19] Coultrap-McQuin, 177.

[20] Phelps, *Chapters*, 263. This definition might surprise contemporary readers, but, in order to interpret it appropriately, we must once more place ourselves in the literary context of the 19th century, because, as Jane Tompkins recognizes, "In the 1850s the aesthetic and the didactic, the serious and the sentimental were not opposed but overlapping designations" (17).

[21] Phelps's nonfiction articles—most of which were given over to the woman question—appeared in distinguished periodicals, among them: *The Independent, Harper's New Monthly Magazine, Harper's Bazaar, McClure's Magazine, Century*, the *North American Review*, the *Atlantic Monthly*, the *Congregationalist, Forum*, the *Ladies' Home Journal*, and *Good Housekeeping*.

[22] Barbara Welter, *Dimity Convictions: The American Woman in the Nineteenth Century* (Athens: Ohio University Press, 1985), 180.

[23] Phelps, *Story of Avis*, 32.

[24] Becky Lewis, "'That Idyl of the June, that Girls' Gospel': Elizabeth Stuart Phelps and Browning's Aurora Leigh" (paper presented at the American Women Writers & The Literary Marketplace Conference, South Carolina, December 15, 1994), 19.

[25] Elaine Showalter, *Sister's Choice: Tradition and Change in American Women's Writing* (Oxford: Clarendon, 1991), 108. Emily Dickinson was one the poets influenced by Browning. Sandra Gilbert and Susan assert that *Aurora Leigh* provided an important apostate text for Dickinson in its depiction of a strong women character who pursues her ambition outside the domestic sphere. Sandra M. Gilbert and Susan Gubar, *The Madwoman in the Attic. The Woman Writer and the Nineteenth-Century Literary Imagination* (New Haven: Yale University Press, 1979), 559-61.

[26] Kerry McSweeney, introduction to *Aurora Leigh*, by Elizabeth Barrett Browning (Oxford: Oxford University Press, 1993), xiii.

[27] Phelps, *Chapters*, 65-66.

[28] Phelps, *Story of Avis*, 31.

[29] Phelps, *Chapters*, 65; *Story of Avis*, 31.

[30] McSweeney, xviii-xix.

[31] Welter, 21.

[32] "Middle-class women were encouraged to develop taste rather than knowledge; and a tentative interest in fine art, music and poetry, content to stay on the amateur side of the fence, was a sign of desirable refinement." Clarissa Campbell Orr, ed., *Women in the Victorian Art World* (Manchester: Manchester University Press, 1996), 110.

[33] This theme can be found in many 19th-century poems, for example in William Wordsworth's "Elegiac Stanzas," and Alfred Lord Tennyson's *In Memoriam*.

[34] Phelps shows in her novels her conception of marriage as another profession for women. See *The Story of Avis*: "'Marriage,' said Avis, not assertively, but only sadly, as if she were but recognizing some dreary, universal truth, like that of sin, or misery, or death, 'is a profession to a woman. And I have my work; I have my work!'" (71).

[35] Phelps, *Chapters*, 15.

[36] Coultrap-McQuin, 170.

[37] Phelps, *Chapters*, 15.

[38] Phelps, *Story of Avis*, 249.

[39] "Guinevere" in *Songs of the Silent World and Other Poems* (Boston: Houghton & Mifflin, 1885).

[40] Alan Lupack and Barbara Tepa Lupack, eds., *Arthurian Literature by Women* (New York and London: Garland Publishing, 1999), x.

[41] Ibid., ix.

[42] Ibid., 4.

Chapter 10

The Hegemonic Body: Politics of a Black Peruvian Dance

Marcia M. Loo

Any epistemological approach to reality involves providing meanings to objects, actions, and relations. The closer that objects are related to subjectivity, the more varied and intricate their meanings become. Human bodies and their parts constitute subjective entities that are often deprecated in Western societies. They are loaded with cultural symbolism: they become public and private; acquire political as well as economic status; and are seen as sexual, moral, and very often controversial objects. The body and the senses are not objects *per se*; rather, they are socially constructed. Therefore their meanings vary and change through time, from one society to another, from person to person. However, no matter what meanings are attached in the construction of the body, we cannot but recognize that we are all embodied, and that the body is primarily a symbol of the self. When bodies are deprived of freedom and owned by others, they strive for liberation. When such deprivation involves violation and physical cruelty that is executed systematically through generations, the struggles become internalized ideological contests. Rituals and performative utterances such as music and dance are the means for ideological expression, and bodies enacting rituals become political sites for manifesting resistance against hegemonic domination.

Spaniards took Africans to Peru and instrumentalized their bodies as tools to fulfill a greed for riches. Some African bodies survived and created a Peruvian subculture with an ideology of its own. Nowadays, although only 2% of the Peruvian population is black, and that percentage is shared with Asian descendants, Japanese and Chinese for the most part, the presence of black music is broadly spread along the coastal cities of Peru where it contains undeniable African influence. It has developed an original style that makes it identifiable among the varieties of the African musical legacy disseminated all around the world. An intriguing feature of this subculture is the fact that Black-Peruvians do not identify themselves as African descendants, nor do they seem *en masse* to possess relevant information about their cultural and racial origins. Strongly nationalistic, their primary identification is as Peruvians; nevertheless they recognize their ethnic group as distinct from those of Whites, Andean, Mestizo and Asian Peruvian, by calling themselves *Peru Negro* or "Black Peru."

The beginnings of African origins in Peru were varied and differed from those elsewhere in the Americas. Unlike Brazil or Central and North American countries, where large groups of slaves with the same African ethnicity were imported, only small and diverse groups were transported to Peru, which discouraged the preservation of communal traditions.[1] Lacking common language and ethnicity, and without social organization to maintain their roots, African slaves were progressively integrated into the culture and language of their new country. European intentions to establish a hegemonic rule, both culturally and politically, were paradoxically surmounted by their own colonizing regulations. What the European conquerors were not able to foresee was the political and cultural potential they were transporting; they thought only of bodily strength. African slaves grew up culturally stronger as time passed, and became a generating source for the building of New World identities. This chapter aims to demonstrate that the performance of an Afro-Peruvian dance called *El Alcatraz* is an enactment of the counter-hegemonic ideology of the Black Peruvian subculture. This chapter explores, through Foucault's discussion of the politics of the body, the non-discursive languages and non-official discourses that are present in the performance—languages and discourses that are witness to intricate processes of transculturation, creolization, and syncretism.

Cultural Interconnections

Black Peruvian music shares characteristics with its African roots but also displays those that typically express its new identity. The most prominent aesthetic characteristic of African music—the emphasis on rhythm and percussion—is exhibited in most Black Peruvian music through richly syncopated rhythmic varieties, contrasting meters, combinations of different rhythms, and offbeat or cross-accent patterns. African rhythm and African drumming help to reinforce a sense of community;[2] this ideological function of music might be traced in the resistance of Black Peruvian percussion to challenges that have threatened its survival.

The rigors of slavery precluded the preservation of African instruments. The desert coastline naturally denied the materials to preserve African membranophones. Drums and marimbas disappeared, but the descendants of African slaves in Peru developed original substitutes. First they used ceramic vessels to keep their rhythms alive. Later, a more effective rhythmic device superseded the ceramic drums: the *cajon*, a simple wooden box, was born as a transculturated instrument to keep the rhythms alive while conveying a new "soundscape."[3] Its creation and permanence needs to be regarded as an objectification of the ancestral impulses of cultural identity. The absence of drums fueled just such an incentive to create a singular percussion instrument. The popularity of the Peruvian *cajon* has notably increased, to the extent that today it is an indispensable rhythmic element of Peruvian coastal music.

In African music, the audience must be actively engaged in making sense of the whole by helping to provide the beat, so that performers and audience are integrated in a participatory music. Black Peruvian music thus does not convey a radical separation between performers and audience. Many Black Peruvian musical genres display a notable repetitive function developed through a dominant conversation with a clearly defined alternation, a swinging back and forth from solo to chorus, or from solo to an emphatic instrumental reply. This type of musical structure, known as *call and response*, is a major characteristic of most African musical idioms.[4]

Equally recognizable and strongly representative of African cultures is the involvement of the body in musical performances. Every participant in the performance stresses the rhythms with bodily motion. As well as the musicians and dancers, the whole community uses their bodies as rhythmic instruments, displaying intense corporeality and sensuality. The musicians perform polyrhythmic features by moving some part of the body while they are playing, so as to keep an additional beat. Most Black Peruvian dances include corporal movements such as shoulder shaking, hip bouncing, the striking of the heels and toes of the shoes against the floor, and brushing movements of the shoe or bare foot along the floor or ground.[5] Black Peruvians also perform rhythmic clapping to provide counter-rhythmic elements, and supportive shouting to encourage corporal involvement. Africans used bodily motion as an undercurrent providing the pulse of the dance; the Peruvian descendants of the transported Africans kept the same use but added another aspect—a political dimension.

Politics of the Body

Anthropology has increasingly concerned itself with the body because, in pre-modern societies, the body was an important surface on which the marks of social status, family position, tribal affiliation, age, gender, and religious conditioning were easily and publicly displayed. While it is obviously the case in modern societies that bodily displays (dress, posture, cosmetics) are crucial for indicating wealth and life-style, in pre-modern societies the body was a more importantly a site of public symbolism, often through decoration, tattooing, and scarification.[6]

Nietzsche makes it evident that the body is crucial in understanding the dilemmas of modernity. He showed that aesthetic experience had more in common with sexual ecstasy, religious rapture, and the frenzy of primitive dance than it did with the quiet, individualistic contemplation of a work of art.[7] Thus, the sensual and erotic response of the body, rather than the neutral inquiry of the mind, becomes for Nietzsche the core of artistic experience. A key notion beyond dispute is Nietzsche's criticism of rationality as a "perspective" or a way of life that obscures the importance of emotion and feeling in the human perception of reality.[8] In order to restore this emotionality, which involves the realities of touch, taste, motion, and the senses, Nietzsche ascribed a singular importance to artistic activity as a simultaneously political and therapeutic practice. He saw human evolution in terms of dialectic. Every period in the human history is characterized by the transformations that humans impose upon nature, which conversely promotes a transformation of human nature itself, thus giving rise to a new ideal of humankind, manifested simultaneously in a new body. In this evolutionary process, art is for Nietzsche a major mechanism, an engendering source.

In Foucault there is a parallel theme: the modern epoch was inaugurated by the discovery of a new regime of surveillance, which has produced the useful and disciplined body. The modern state is characterized not only by different practices of regulation, but also by the fact that human beings have developed internal techniques of self-mastery and restraint. The necessity of vindicating the body, of giving back its human rights, has generated "oppositional writing"—critical writing that opposes hegemonic discourse and restores the status of the body as the seat of desire, irrationality, and emotionality; thus, the body emerges as a symbol of protest, interrogating the rationality and regulations of official culture.

The starting point for any examination of the human body is the relationship between the body and something else. Being a "dialogical" confrontation, it provides the foundation for a historicity of the human body by contrasting, opposing, or comparing it to something taken to be different.[9] In addition to this consideration, recent philosophical inquiries of the general concept of the body have increasingly focused on humankind as a central problem; thus the need for conceptualizing the *human* body in particular becomes apparent. The social relations and cultural meanings of colonial Peru did not allow African slaves' bodies to become *human* bodies. At that time, the importation of African slaves introduced a racial, ethnic component supposed to be irrelevant as historical agent. Considered just as working tools for mining and agricultural labor, African bodies were not viewed in human terms. Spanish colonization imposed a socio-cultural system strongly influenced by the Catholic religion, whose basic oppositions were life and death, sacred and profane; the human body acquired meaning in its relation to the soul. Body and soul were hierarchically tied, and while the body was not necessarily something negative, it was by definition inferior in relation to the soul. Spanish colonial hegemony implicitly denied the status of human bodies to African slaves since the Catholic religion did not recognize slaves' bodies as qualified containers for souls. Therefore, the inability to relate African bodies to anything else—soul, spirit, or anima—left them out of any possible conceptualization as human bodies.[10]

The soul is thus the principle that provides the body with its human quality. The foundation of this statement is not religious, though; Foucault's theories on the domination of the body provide us with the political significance of interconnecting body and soul. The body is simply a body—more precisely, a living body with its own rhythms, flows and intensities, its pain and its pleasures. Foucault argues that the soul really does exist, and that its existence is produced perpetually. Therefore, it is the political context of the body that generates the soul. Foucault's view stands Plato's conception on its head, for if the soul is an effect and a tool of a political anatomy, then the soul is in fact the prison of the body.[11]

> It is produced permanently around, on, within the body by the functioning of a power that is exercised on those punished—and, in a more general way, on those one supervises, trains and corrects; over madmen, children at home and at school, the colonized, over those who are stuck at a machine and supervised for the rest of their lives.[12]

It was not until the 17th and 18th centuries that a general Western concept of the body began to take shape, pushed by the emerging technology of power. This concept was forged through what Foucault called the disciplining of the body, characterized by the usefulness (the body as a tool) and manageability (controllability) of the body. The emergence of a concept of the body in Peru was subordinated to the liberation of the country from colonization, which occurred in 1821. A conceptualization of Black Peruvian bodies had to wait even longer, until 1845, when Peruvian president Ramon Castilla's proclamation to unchain the slaves allowed for the evolution of Black Peruvian hegemonic bodies, which today are capable of enacting political statements through the performance of dances such as *El Alcatraz*.

Bodies can be read as discourses, and discourses can in turn construct bodies. Rhetorical puzzle or philosophical paradox, this dichotomy probably reflects two sides of the same coin. When thinking about discourses, the usual associations generally concern the display of speech, the content of the speech itself, the text of printed material, the arrangement of sentences within a text, and so on. What they all have in common are "words," so words typically characterize discourses. But Foucault projects discourses beyond words. His definition of discourse introduces the supporting social constructionism needed to elaborate his extreme version. However, defining discourses as "practices which form the objects of which they speak" conveys a far more relevant meaning for power-knowledge relations.[13] Such a definition does not imply that all the objects of our consciousness are created out of discourses, or that nothing has an independent existence outside of language. It rather relies upon the frame of reference that a discourse provides in order to construct the meanings of the objects to which it refers. A discourse refers to a set of meanings, metaphors, representations, images, stories, statements, and so on that together to produce a particular version of events. The general association with words allows a discourse to manifest itself in written text as well as in speech. But a discourse can go beyond the scope of language to express meanings in visual images like advertisements, films, clothes, or bodies. The body and its movements can thus be read as a "text."

El Alcatraz: A Discursive Dance

El Alcatraz is a varied form of another important Black Peruvian musical genre called *Festejo*. Both share common musical characteristics, though the performance of the dances is different. The music displays a considerable metric variety and even the simultaneous use of two different meters, but the underlying meter is essentially 6/8. The tempo is a bit faster in the *Festejo*, whereas *El Alcatraz* exhibits greater syncopation. The character of both dances is festive and contagious; however, the syncopation gives a warm sensuality to the latter. The form is cyclical, with a rhythmic pattern constantly repeated yet enriched by the syncopated hand-clapping. The melody consists of short phrases, with a surging rhythm frequently interrupted at phrase-endings by a sudden pause or by a tone of longer duration. The "call and response" character of the melodic line in consecutive phrases is exaggerated in the final section, composed of melodic fragments sung in response by soloist and chorus. The texts of *El Alcatraz* often follow a set of strophic forms. They usually treat a festive theme, or reflect the painful conditions of slavery. Texts and melodies are sometimes interchanged between *Festejos* and *Alcatraces*, and texts may even be borrowed from another musical genre.

The instrumentation of *El Alcatraz* includes the typical elements of a traditional Black Peruvian ensemble: guitar, *cajon*,[14] *quijada*,[15] hand-clapping, shouting and voices, a soloist, and a chorus. The instrumentation progressively increases the musical density by introducing each instrument one after the other. The acoustic guitar starts with a stressed, syncopated rhythm that shows the result of a creolization of Spanish, Andean, and African legacy, by bringing together the instrument, the scale used, and the syncopation. A polyrhythmic fabric is woven by means of hand-clapping, and a cross-accented rhythm is provided by the *cajon*.

The performative features of *El Alcatraz* dance are different from those of the *Festejo*. *El Alcatraz* takes its name from the sea bird whose walk is imitated in the steps of the dance. But the name also refers to the human buttocks through the similarity of the words *alcatraz* and *acá atrás*, the latter Spanish expression meaning "here, my tushy." *El Alcatraz* is performed in a circle, alternating between male and female. In the center of the circle, one male-female couple dances at a time. Either or both dancers carry a flaming stick or candle with which he or she tries to light a paper streamer attached like a tail behind the partner, while the other makes such pelvic movements that the streamer flicks about, dodging the flame. Strongly symbolic, the contents of the dance have been for the most part interpreted as an expression of exuberant eroticism, in colonial terms a characteristic usually associated with blacks in Peru. The variety of body movements that accompany the music were read as unrefined, primitive, immoral, or promiscuous—these were the common colonial discourses attached to it. Although the presence of sensuality is undeniable, it does not constitute the main ideological purpose of the dance. The white master's fire burned countless black slave bodies on the basis of colonial rights. Postcolonial Black Peruvians enabled themselves to extinguish the colonial fire by means of corporal movements; the "obscene" bodies that had experienced the hegemonic violence learned how to react counter-hegemonically.

The discourses present in any culture—those of age, gender, education, sexuality, and others—are constructed differently, depending on the implications each component has for each other. Individuals sharing ethnicity, social status, education, and nationality for the most part share some common discourses. However, alternative discourses are available when a critical reading looks for deeper connections not overtly exhibited on the surface of a text. An alternative discourse of the dance, *El Alcatraz*, requires paying attention to a variety of performative characteristics that reveal the potent interconnections between them.

The same discursive mechanisms that turn objects and events into texts to be read can reverse the process and turn discourses themselves into beings, whose existence is commonly assumed to be real. Thus, as Ian Parker argues, "discourses allow us to see things that are not 'really' there, and ... once an object has been elaborated in a discourse it is difficult not to refer to it as if it were real."[16] This discursive transformation is precisely what has occurred in the case of abstract qualities and entities such as "beauty," "justice," "intelligence," "marriage," and "love," among others; we tend to treat them as if they have the same kind of presence as physical objects. Discourses, then, convey the awesome potential to switch the ontological status of words.

Multiple cases of ontological permutation can be detected in official discourse, wherein patterns for "healthy," "normal," "beautiful," and "moral" people are constructed. Such discursive constructs match the traces left by Spanish domination as it was imposed upon African slaves. Black Peruvian subculture was marked by its own slave history, the remnants of which continued to influence Peruvian social and cultural organization long after the end of slavery. Official discourse attached to Black Peruvians meanings of "less intelligent," "less beautiful," "less sensitive," and "less morally capable" than "normal people." In this manner, the bodies of the Africans and their descendants were considered to be "naturally" equipped for hard labor, for popular, "unrefined" sports involving physical strength—like boxing and soccer—and for "obscene" and "evil" dance.

But the performance of *El Alcatraz* dance cannot be regarded as official discourse. *El Alcatraz* is a performance of popular music and dance, at its most popular level, the music and dance that Black

Peruvians use for entertainment, to enliven parties. However, from the *perspective* of official culture, *El Alcatraz* cannot be regarded even as legitimate knowledge, so the discourse encapsulated in *El Alcatraz* text is taken to be simply popular and meaningless lyrics. Yet, through Foucault's genealogy, non-official discourses can indeed be read as legitimate knowledge. *El Alcatraz* legitimates its own discourse by denouncing the violation and physical abuse perpetrated on slave bodies. It challenges the official perspective by saying "*A que no me quemas*"—"I bet you can't burn me"—and affirms a commitment to a radical opposition to slavery when stating, "*A mi no me quema nadie*": "I will be burned by no one."

It is worthwhile here to consider Foucault's construction of a "counter-memory," or "non-discursive" language.[17] In the performance of *El Alcatraz*, each movement and gesture can be read as a counterpart to the traditional dancing style officially accepted as expressive of a "refined" education. Here, the non-discursive language of the body actually speaks of resistance to the official patriarchal culture. In *El Alcatraz*, female and male bodies are detached from each other, as opposed to the more elegant interlacing of couples. Female bodies move freely, where in the bourgeois dance they must be restricted. Female body motion conveys self-initiative, while "dignified" dancing suggests that women must be subordinated to male leadership. Vigorous shaking of the hips and shoulders is the norm, whereas decorous and refined dancing requires a controlled body motion. The hands and arms are detached and free, as opposed to moderately policed and controlled. The free hands and arms belong to the women, untrammeled by male hands and shoulders.

These features illustrate how the body in *El Alcatraz*—in particular, the female body—becomes a key site of resistance to the dominant culture. Black Peruvians, it can be argued, could not linguistically or through writing express their will as a collective until they had developed a post-colonial discourse of their own. Meanwhile, the body made statements of affirmation of cultural identity, of racial pride, and vital sensuality. By performing *El Alcatraz*, Black Peruvians challenged the master's fire and official power by blowing out the fire with hip shaking. Moreover, the dance mocked and laughed at hegemonic rule, even when attacking by the flank. Black Peruvian voices may not have had representation in the channel of official discourses, but notwithstanding this, their bodies have learned to communicate their oppositional power. Black Peruvian identity maintained the ancestral vestiges of its African legacy, and processed them with the fuel of oppression and resistance. Yet it adopted a rich, hybrid Peruvian cultural tradition as well. In intermingling such varied cultural threads, it gave birth to sounds and performances unique in their style, and promoted a new ideology, a particular way of thinking and feeling not identifiable as African or Peruvian, but proudly Black Peruvian.

---

[1] See Maria Rostworowski, *Pachacamac y el Señor de los Milagros* (Peru: Pontificia Universidad Católica del Peru, 1992).

[2] John Chernoff, *African Rhythm and African Sensibility* (Chicago: The University of Chicago Press, 1979), passim.

[3] "Soundscape" is a cultural soundprint, or the particular "sound-taste" of the music of a given culture.

[4] William David Tompkins, "Afro-Peruvian Traditions," in *The Garland Encyclopedia of World Music* eds. Dale A. Olsen and Daniel Sheehy (New York: Garland Publishing, Inc., 1998), 2: 491-502.

[5] William David Tompkins, *The Musical Traditions of the Blacks of Coastal Peru* (Los Angeles: University of California Press, 1981), passim.

[6] Robert Brain, *The Decorated Body* (London: Hutchinson, 1979), 106-37.

[7] See Friedrich Nieztsche, *The Birth of Tragedy and the Genealogy of Morals* (Garden City, NY: Doubleday, 1956).

[8] According to Nietsche's *Perspectivism*, "knowledge" is a point of view, and "truth" is a matter of the perspective one adopts.

[9] Mikhail Bakhtin, *The Dialogic Imagination: Four Essays* (Austin: University of Texas Press, 1981), 420-22.

[10] See Pasi Falk, *The Consuming Body* (London: Sage Publications, 1994).

[11] Ibid., 30.

[12] Michel Foucault, *Discipline and Punish* (Harmondsworth: Penguin Books, 1979), 29.

[13] Michel Foucault, *The Archeology of Knowledge* (London: Tavistock, 1972), 49.

[14] The *cajon* is the Black Peruvian idiophone most widely used in the performance of Peruvian coastal music. It is a simple wooden box about 50cm x 30cm x 25cm, with a sound hole about 10cms in diameter in the back. The player normally sits on top of the instrument, rhythmically striking the front and sides of it with his hands.

[15] The *quijada* supplies a buzzing effect produced by numerous African instruments. Also called *carraca* or *carachacha*, the *quijada* is the lower jawbone of an ass, mule, or horse, and one of the most popular Black Peruvian idiophones. To be used as a percussion instrument, the jawbone is stripped of its flesh and the teeth are loosened so they can rattle in their sockets when the player scrapes a piece of sheep's rib across the face of the jaw or the surface of the molars.

[16] Ian Parker, *Discourse Dynamics: Critical Analysis for Social and Individual Psychology* (New York: Routledge, 1992), 5.

[17] Scott Lash, "Genealogy and the Body: Foucault/Deleuze/Nietsche," in *The Body: Social Process and Cultural Theory*, ed. M. Featherstone (London: Sage, 1991), 256-78.

Part Four:
Transatlantic Economies

Chapter 11

Exporting the Industrial Revolution: The Migration of Cornish Mining Technology to Latin America in the Early 19th Century

Sharron Schwartz

Situated at the extreme southwest of Britain, Cornwall is a narrow peninsula surrounded on three sides by the Atlantic Ocean and bounded from neighboring Devon by the River Tamar in the east. It covers an area of no more than 1,365 square miles, and at no time during the first half of the 19th century could it boast a population greater than 375,000. Yet its size is disproportionate to the influence the Cornish people have exerted upon the world in the field of metalliferous mining and engineering.

Shifts in spatial focus exploring the combined and uneven regional patterns of industrialization in Britain have drawn attention to Cornwall's leading role in the industrial revolution in the field of metal mining and steam engineering.[1] Important advances, too, have been made in the field of area studies.[2] Instead of viewing the world as being divided into a set number of large, quasi-continental regions, new, less rigid models of global scholarship are re-framing area studies around ocean and sea basins.[3] We are increasingly being encouraged to look at the world not as divided into knowable, self-contained "areas," but as part of an inter-linked whole in which people, ideas, capital, and technology are connected across great physical divides.[4] The importance in this spatial shift in area studies is that it highlights the significance of littoral societies—such as Cornwall—and enables us to view them not as peripheries of nation-states or territorial civilizations, but as communities in their own right.

With this advance in area studies and the new epistemological approach to industrialization outlined above, it is perhaps timely to investigate the role of *regional* contributions to the overseas expansion of British industrial prowess in the early 19th century. This chapter therefore concentrates on the pioneering exportation of metalliferous mining skills and steam technology to Latin America by Cornish miners, or "Cousin Jacks" as they were colloquially known,[5] which heralded the transatlantic migration of the industrial revolution. Latin America, as an early recipient of British industrial technology, was the birthplace of the modern, integrated global mining economy with its attendant capital and labor markets. In the first half of the 19th century, Cornwall formed the hub of this developing international mining market, initially connected by dense transatlantic trade and migration networks with South and Central America. These networks soon radiated throughout the world as Cornwall's miners and engineers, "the light infantry of capital," developed mining fields across the globe.[6]

Cornwall: Engine House of the Industrial Revolution

By the late 18th century, Cornwall had emerged as a center of technological innovation in deep lode mining and engineering. Sidney Pollard has identified Cornwall as one of Britain's earliest industrial regions, with a distinct and specialized extra-regional commodity export: copper ore.[7] This, together with tin and some lead, provided the main output of Cornwall's mining industry. The marshalling of large quantities of fixed capital and the rise of semi-joint stock forms of organization, with a brisk informal share market and a hierarchically-structured labor force, made Cornish mines among the most sophisticated industrial enterprises in Western Europe in the early 1800s.[8] By then, Cornwall had established a clear comparative advantage in metal mining in a similar way that Lancashire had in cotton textile manufacture.[9] More than a century of specialization in metal mining had resulted by 1851 in an occupational structure dominated by mining and quarrying. With 29% of its men employed in these categories, Cornwall had a higher level of occupational specialization in metal mining than did South Wales in coal mining

(25% of men employed) or the northwest of England in textiles (27%).[10]

Deep lode mining was facilitated primarily through the advances made in the field of steam technology. The expiry of the Boulton and Watt patent on the low-pressure engine in 1800 ushered in a period of creativity that lasted into the 1840s, when many of Britain's top engineers made Cornwall their base. This resulted in the manufacture by Richard Trevithick, the son of a Cornish mining captain, of the high-pressure Cornish beam engine. This was a clear advance on the Boulton and Watt design with its separate condenser, and was found to perform much more efficiently than contemporary physics said was theoretically possible.[11]

Moreover, Cornwall's rapidly deepening mines called for ingenuity in other aspects of engineering and science, and advances were made in ore extraction techniques, surface crushing and dressing operations, methods of shaft sinking and timbering, and mine safety. The safety fuse, for example, was invented and manufactured by William Smith at Tuckingmill in 1831. At the beginning of the 19th century, the Cornish mining industry was at the cutting edge of technology and was arguably the most advanced mining region in the world. By contrast, the once great mines of Latin America were in decline in the politically unstable aftermath of the collapse of Iberian hegemony. Mine owners, alarmed at the decline of their once mighty industry, began to consider the introduction of British technology as a possible means of reviving their fortunes.

Trevithick and the Transatlantic Migration of Steam Technology

One of the earliest examples of the transatlantic migration of British engineering technology could be found in the celebrated mines of Cerro de Pasco, a Peruvian venture formed in 1812 by the prominent Lima merchants Pedro de Abadía and Joseph de Arismendi, along with their Swiss partner, Francisco Uvillé. After numerous attempts to drain the Pasco mines by *socavónes* (tunnels, or adits) with limited success, this new company proposed to de-water the mines with British-made steam engines in 1812. Uvillé, sent on a scouting mission to Britain in 1811, had discovered and purchased a model of a Cornish engine in London manufactured by Richard Trevithick, who had invented the world's first practical steam carriage in 1801.[12] When Uvillé set Trevithick's model engine to work at Pasco, it defied critics who claimed it would not function at over 14,000 feet in the rarefied atmosphere of the Andes.

In 1813, Uvillé returned to Britain to find Trevithick, to purchase several steam engines and employ the workmen to construct them.

Trevithick enthusiastically agreed to design the engines with the necessary auxiliary equipment, and undertook to organize their construction. The level of his interest is evidenced through his investment of about $3,000 in the Pasco Mining Company when Uvillé commenced selling shares in London to help finance the enterprise. In 1814, 15 months after his arrival in Britain, Uvillé sailed from Portsmouth bound for Peru with 4 Cornish pumping engines complete with pitwork, 4 winding-engines, a portable rolling-mill engine, two crushing mills and 4 extra Cornish boilers. Several Cornishmen who were to install and maintain the machinery were instructed by Trevithick to join the voyage. The machines had been manufactured at the Bridgnorth Foundry, Shropshire, and at Holman's of Camborne, soon to be one of Cornwall's foremost foundries and manufacturers of the first machinery to leave British shores for Latin America.

The scale of the operation in an era that preceded modern communication and transportation systems is truly remarkable. After a long sea voyage via Cape Horn to Callao and a tortuous 12-18 month trek inland through difficult terrain over which no wheeled vehicle could travel, most of the equipment arrived at Pasco—at the immense cost of £10,000. The engines and boilers had been specially cast in sections to allow the parts to be transported more easily to the mines by mules, where they were to be assembled. In 1816, one of the engines was set to work at the Santa Rosa Mine, where it rapidly drained a pit below adit level (the level at which water will flow from a mine naturally). This astonished a local official who described the innovation as "the most significant for the mining industry since the conquest of Peru."[13]

The celebrations, however, were premature. Further progress was impeded by difficulties in component assembly, highlighting the problems of technology-transfer to regions lacking the infrastructure of proper roads, improvising engineers, foundries, and workshops—all of which had been taken for granted in Cornwall. The problems arose with the boilers that were designed to burn coal, and not peat, and which had to be modified; for this purpose Trevithick traveled to Peru in 1817 with a Cornish boiler-maker. Upon his arrival the problems were eventually surmounted, aided in part by the discovery of a seam of coal in the vicinity of the mines. By the end of 1819, three engines were at work at the mines of Santa Rosa, Caya and Yanacancha.

Figures for silver production at Cerro de Pasco suggest that the application of Trevithick's steam engines had a dramatic, immediate effect on silver mining, enabling rich ores lying below adit level to be exploited for the first time.[14] Silver registration at Pasco rose by 350% in 1820, the greatest increase since 1811 and the second highest figure ever recorded for Pasco, representing over 65% of Peru's total registered silver production for 1820.[15]

Fig. 1. Registered Silver Production for the Caja of Pasco, 1800-1824[16]

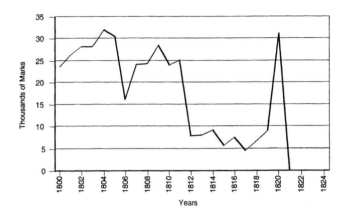

Another technological advance was made in metallurgy, when a party of Cornish lead smelters who had arrived at Lima in 1819 made a significant breakthrough in the recovery of lead, formerly lost in the native silver smelting process. The setting up of a furnace at Pachachaca near Pasco promised success until the wars of emancipation intervened. Battles raged in the Pasco area for over 4 years, bringing silver production to a virtual halt; valuable machinery was smashed and Trevithick fled to Central America.[17] Trevithick's enterprise in the Andes has been described as a failure, but the figures for silver production at Pasco suggest otherwise.[18] Had it not been for the war, the promising foundations laid by the introduction of British technological skill would doubtless have been built upon.

A New World Order: The 1820s "Boom"

For 300 years Latin American mines had been the principal source of precious metals and the envy of the world. But by the 1820s, the volatile political situation had sent them into dereliction. The mining infrastructure had collapsed; apparatus was left to decay; capital was withdrawn as financiers, fearing reprisals, fled to Spain; and the mining villages steadily depopulated. Great Britain—then the economic powerhouse of the world, with surplus capital to invest—had long cast a covetous eye on Latin America; as one British paper intoned, "The imagination can scarcely encompass the field of speculation that opens to the enterprises of British industry and the employment of British capital."[19] The newly independent Latin American countries courted Britain with the promise of trade (albeit with duties) and opened up their interiors to commerce, ownership, management, and above all, investment. The resulting investment "boom" in the early 1820s saw large-scale capital outlay in Latin American government bonds and in joint stock companies. Of the 127 new companies added to the London Stock Exchange, 44 were mining companies—a highly significant number, given that practically none had existed before. Moreover, more than half of these new companies were formed to work mines in Latin America.

Table 1. British Mining Companies operating in Latin America 1824-25[20]

Name of Company	Country of operation	Capital	
		£ Authorized	£ Paid Up
Anglo-Chilean	Chile	1,500,000	120,000
Anglo-Mexican	Mexico	1,000,000	750,000
Anglo-Columbian	Colombia	1,500,000	75,000
Anglo-Peruvian	Peru	600,000	30,000
Bolaños	Mexico	200,000	87,500
Bolívar	Venezuela	500,000	50,000
Brazilian	Brazil	2,000,000	20,000
Castello	Brazil	1,000,000	50,000
Chilian	Chile	1,000,000	75,000
Chilian & Peruvian	Chile & Peru	1,000,000	50,000
Colombian	Colombia	1,000,000	150,000
Famatina	Argentina	250,000	50,000
Guanajuato	Mexico	400,000	6,000
General South American	Primarily Brazil	2,000,000	100,000
Haytian	Haiti	1,000,000	50,000
Imperial Brazilian	Brazil	1,000,000	200,000
Mexican	Mexico	1,000,000	150,000
Pasco-Peruvian	Peru	1,000,000	150,000
Potosí-La Paz & Peruvian	Peru & Bolivia	1,000,000	50,000
Real del Monte	Mexico	400,000	325,000
Río de la Plata	Argentina	1,000,000	75,000
Tlalpuxahua	Mexico	400,000	120,000
Tarma	Peru	200,000	5,000
United Chilian	Chile	500,000	50,000
United Mexican	Mexico	1,240,000	775,000
United Provinces	Central America*	1,500,000	15,000
TOTAL		24,190,000	3,508,500

This period can be said to mark the real commencement of British investment in independent and semi-independent foreign nations.[21] The new Latin American governments acted quickly to create the prerequisite conditions for foreign intervention in the mining industry, believing this to be the touchstone of prosperity and the basis on which foreign trade would rest.[22] Highly inflated prospectuses were issued by companies set up to work mines across Latin America. Their claims were based more on the myths of their colonial past than on fact or scientific grounds, many drawing heavily on the writings of the celebrated German naturalist and explorer, Alexander von Humboldt. These prospectuses hammered home two basic points: first, the mines worked in colonial Latin America had been profitable, but were hampered by the lack of modern technology and a dearth of geological knowledge; second, and more important, the introduction of British capital, technology, and skilled labor would surmount any difficulties in developing a modern metalliferous mining industry in Latin America:

> [By introducing] English Capital, skill, experience, and machinery, the expenses of working these Mines [of the Anglo-Mexican Mining Association] may be greatly reduced, and their produce much augmented.... With the advantage of English assistance ... the benefit to be derived from the investment of Capital in the performance of these Contracts promises to be very ample.[23]

Exporting the Industrial Revolution
In order to fulfill such claims, the operators of the new companies looked, as the Pasco Peruvian Company had done, primarily to Cornwall. Almost a third of the mining companies set up in the 1820s had Cornish directors, who were also key investors. Although miners from other parts of Britain were recruited, as well as men from America and Europe, miners from Cornwall far outnumbered them; Cornish directors tended to appoint Cornish mine managers, who in turn recruited Cornish workers from Cornish mines. The head offices and annual general meetings may have been located in London, but most of the logistical arrangements were conducted in Cornwall, as was the manufacture of machinery and equipment. Here the great foundries such as Sandy's, Carne and Vivian, and Harvey's—both of Hayle—Holman's of Camborne, and the Perran Company Foundry of Fox-Williams built the Cornish steam engines, boilers, pumps and stamps (ore crushing machinery) for Latin American mines. Cornwall thus spawned a world-class export market in mining machinery that lasted into the 20th century, while smaller Cornish manufacturers made

everything from safety fuses, theodolites and ropes, to miners' tools and clothing.

The export of men, machinery, and equipment was facilitated by Cornwall's extensive network of ports. Primarily a maritime area, Cornwall had a long and historic association with the Atlantic, and in Falmouth, could boast the third largest and deepest natural harbor in the world. One of Britain's premier naval ports, with ships calling there "for orders," Falmouth was also home to the packet ships, by virtue of its being granted official Packet Status in 1688.[24] At first operating ships to the Iberian Peninsula, Falmouth's packet fleet soon commanded routes to the West Indies and North and South America, forming far-reaching transatlantic trade and communication networks. Through these networks, Falmouth became the main port of export for the mining companies. Its streets in 1825 were described as "thronged with people ... the hotels and principal houses consequently filled ... as the agents and others engaged for the different mining speculations abroad are assembled and wait to sail for their various destinations."[25]

Technology Transfer: A Transatlantic Success Story?

It is difficult to assessing whether or not the transfer of Cornish mining technology to Latin America was ultimately a success. The process has to be viewed not in the short-term, but over a period of several decades. Considerable differences in the acceptance of the technology existed across Latin America, with some mining regions embracing the Cornish steam engine whilst rejecting Cornish mine management. Other regions accepted the hard rock mining skills of the Cornish and their *modus operandi*, yet found that steam technology was impractical. Certainly the beginning for British-backed mining companies in Latin America was anything but auspicious; many accounts of the introduction of Cornish miners and their technology are pessimistic as a result.[26] The reason for the uncertain start was primarily due to the collapse of the London stock market in 1826, which deprived the fledgling mining companies of finance. Only a fraction of the authorized capital for the mining companies was ever paid in (see Table 1); J. F. Rippy estimated that total losses probably amounted to over 3 million pounds sterling.[27]

Although the stock market crash was undoubtedly the prime cause of failure, other factors contributed. The sheer novelty of transporting heavily capitalized, mechanized enterprises to regions that did not have the economic, social, or political infrastructure to support them led to great problems. Steam engines landed at Tampico, Mexico, sank in the sand, whilst ironwork and other equipment was lost offshore, never to be recovered. As the Pasco-Peruvian Company discovered, getting heavy equipment to remote areas through regions with no proper roads was a logistical nightmare. Climatic conditions and disease depleted imported labor, which was costly to replace. The fickleness of local governments who prevaricated over mining concessions to foreign companies did not help either. Cornish miners sent to Argentina in 1825 by the Río de la Plata Association were sent back home by the company due to a volte-face by the local government, which prevented the association from securing the mines it had planned to work[28] The over-hasty purchase of mines—founded on wildly inaccurate descriptions in prospectuses of mineral potential and locations—also precipitated failures.

Here, then, we must critically analyze the role and contribution of Cornish miners and their British-made technology to the development of Latin American mines, in order to avoid the excesses of filiopietism that has marred scholarship of ethnic migrations in the past. Evidence suggests that the pre-eminent role the Cornish came to play in Latin American mining fields was by no means a foregone conclusion. The British incursion into Latin American mining was sudden and dramatic; the introduction of pioneering technology involving heavily capitalized and centralized methods of working held great potential for conflict, especially in regions that already had a long and successful mining history built on age old traditions. As "the light infantry of British capital," Cornish miners were uprooted from familiar surroundings, shipped half way around the globe and transported to some of the most difficult environments on earth. The miners themselves inevitably bore the brunt of official criticism.

In the early 1820s, their suitability as "practical" miners was called into question when they were shown to be deficient in their knowledge of the geology of complex ore bodies of gold and silver. We learn, for example, in Charles Lambert's letter of 1825 to the directors of the Chilian [*sic*] Mining Association in London, that he considered the Cornish of little use until they had been in Chile for some time: "[T]hey are still misled by the different mineral deposits in this country."[29] Initial problems also arose between the fiercely independent Cornish miners and the military men who had been selected by the mining companies to direct affairs, and who often knew little about mining. Antagonisms quickly arose, for instance, between a Scotsman, Captain James Vetch, and the Cornish miners at Real del Monte, who the former found to be "the most difficult we have to manage ... and the most ungrateful."[30] Captain J. Andrews of the Chilian and Peruvian Mining Association also found the Cornish (who were constantly bickering with a group of Welsh miners) objectionable, preferring miners from Germany who were "more hardy, patient, and enduring, and far less nice and punctilious about trifles. Cornishmen are intractable if put the least out of their way. They harmonize together 'one and all,' but not with strangers."[31] We must also ask how suitable, in the end, was British technology to Latin American mines? The most visible sign of British industrialization was the arrival of stream technology, with the engines encased in characteristic houses that may still be seen in Cornwall today. In terms of success, the picture is somewhat mixed. Cuba and Mexico—with its deep and flooded silver mines—proved to be most predisposed to steam. Engines were employed at the mines of the Real del Monte and Bolaños companies, over which the mining doyen, John Taylor, exercised control. Taylor, who had managed mines in Cornwall, was convinced that steam engines were vastly more efficient and cheaper than the native system of using *malacates* (horse-powered machines for raising ore and dewatering mines). At Bolaños, 44 *malacates* employing 2,000 mules (50 to each) overseen by 384 drivers, stable boys and others, had cost, between 1791 and 1798, £79,552 each year. By the late 1820s, the mine was being drawn by one steam engine and one waterwheel. At Real del Monte, the expense of drainage by steam was about £8,000 a year, effecting an annual saving of £62,000 over that of *malacates*, although the mine was being worked at far greater depths.[32] In Cuba, engines ordered by the Royal Santiago Mining Company were cast at Cornwall's Perran Foundry, and the neighboring mining set of the Cobre Mining Association ordered their engines from Harvey's Foundry, Hayle. The arrival of these engines at Cobre provided the means by which a large supply of copper found its way onto the international market in the 1840s, challenging Cornwall's own hegemony in copper production.

There were drawbacks, however, with steam technology, particularly with regard to maintenance. The transatlantic nature of the mining operations meant that replacement engine components were often delayed for several months while Cornish foundries received, made, and dispatched the orders. There was also concern over the suitability of using engines in areas where there was no coal and a shortage of timber or alternative fuel. The Anglo-Mexican Company initially installed steam engines at their Guanajuato mines during a shortage of mules to work *malacates* in 1825, but were forced, by a lack of good timber, to rely primarily upon local, pre-industrial methods.[33] In Chile, steam engines never made a huge impact; only one mine in 23 was worked by steam in the 1870s, it being far cheaper to use *apires* (workmen hired to convey the ore) in mines worked on shallow copper deposits.[34] In Brazil, steam technology made very little impact. Much of the de-watering, stamping, and amalgamation was effected through a sophisticated system of waterwheels (employed by the British on an unprecedented "rational, large-scale and systematic basis").[35] The Cornish-style engine houses built to accommodate these steam engines remain potent symbols of British industrial prowess, particularly in the districts of Real del Monte and Zacatecas, Mexico, today. They mark the arrival of the industrial revolution in Latin America. Yet, in the aggregate, steam technology proved less of a panacea for Latin American mines than for those in Cornwall, due to the lack of foundries capable of building and maintaining Cornish-style mining equipment, as well as the absence of the large, high quality coal reserves that Britain enjoyed.

The picture is also mixed as regards the introduction of Cornish methods of working mines. In Mexico, for example, Cornish miners and managers were initially welcomed as heralds of economic rejuvenation and progress, particularly in areas where war had led to depopulation and a shortage of skilled miners. However, Cornishmen soon encountered resistance from native miners whose refusal to accept changes to the traditional labor structure frustrated their plans. Particularly contentious was the introduction of the Cornish *tribute* system for working mines. This meant abandoning long-established modes of operation—in this instance, the *partido* system, which the British believed to be inefficient, unprofitable, and unsafe.[36] J. W. Williamson, the director of the Anglo-Mexican Mining Association, concluded that all the British companies could reasonably expect was a modification of the traditional Mexican practice. He was proven right in the late 1820s, when native miners were provoked into strike action upon the abandonment of the *partido* at the mines of Real del Monte, Zacatecas, and Guanajuato. This unrest provided a salutary reminder to the Cornish mining captains of the danger of trying to graft a foreign system onto an industry equally as old and proud as their own. In Chile, Cornish superintendents found that the introduction of windlasses and *kibbles* for raising ores were often dismantled because the native proprietors preferred the ancient Chilean mode of raising ore: in bags on the backs of *apires*.[37]

However, the Cornish did successfully introduce a variety of other hard-rock skills and innovations. They brought with them sophisticated methods of deep-shaft mining known as "single-" or "double jacking," for boring and blasting through hard rock hundreds of fathoms underground. They also introduced the miners' safety fuse that reduced the number of accidents due to mistimed or misfired holes. Moreover, "English labourers" were "less expensive in proportion to the work performed," commented a Captain Cotesworth of the Cata Branca Mine in Brazil, "and preferable in every respect to other nations or

Negroes."[38] Echoing this imperial sentiment was the mine manager of the Colombian Mining Association. He had introduced the tribute system, having concluded that the Cornish miners could work far more cheaply and efficiently than native laborers, whom he deemed "but inferior miners, being but little accustomed to blast and break the ground."[39] At the Imperial Brazilian Mining Association's mines at Gongo Soco, G. V. Duval agreed that the native workforce could not "supersede the necessity of a supply of good miners from England."[40] In 1837 he was forced to admit "that it will never be possible to render [the company] entirely independent of English labour and of home engagement."[41]

The Cornish were highly valued for their skill as ore dressers, masons, and carpenters. Much of the machinery installed at the surface of Brazilian gold mines at Gongo Soco and Morro Velho was the work of Cornish carpenters who constructed the huge waterwheels and stamps. However, the Cornish could not greatly improve upon the native method of silver amalgamation, the ancient *patio* process. (Nor, it has to be said, could the Germans. It was only with the introduction of cyanide treatment of ores by American mining companies in the early 20th century that any major advances in amalgamation occurred.) The Cornish did produce successful innovations in gold and copper refining. In the Colombian gold mines in the 1830s, for instance, the introduction of a new system of dressing in a Cornish "tye"—a long trough in which to separate roughs from slimes by washing—had resulted in a reduction of gold loss from 60-70% to approximately 37%. This system offered decided advantages over every other method previously employed.[42] In the Aroa copper mines of the Bolívar Mining Company, Cornishmen in the reduction department likewise made significant advances in the calcination process of copper ore.[43]

Although many of the early mining ventures failed, the combination of British capital and Cornish skill did enable a renaissance in mining in many Latin American regions. Indeed, C. Veliz has concluded that had it not been for the financial disaster of 1826—from which the Copiapó Mining Association was to rise phoenix-like in the 1830s— the other mining companies in Chile would have prospered (see Table 1).[44] And although the British mining venture in Real del Monte, Mexico, has been described as a failure, R. W. Randall argues that the modern, structured company that reverted back to Mexican ownership in 1848 was unrecognizable from the run-down enterprise that the British had acquired a quarter of a century before. He concludes that the British company and its Cornish miners did, in fact, lead in the expansion and development of mining in the Real del Monte region.

Ironically, soon after the end of the British period of management, one of the mines they had controlled went into bonanza.[45]

Undeniably, the incursion of British industrial technology in Latin America helped to pave the way for further developments over succeeding decades, in industries such as engineering, foundries, smelting, railway construction, nitrates, coal, shipping, and ultimately in banking, trade, and commerce.[46] This facilitated the modernization of Latin America's transportation and communications systems in order to maximize the new technologies the industrial world had to offer. The development of roads, railways, bridges, and new national and international shipping networks anticipated an "age of connexity" that challenged the spatial frameworks in which people on both sides of the Atlantic had hitherto lived and worked.[47] Amidst these developments, the Cornish dimension is crucial, for the transatlantic relationship between Cornwall and Latin America was clearly a symbiotic one. By migrating to mining fields across South and Central America, Cornish miners acquired new skills in mining and dressing gold and silver to add to their knowledge of tin, lead, and copper. This enabled them to enhance their skills still further and acquire the reputation of the foremost hard rock miners in the world.

By the mid-19th century, Cornish miners and their technology could be found in virtually every developing mining field, as the seeds of the international mining economy sown in Latin America took root and flourished in the mining fields world wide. The Cornish miners had already established their place at the center of an increasingly complex web of transnational and global connections. Cornwall, an important littoral region at the heart of the Atlantic world, became a major migration center for mining technology and a skilled and mobile work force. This gave rise to the trans-migrant Cornish communities that spanned the globe by the early 20th century. As markets became increasingly interdependent, an integrated labor market emerged in which the Cornish dominated, they being the most visible imported workforce since the very beginnings of the global mining market in Latin America. For Cornwall, this process resulted in the international recognition of a small yet unique region of the British Isles, marked as much for its migration as for its skills in hard rock mining.

---

[1] Sidney Pollard, *Peaceful Conquest: The Industrialisation of Europe 1760-1970* (Oxford: Oxford University Press, 1981); N. Von Tunzelmann, "Technical Progress During the Industrial Revolution," in *The Economic History of Britain Since 1700*, eds. Roderick Floud and Donald McCloskey (Cambridge: Cambridge University Press, 1981), 1: 150-151; B. Deacon, "Proto-Regionalisation: The Case of Cornwall," *Journal of Regional and Local Studies* 18, no.1 (1998): 27-41.

[2] University of Chicago Globalization Project, *Area Studies, Regional Worlds: A White Paper for the Ford Foundation* (Chicago: Center for International Studies, 1997); Ford Foundation, *Crossing Borders: Revitalizing Area Studies* (New York: Ford Foundation, 1999).

[3] M. W. Lewis and K. Wigen, "A Maritime Response to the Crisis in Area Studies," *The Geographical Review* 89, no. 2 (1999). The authors are currently engaged in research for a project entitled "Oceans Connect: Culture, Capital, and Commodity Flows across Basins" at Duke University, USA, funded by the Ford Foundation.

[4] T. A. Volkman, "Crossing Borders: The Case for Area Studies," *Ford Foundation Report* 29, no. 1 (1998): 28-29.

[5] There is no clear consensus on how the Cornish miners acquired the name of "Cousin Jacks," but evidence seems to point to the mines of Devonshire in the 18th century, where migrant Cornish miners sought work. The term "Cousin Jack" is also thought to have been used to express an "otherness," the Cornish considering themselves a distinct people with specific mining skills that they jealously guarded.

[6] G. Burke, "The Cornish Diaspora of the Nineteenth Century," in *International Labour Migration: Historical Perspectives,* eds. Shula Marks and Peter Richardson (London: Temple Meads, 1984), 57-75.

[7] Pollard, 14.

[8] R. Burt, "The Transformation of the Non-Ferrous Metals Industries in the 17th and 18th Centuries," *Economic History Review* 48 (1995): 42.

[9] Deacon, 27-41.

[10] Ibid.

[11] J. Griffiths, *The Third Man: The Life and Times of William Murdoch, 1754-1839* (London: Andre Deutch, 1992), 239-242; J. Kanefsky and J. Robey, "Steam Engines in 18th-Century Britain," *Technology and Culture* 21 (1980): 176-177.

[12] Biographies of Trevithick are: F. Trevithick, *Life of Richard Trevithick* 2 vols. (London, 1872); H. W. Dickinson and A. Titley, *Richard Trevithick: The Engineer and the Man* (Cambridge: Cambridge University Press, 1934); J. Hodge, *An Illustrated Life of Richard Trevithick, 1771-1883* (Aylesbury: Shire Publications Ltd, 1973); A. Burton, *Richard Trevithick: Giant of Steam* (London: Aurum Press, 2000).

[13] J. R. Fisher, *Silver Mines and Silver Miners in Colonial Peru, 1776-1824* (Liverpool: Liverpool University Press, 1977), 115.

[14] Ibid., 122.

[15] Fisher, 114.

[16] Taken from figures given by Fisher.

[17] J. Miller, *Memoirs of General Miller in the Service of the Republic of Peru* (London, 1829), 2: 143-44; Dickinson and Titley, 185-86.

[18] M. J. Fenn, "British Investment in South America and the Financial Crisis of 1825-26," (Ph.D. diss., Durrham University, 1969), 100.

[19] *Western Luminary,* 8 March 1825.

[20] Extracted from Henry English, *A General Guide to the Companies formed for Working Foreign Mines* (London, 1825). Venezuela was then a part of the

state of Gran Colombia; the activities of the United Provinces company were focused on the *Provincias Unidas del Centro América*—Guatemala, Honduras, El Salvador, Nicaragua and Costa Rica.

[21] J. F. Rippy, "Latin America and the British Investment 'Boom' of the 1820's," *Journal of Modern History* (1947): 122-29.

[22] R. W. Randall, *Real del Monte: A British Mining Venture in Mexico* (Austin: Texas University Press, 1972), 28-29; N. R. Gillmore, "British Mining Ventures in Early National Mexico" (Ph.D. diss., University of California, 1956), 90; H. English, *A General Guide to the Companies Formed for Working Foreign Mines* (London, 1825), 11.

[23] English, 5

[24] *Western Morning News*, 28 August 2000. Other important ports included Portreath and Hayle.

[25] *Royal Cornwall Gazette*, 19 February 1825.

[26] Many of the contemporary accounts of the British incursion into Latin American mining fields with imported Cornish labor and technology are pessimistic, to say the least, and are summarized in D. Gregory, *Brute New World: The Rediscovery of Latin America in the Early 19th Century* (London: British Academic Press, 1992).

[27] See Rippy, 1947. Companies that survived included Real del Monte, Bolaños, Anglo-Mexican, Colombian, Imperial Brazilian, and Bolivar.

[28] *Quarterly Mining Review* (1830): 81-106.

[29] J. Mayo and S. Collier, *Mining in Chile's Norte Chico: Journal of Charles Lambert, 1825-1830* (Boulder: Westview, 1998), 15.

[30] A. C. Todd, *The Search for Silver: Cornish Miners in Mexico, 1826-1947* (Padstow: Lodenek, 1977), 36.

[31] Captain J. Andrews, *Journey from Buenos Ayres through the Provinces of Cordova, Tucuman and Salta, to Potosi, Thence by the Deserts of Caranja to Arica, and Subsequently, to Santiago de Chili and Coquimbo, Undertaken on Behalf of the Chilian and Peruvian Mining Association, 1825-26* (London, 1827), 1: 209-210. The reference to "one and all," the Cornish motto, is clearly meant to be cutting and emphasizes the Cornish propensity to clannishness.

[32] *Quarterly Mining Review* (1836): 359.

[33] M. E. Rankine, "The Mexican Mining Industry in the 19th Century, with Special Reference to Guanajuato," *Bulletin of Latin American Research* 2, no.1 (1992): 29-48; Gilmore, 1956.

[34] L. R. Pederson, *The Mining Industry of the Norte Chico, Chile* (Evanston: 1966), 191-92.

[35] M. Eakin, "The Role of British Capital in the Development of Brazilian Gold Mining," in *Miners and Mining in the Americas*, eds. Thomas Greaves and William Culver (Manchester: Manchester University Press, 1985), 13.

[36] Cornish tributers contracted to work a "pitch," an area in the mine that had been examined by the Mine Captain, for a previously agreed price. They received a proportion of the value of the ores raised. The Mexican mining system was ancient and complex. Put simply, *buscones* mined the ore wherever it looked promising, and hired *tenateros* to carry it to the surface. Mexican miners received half the ore raised in this way—the *partido*. The ad

hoc methods of working under the *partido* system often resulted in a maze of unstable galleries and tunnels, a matter that greatly concerned the British management of Mexican mines, who thought that it militated against mine safety and correct management.

[37] W. J. Henwood, "On the Mining District of Chañarcillo in Chili," *Transactions of the Royal Geological Society of Cornwall* 8, no. 1 (1871): 169-153. Kibbles were large metal buckets used to convey ore.

[38] *Mining Journal*, 22 July 1837.

[39] *Mining Journal*, 22 April 1837.

[40] *Mining Journal*, 4 June 1837.

[41] *Mining Journal*, 29 July 1837.

[42] *Quarterly Mining Review* (1830): 516.

[43] HJ/1/17, Royal Institution of Cornwall, Truro.

[44] C. Veliz, "Egaña, Lambert, and the Chilean Mining Associations of 1825," *Hispanic American Historical Review* 55 (1975): 637-663.

[45] Randall, 219.

[46] For a critique of railway building in the Pacific Littoral, see R. Miller and H. Finch, "Transferring Techniques: Railway Building and Management on the West Coast of South America," *Technology Transfer and Economic Development in Latin America, 1850-1930* (Liverpool: University of Liverpool, Institute of Latin American Studies, 1985). See also Katherine de la Fosse, *Los Primeros Cien Años: Industria y Comercio Británicos en México: 1821-1921* (Mexico, n.d.); B. A. Tenenbaum and J. N. McElveen, "From Speculative to Substantive Boom: The British in Mexico, 1821-1911," in *English Speaking Communities in Latin America*, ed. O. Marshall (London: Macmillan, 2000), 51-81.

[47] G. Mulgan, *Connexity: Responsibility, Freedom, Business, and Power in the New Century* (London: Vintage, 1998).

Chapter 12

George W. Ball, Jean Monnet, and the Founding of the European Coal and Steel Community: A Case of Transatlantic Influence

Brigitte Leucht

This chapter focuses on the impact of the personal upon the political—namely, the relationship between an American lawyer. George W. Ball and a French strategist, Jean Monnet. Today, George Ball is probably remembered mostly for his stand against the Vietnam War. As a member of both the Kennedy and Johnson administrations, he recognized early the problem of US extrication from Vietnam. After serving as Under Secretary of State for Economic Affairs from 1961 to 1966, Ball became US Ambassador to the United Nations in 1968.[1] Jean Monnet, for his part, has attained somewhat mythical status as one of the European "founding fathers." Sometimes referred to as "Mr. Europe," Monnet became known for his tireless efforts to bring about European integration.[2] It is remarkable that a man who never held elected office proved, from the 1940s onwards, most decisive in shaping the future of "Europe" as a coherent entity.[3] It is no exaggeration to say the friendship and mutual engagements between these two men, particularly in the year 1950, were instrumental in establishing the earliest political framework that would ultimately lead to the creation of the European Union.

The political frame of the Ball-Monnet relationship of 1950 rests on the Schuman Plan declaration of May 9, 1950, which proposed the pooling of the French and German coal and steel production under "a joint high authority."[4] Introduced by the French Foreign Minister, Robert Schuman, the plan had been developed by Jean Monnet and his (mostly French) advisors.[5] Although directed at the Federal Republic of Germany, the French proposal was open to other European nations. Not only was the area of coal and steel regarded as symbolic in improving the acrimonious Franco-German relationship of the immediate postwar years, but it was also expected by its founders to establish the basis and framework for what was eventually to become a European political union. As Schuman declared, "The pooling of coal and steel production will immediately assure the establishment of common bases for economic development, which is the first state for a European federation."[6] In the period following the Schuman Plan declaration, Germany, France, Italy, and the Benelux countries participated in multinational negotiations in Paris.[7] Nearly a year after Schuman announced the plan—on April 18, 1951—these 6 countries signed the treaty establishing the European Coal and Steel Community (ECSC). The High Authority was finally created in 1952, after the 6 member-nations had ratified the ECSC treaty. Contrary to earlier efforts at European integration—including American initiatives such as the European Recovery Program (the 1948 Marshall Plan) and European attempts like the Council of Europe (1949)—the ECSC proved the first project to truly advance European integration by establishing supranational institutions in the limited area of coal and steel.

Against this backdrop, I wish to discuss selected materials from the George W. Ball papers relating to the Schuman Plan, which are presented here for the first time.[8] The Ball-Monnet relationship is to be viewed in the context of a distinct transatlantic network, designating a group of people from both sides of the North Atlantic who, to varying degrees and for varying reasons, shared a belief in European integration. More importantly, these people were prepared, ultimately, to engage in *accomplishing* European integration. Throughout 1950 and 1951, the constituents of this transatlantic network significantly contributed to the realization of the Schuman Plan.[9]

France Proposes, the US Hesitates

The multinational negotiations following the Schuman Plan declaration were the product of a visibly transatlantic, rather than a discretely European, approach. There were, of course, geo-political reasons for this. In its goal of enlisting a democratic *and* capitalist Western Europe in the fight against Soviet Communism in the early 1950s, the US openly supported efforts at European integration within an Atlantic framework. Historian Geir Lundestad, in particular, has made a strong case for the promotion of European integration as an essential part of US policy in the context of the postwar "American empire."[10] As a powerful occupational force in defeated Germany and as the major transatlantic ally of victorious Britain and France, the US held a unique position in post-World War II Europe.

The official US reaction to the Schuman Plan was favorable and praised France's attempt at reconciliation with Germany in a European framework. This was a remarkable position for two reasons. First, it was evident that America's traditional European partner, Great Britain, was not going to participate in a European enterprise that would demand them to abnegate part of their national sovereignty. With its endorsement of the Schuman Plan proposal, the US thus confirmed that France would now be expected to take the lead in advancing European integration.[11] Although not officially represented at the talks, the US (through its embassy in Paris) was at all times informed in great detail about the proceedings of the negotiations and was regularly provided with updated versions of the draft treaty.[12] Second, the Americans at the outset were deeply concerned with the economic concept underlying the Schuman Plan. To comprehend these concerns, it is necessary to point out that the American understanding of European integration always comprised a political as well as an economic component. Consequently, although the US most warmly welcomed the plan for its political implications—particularly the attempt at Franco-German reconciliation and the integration of the Federal Republic of Germany—American doubts were voiced regarding the "super cartel" that the Schuman Plan might in fact set up by pooling national coal and steel production. Notably, Secretary of State Dean Acheson's official response approving the Schuman Plan represented a substantial departure from his initial reaction to the proposal. Acheson and the American ambassador to France, David Bruce, had not been at all convinced when introduced to the idea by Schuman. Only in the course of talking to Monnet and his friend, John J. McCloy, the US High Commissioner to Germany, did Acheson warm to the idea.[13]

The American press also voiced their concerns. In the eyes of some commentators, European integration would be advanced at the expense of the American ideal of free markets and unrestricted competition. "The Schuman proposal," lamented the *Newsweek* journalist Henry Hazlitt, "was followed by a chorus of unqualified praise and endorsement." Decisions were to be made by a joint high authority, which, to Hazlitt, implied "that the industries as a whole would be directed in the same unified way as a monopoly or a typical international cartel.... The plan brings out the ambiguity of the newly fashionable word "integration." What is proposed is a cartelized, state-dictated "integration"....[14] *Newsweek*'s criticism was thus not targeted at European integration as such, but at the fact that American diplomats had declared their nation's support even though integration would clearly not proceed under terms and ideas envisioned by the US.[15]

Amidst such negative public currents, George W. Ball and Jean Monnet established a unique friendship that was based on a sound working relationship. In the course of the Schuman Plan conference, Monnet could draw on Ball for legal advice precisely because the two of them had developed a shared vision. Hence the importance of considering the personal, informal nature of specific relationships within the broader transatlantic network.

Ball and Monnet: A Transatlantic Biography

In 1950, both George Ball and Jean Monnet could look back on various significant transatlantic encounters. At the time of the Schuman Plan proposal, Ball was working as a lawyer for Cleary, Gottlieb, Steen, and Hamilton, a New York-based law firm that he had joined in 1946. Behind him were his Midwestern origins in Des Moines, Iowa, where he was born in 1909, the third of three children. He received his bachelor and law degrees from a Midwestern institution, Northwestern University in Illinois. Following a spell in Washington, DC, where he had been attached to the Farm Credit Administration and then to the Treasury (and where he gained first-hand experience with the New Deal policies that he championed), Ball retreated to the Midwest where he practiced law. It was his friend, fellow lawyer, and future Democratic presidential candidate, Adlai Stevenson, who convinced him to return to Washington as the US became involved in World War II. Ball shifted his attentions from the American Midwest to Europe, as he was appointed the operating head of the General Counsel's Office of the Lend Lease administration. In this capacity, Ball first met the Frenchman Jean Monnet, who was at that time working with the British Supply Council. Before he was to collaborate with Monnet, however,

Ball accepted an assignment in 1944 that would involve him even further in European affairs. He served as a civilian member on the board of the US Strategic Bombing Survey, whose task was to evaluate the effectiveness of the Allied air strikes. His duties on this board, based in London, led at the end of the war to Ball's meeting and interview with Albert Speer, "the czar of German war production."[16] Upon returning to the US, Ball, as legal counsel, closely collaborated with Monnet for the French Supply Council. On behalf of the French government, Monnet retained Ball's law firm, which ensured that Ball and Monnet would continue working together.[17] Thus did this son of the American Midwest become intimately connected with European, and particularly French, affairs.

In 1950, Monnet was at a more advanced point in his career than Ball, and as head of the French delegation in the Schuman Plan conference, he could activate his personal transatlantic network. Born in 1888 in Cognac to a family that was into the brandy business, he was also 20 years older than Ball. Monnet's first transatlantic experiences stretched back to the pre-World War I era, through representing his family's company in Canada and the US. At the age of 26, he was appointed French representative at the Inter-Allied Supply Committee in London. It was then that he first came to understand the importance of international coordination of economic and political policies of the European countries to guarantee their mutual survival. In the inter-war period, among other appointments, Monnet served as Deputy Secretary-General to the League of Nations, and was affiliated with the New York investment banking firm, Blair and Co., where he specialized in corporate reorganizations. This enabled Monnet to intensify his acquaintance with an American whose networking capabilities equaled his own, namely John J. McCloy, the future US High Commissioner to Germany.[18] After having held the positions of chairman of the Anglo-French Coordinating Committee in London and deputy chairman of the British Supply Council in Washington during World War II, Monnet returned to the US as the president of the French Supply Council, which coordinated French imports from the US under Lend-Lease. His belief in mobilizing the economy that he had helped to develop in World War I was further strengthened by the "American production miracle" of World War II. He served as head of the newly established *Commissariat Général du Plan* that oversaw the reconstruction of the French economy. The first step to revitalize France's economic resources in order to achieve peace and prosperity after the war was Monnet's *Plan de Modernisation d'Equipement*, which became known as the "French Plan" or the "Monnet Plan." The second step in this direction would be the Schuman Plan.[19] In connection with the "French Plan," Monnet also worked with later Ambassador to France, David Bruce (then the head of the Marshall Plan Mission in France), and William Tomlinson, the American Treasury representative in Paris.[20] Monnet had thus acquired considerable planning experience, on both a European and transatlantic basis, which was to prove especially significant for the Schuman Plan negotiations.

Ball, Monnet, and the Schuman Plan Conference

Throughout the years in which the foundations of European integration were successfully laid, Monnet relied on and regularly consulted American friends and officials, most notably George Ball. Their joint work on projects throughout the 1940s demonstrates that their basis for working together was well established before the Schuman Plan proposal. Of his actual involvement in the Schuman Plan negotiations that were scheduled to start on June 20, 1950, Ball recollected in his *Memoirs*:

> I felt relieved rather than surprised when Monnet telephoned me on June 18 with his familiar request: "Be here tomorrow." Because my plane was delayed, I did not arrive until evening at rue de Martignac, where I found Monnet, Pierre Uri,… Etienne Hirsch,… and Professor Paul Reuter.[21]

During the first period of the negotiations, from June 20 to August 10, 1950, the delegates from the 6 European nations were concerned with institutional questions, in particular Title II of the ECSC Treaty. By early October 1950, they had finished the outline of the community's institutional framework and the functions of its organs— the High Authority, the Council of Ministers, the Court of Justice, and the Common Assembly.[22] George Ball emphasized that Monnet needed other people to assist him in the process of developing concepts and putting them into words. Just as Monnet used to collaborate with his European advisors, Uri (who was at his staff at the *Commissariat du Plan*), Hirsch (with whom he had already worked during the war), and others, he relied to a great extent on Ball's expressive skills, as the latter recalled: "My role was essential, for Monnet himself was no writer. I never knew him to draft a document; he evolved letters, papers, plans, proposals, memoranda of all kinds by bouncing ideas against another individual,"[23] Monnet had, in fact, summoned George Ball on June 18, 1950, at a very critical point before the start of the

Schuman Plan conference. Asked in an interview in 1981 whether he thought Monnet was looking for "reassurance from a friend" or for "somebody on the other side of the ocean to say this was okay," Ball answered, "Oh, no ... he wanted to put me to work.... You know, we were used to working together, and he wanted somebody with a certain facility for writing and for arguing."[24] As Monnet declared in an interview in 1974, he appreciated Ball's "great capacity to analyze" and the passion Ball had for the questions with which he dealt. Most of all, however, Monnet was impressed with what he called Ball's "good will": "George is primarily, I think, a man of good will and the reason why we work together was that he impressed me with that feeling."[25]

Judging from Ball's accounts, collaborating with Monnet must have been a tiring, while at the same time highly inspiring, enterprise. He recalls long talks after which Monnet expected him to produce a draft paper quickly. Monnet never hesitated to let his colleagues redraft proposals. Ball had difficulties, however, in coming to terms with Monnet's assumption that all human needs, such as sleeping and eating, would have to be put aside as long as the result of a drafting session had not proven satisfying. In a letter written during the Schuman Plan negotiations, Ball complains, "I have been working night and day on several matters here, principally the Schuman Plan. Jean Monnet has not improved his habits any and he does not respect the working hours of normal people."[26]

Assessing Ball's Role in the Schuman Plan Conference

An assessment on Ball's role in laying the foundations of the European Community needs to address two questions: what was his contribution to the outcome of the Schuman Plan negotiations (namely the ECSC treaty), and what was significant about his status as an American advising Monnet and the French delegation? Unfortunately, the George Ball papers do not satisfactorily answer the question of his actual input regarding the ECSC treaty. In his correspondence, Ball frequently referred to "working literally day and night with ... Monnet, on the Coal and Steel problem,"[27] or he dropped remarks such as, "The Schuman Plan has reached the drafting point."[28] There is, however, no substantial discussion of what exactly was being negotiated at which point, or of Ball's particular role in the process. The typed diaries merely contain information on Ball's whereabouts and occasionally acknowledge what he was working on. What *can* be confirmed from the diaries is that Ball was in Paris for some months during the Schuman Plan negotiations, including the most decisive moments of the negotiating process. Despite obvious difficulties in establishing

Ball's direct impact on the ECSC treaty, his correspondence and diaries allude to his working on two specific problems in the course of the proceedings: first, the institutional framework (July 1950) and second, the anti-cartel articles (November-December 1950).[29] Previous Monnet-Ball collaborations imply that the former expected the latter to vigorously bring his American legal background into the negotiations—or rather, into the informal sessions accompanying the conference. Moreover, those problems specifically mentioned, such the institutions and the anti-trust laws, suggest that Ball could present relevant ideas to Monnet and those other Europeans who were interested in the US experience and precedents. Ball also records the influence on the second part of the negotiations of other American constituents of the transatlantic network, such as Robert R. Bowie, the head of the Office of General Counsel of the US High Commissioner for Germany, and William Tomlinson. This period of the negotiations resulted in the acceptance of articles concerning the "economic and social provisions" (ultimately Title III of the ECSC Treaty) and included the discussion of anti-cartel provisions.[30]

Ball's presence during the first period of the Schuman Plan conference, when the political questions were discussed, was not *officially* recognized. This, however, had changed by the time he returned in late October: "I am here officially this time, as my designation as an advisor to the French Delegation was cleared with Mr. Schuman before my departure from the States."[31] From the beginning, Ball worked closely with a host of people behind the scenes of the conference. On the European side these included, among others, Robert Marjolin, Etienne Hirsch, and Pierre Uri. This indicates that Ball's European contacts were more or less Monnet's "inner circle." On the American side, Ball interacted with the staff at the American embassy in Paris. This included, among others, William Tomlinson, Stanley Cleveland, consul at the embassy, and Wayne Jackson, the officer in charge of UK and Ireland affairs. Moreover, Ball—partly, no doubt, due to Monnet's friendship with the US High Commissioner, John J. McCloy—collaborated with the latter's general counsel, Robert R. Bowie.

In terms of the *de facto* processes of political organization, it is important to remember that at no point during the Schuman Plan negotiations was George Ball representing the US government, although officials at the US embassy in Paris were indeed informed of Ball's advisory capacity to Monnet and the French delegation. One particular incident provides evidence of Ball's attempt to influence US officials on behalf of the French government. This involved an early

Cold War event that was to have a decisive impact on the negotiations in Europe—namely, the South Korean invasion. Only a couple of days after the start of the conference, on June 25, 1950, the North Korean Army crossed the 38th parallel. Ball, who was at Monnet's house in Houjarray on that day, recalls that Monnet quickly realized that this would provoke a discussion of German rearmament. The US would be eager to see a potentially strong Federal Republic of Germany as part of a Western military alliance. This, in turn, could lead the French to back away from the Schuman Plan and could therefore endanger the realization of the project. In a letter of late August 1950, Ball states, "I think it should be kept in mind that the French will be willing to face up to the problem of rearming Germany only after the Schuman Plan is in operation."[32] The Korean attack did, in fact, lead the US to propose bringing West Germany into NATO on September 12, 1950. On September 7, 1950, shortly before the scheduled Foreign Ministers' meeting in New York—during the course of which Acheson would announce this proposal—a worried Ball visited the US embassy in Paris. Wayne G. Jackson, who had been part of the US delegation involved in the preparatory meetings for the New York conference, noted:

> George Ball, a Washington lawyer who does a great deal of work for the French Government, and who has been acting as a consultant to Monnet in Paris in connection with the Schuman Plan, came in to see me this morning. He reported that the French Government is worried that the Germans may cool off on the Schuman Plan...."[33]

Jackson surmised that the French fears were based on the possibility that once German rearmament seemed within reach (and with it, a greater degree of equality and independence), the Federal Republic would no longer regard integration into a supranational community as essential for "removing economic limitations and ... enhancing their political position." Jackson concluded, "While I do not think that George Ball was specifically instructed to make these comments to the Department, I have no doubt that he is in substance acting for the French Government."[34] If Monnet knew of, or even initiated, Ball's visit, it is perfectly arguable that, in addition to his drawing on Ball's legal expertise and drafting abilities, he had hoped to utilize Ball to ensure continuing American support for the ECSC project. While this may be mere retrospective speculation, it is true to say that the French, in the autumn 1950, were justifiably concerned. To the Americans, the establishment of the ECSC indeed had become subordinate to the problem of German rearmament, and the momentous issue of European integration diminished to one of many elements of the larger concerns of Western defense. In his memoirs Acheson confirms the validity of the French fears as expressed by Ball: "Perhaps the most important issue came in autumn when, to anticipate, American proposals for German participation in the defense of Europe gave Bonn a stronger bargaining position than it had as an occupied country."[35] This observation applied to the Schuman Plan conference in particular and accounted for difficulties regarding the second part of the negotiations, involving the re-organization of German industry—difficulties that ultimately were only to be resolved through the intervention of High Commissioner McCloy and his staff.[36]

What might be said in conclusion? This is a case study with significant implications, drawing our attention to the impact of personal relations on national and supranational events. George Ball and Jean Monnet were two members of a transatlantic network that provided the context for a particularly fruitful working relationship and a productive friendship. Their mutual engagements at the time of the Schuman Plan conference led to a decisive inauguration; theirs was thus a transatlantic relationship that truly left its mark upon history.

---

[1] George W. Ball, *The Past Has Another Pattern: Memoirs* (New York: W. W. Norton and Company, 1982).

[2] "Mr. Europe at Work," *Newsweek*, 27 January 1958, 38, 40.

[3] For a balanced assessment of Monnet's influence, see Gérard Bossuat and Andreas Wilkens, eds., *Jean Monnet, l'Europe, et les chemins de la Paix: Actes du Colloque de Paris du 29 au 31 mai 1997* (Paris: Publications de la Sorbonne, 1999).

[4] Translation of Schuman's statement; May 9, 1950, in *Foreign Relations of the United States*, vol. 3 (Washington: US Government Printing Office, 1977), 692-694.

[5] The idea of the coal-steel pool was not a novel one. However, as historian John Gillingham shows, it was Monnet who launched the proposal at the right moment. John Gillingham, "Jean Monnet and the European Coal and Steel Community: A Preliminary Appraisal," in *Jean Monnet: The Path to European Unity*, eds. Douglas Brinkley and Clifford Hackett (New York: St. Martin's Press, 1991), 129-162 (135). For the context of the proposal see also Hanns Jürgen Küsters, "Die Verhandlungen über das institutionelle System zur Gründung der europäischen Gemeinschaft für Kohle und Stahl," in *Die Anfänge des Schumanplans: 1950/51: Beiträge des Kolloquiums in Aachen, 18-30 Mai 1986*, ed. Klaus Schwabe (Baden Baden: Nomos Verlag, 1988), 73-102 (74).

[6] Translation of Schuman's statement, 693.

[7] For the history of the Plan and the Schuman Plan negotiations, see various contributions in Schwabe. Focusing on the positions of the French and Federal German governments is Ulrich Lappenküper, "Der Schuman Plan: Mühsamer

Durchbruch zur deutsch-französischen Verständigung," *Vierteljahreshefte für Zeitgeschichte* 42 (1994): 403-445.

[8] The *George W. Ball Papers* (Public Policy Papers, Department of Rare Books and Special Collections, the Seeley S. Mudd Library, Princeton University Libraries, Princeton, NJ). Citations from the George W. Ball Papers (hereafter cited as *GWB*) contain identification of a specific item; the date (if known); the box containing a specific document. Not included in this article are those materials from *GWB* that concern the so-called Schuman Plan book that Ball started writing in December 1950. This "book" (preserved in manuscript form alone) never reached the stage of publication. It is the subject of a separate article in preparation.

[9] This particular transatlantic network has to a considerable extent been reconstructed by Pascaline Winand, *Eisenhower, Kennedy, and the United States of Europe* (New York: St. Martin's Press, 1993). However, Winand does not focus on the Schuman Plan negotiations. This also holds true for a more recent article in which Winand again acknowledges Ball's significance for Monnet. See Pascaline Winand, "European Insiders Working Inside Washington: Monnet's Network, Euratom, and the Eisenhower Administration," in *The United States and the European Alliance since 1945*, eds. Kathleen Burk and Melvyn Stokes (Oxford and New York: Berg, 1999), 207-238 (209). From the perspective of Jean Monnet, see Holger Schröder, *Jean Monnet und die amerikanische Unterstützung für die europäische Integration 1950-1957* (Frankfurt am Main et. al.: Peter Lang, 1994).

[10] Geir Lundestad, *"Empire" by Integration: The United States and European Integration, 1945-1997* (Oxford: Oxford University Press 1998), 1-4. That this "empire" in the case of France was consensual and beneficial to both the US and France is emphasized by William I. Hitchcock, *France Restored: Cold War Diplomacy and the Quest for Leadership in Europe, 1944-1954* (Chapel Hill: The University of North Carolina Press, 1998), 9.

[11] Secretary of State Acheson's attitude towards France had developed over the preceding year. See Edmund Dell, *The Schuman Plan and the British Abdication of Leadership in Europe* (Oxford: Oxford University Press, 1995), 9-13. Wilfried Loth argues that British non-involvement in the Schuman Plan project and the ECSC put an *end* to the idea of Europe as a "third force" (after Soviet communism US capitalism). See Wilfried Loth, "Der Abschied von Europarat. Europapolitische Entscheidungen im Kontext des Schuman-Plans," in Schwabe, 183-195.

[12] Dirk Spierenburg and Raymond Poidevin, *The History of the High Authority of the European Coal and Steel Community: Supranationality in Operation* (London: Weidenfeld and Nicholson, 1994), 26-28; Klaus Schwabe, "'Ein Akt konstruktiver Staatskunst'—die USA und die Anfänge des Schuman-Plans," in Schwabe, 211-239.

[13] Dean Acheson, *Present at the Creation: My Years in the State Department* (New York: W. W. Norton, 1969), 383.

[14] "Business Tides—Towards State-Managed Cartels?" *Newsweek*, 5 June 1950, 70. Even harsher in its criticism is *Fortune*, July 1950, 58-60. See also

Schwabe, "Ein Akt konstruktiver Staatskunst," 225-228; Spierenburg and Poidevin, 26-28. For other discussions of political approval and economic concerns, see *Commonweal*, 26 May 1950: 165; Howard C. Gary, "French Steel Opens Debate on Europe's Economy," *Foreign Policy Bulletin*, 19 May, 1950, 4; "A Move Toward French-German Amity," *New Republic*, 22 May, 1950, 6.

[15] For matters of brevity, this account omits opposition in the US to the policy of actively promoting free-market economy abroad and the larger discussion of the proper role of American foreign policy.

[16] Ball, *Memoirs*, 51. George Ball's biographical sketch relies on his autobiography, 1-68.

[17] Ibid., 77.

[18] Kai Bird, *The Chairman: John J. McCloy: The Making of the American Establishment* (New York: Simon and Schuster, 1993); Jean Monnet, *Memoirs* (Garden City: Doubleday, 1978). Moreover, see the excellent biography by Francois Duchene, *Jean Monnet: The First Statesman of Interdependence* (New York: W. W. Norton, 1994). The foreword to this biography was written by none other than George Ball.

[19] Gillingham, 129; Irwin M. Wall, "Jean Monnet, the United States and the French Economic Plan," in Brinkley and Hackett, 86-113.

[20] Wall, 100.

[21] Ball, *Memoirs*, 84. 18 rue de Martignac was the seat of the French *Commissariat du Plan*.

[22] Küsters, 80-95.

[23] Ball, *Memoirs*, 73. For an account of Monnet's methodology, see Francois Duchene, "Jean Monnet's Methods," in Brinkley and Hackett, 184-209.

[24] George W. Ball, interview for the Jean Monnet Foundation, New York City, 15 July, 1981, transcript, *GWB*, 146: 15.

[25] Jean Monnet, interview, 5 December 1974, transcript, *GWB*, 146: 1.

[26] Ball to M. E. S. Ziegler; 25 July 1950, *GWB*, 43.

[27] Ball to M. E. S. Ziegler; 27 June 1950; *GWB*, 43.

[28] Ball to Louise Wright, Director of the *Chicago Council on Foreign Relations*, 30 October 1950, *GWB*, 43.

[29] Diaries, 1950; *GWB*, 43.

[30] Ibid.

[31] Ball to Leo Gottlieb; 28 November 1950; *GWB*, 43. Diaries, 1950; *GWB*, 43.

[32] Ball to Marquis W. Childs, 28 August 1950; *GWB*, 43.

[33] Memorandum, 7 September 1950; Jackson to G. W. Perkins: US National Archives, RG 59, 850.33.

[34] Ibid.

[35] Acheson, 389.

[36] A. W. Lovett, "The United States and the Schuman Plan: a Study in French Diplomacy, 1950-1952," *The Historical Journal* 39, no. 2 (June 1996): 425-455. Klaus Schwabe, "Do Personalities Make a Difference? Washington Working with Europeans," in Burk and Stokes, 239-267 (247-249).

Chapter 13

Transatlantic Perspectives on the Euro and the Dollar: Dollarization and Other Issues

Saturnino Aguado

The creation of the euro has been the most important development in the international monetary system since the adoption of flexible exchange rates in the early 1970s. A bipolar currency regime dominated by Europe and the US, with perhaps Japan as a junior partner, is already replacing the dollar-centered system that prevailed for most of the 20th century. In this context, issues like dollarization appear crucial for the understanding of future international monetary economics. Much has been written recently on the issue of the euro and the dollar. The specific purpose of this chapter is twofold: first, it is to shed some light on the important issue of dollarization, and second, it is to study the implications of the appearance of the euro as a great international currency in competition with the dollar.

The International Role of the Dollar: Dollarization
C. Fred Bergsten, the Director of the Institute for International Economics, cites the dollarization of foreign economies as a fairly widespread phenomenon. By his account, foreign dollar deposits in 1998, exceeded 50% of national money supplies in seven countries that had had programs with the International Monetary Fund (IMF) since

1986; accounted for 30-50% in another dozen or so "highly dollarized" countries; "commonly" reached 15-20% in countries where residents were allowed to maintain such accounts. In fact, dollar ratios of 30-60% had prevailed in most transition economies in Eastern Europe and the former Soviet Union during the period 1990-1995 and were prevalent in Latin America as well. The ratios of most countries remained very small: the largest were Turkey (with a foreign currency share of 46%), Argentina (44%), Russia, Greece, Poland, and the Philippines (all about 20%). Mexico's dollar ratio was only 7%, while Bolivia had the highest at 82%. The only fully dollarized countries in this period were Panama and Liberia.[1]

From an American standpoint, it is noteworthy that about two-thirds of all dollar currency are held outside the US. About three-quarters of recent increases in such cash holdings have accumulated beyond the US borders. US exports of dollars totaled $44 billion to Russia and $35 billion to Argentina alone during 1989-1996. But it is important, from the beginning, to distinguish between *de facto* dollarization, where residents of one country seek refuge in the dollar (for whatever the reason, mainly to fight local inflation), and "policy" dollarization, where a government decides to dollarize. This chapter is primarily concerned with the latter.

Emerging market countries have three basic choices in determining the monetary linkage between their economy and the rest of the world:

- They can let their currency float freely in the exchange markets;
- They can fix "convincingly" the price of their currency against a specific foreign currency;
- They can choose intermediate approaches, such as maintaining a "fixed but adjustable peg," or pursue other intermediate approaches such as "managed floating," "target zones," or "crawling bands."

There is increasing consensus that, particularly after the global economic crises of the last decade, options in the third category do not work well for emerging market economies.[2]

Thus, countries should either float or fix "convincingly." There are two ways of achieving this: through a currency board, or through dollarization. Under a currency board arrangement, the monetary authorities commit themselves to the exchange of dollars for domestic currency on demand at a fixed exchange rate. The domestic currency is fully backed by a corresponding stock of foreign exchange. There is no extension of domestic credit to the government or banks, so that the only mechanism the central bank can use to increase the base money supply is to have more dollars supplied—for example, through a surplus in the balance of payments. Dollarization thus shares similarities with currency board arrangements, although there are important differences, the main one being that it is much more difficult to reverse dollarization than to modify or abandon a currency board arrangement.

The issue of dollarization demonstrates the extent to which the process of euroization facing most parts of Europe—in particular, southern countries such as Spain—shares similarities with some Latin American countries attempting to dollarize, such as Argentina. Clearly, it would be much easier for Argentina to exit from its present currency board arrangement than for Spain to leave the euro. However, on a wider scale, the European experience could well demonstrate the benefits that a dollarization strategy could bring to the greater part of Latin America.[3] What, then, are the benefits and costs of dollarization? It is helpful to consider the question from two perspectives—those of Mexico and the US.

Dollarization from a Mexican Perspective

The first and most obvious benefit of Mexican dollarization is that of avoiding currency and severe balance-of-payments crises. Without a domestic currency, there is no possibility of a sharp depreciation, and no likelihood of sudden capital outflows motivated by the fear of devaluation. Another clear advantage is that inflation and interest rates would be aligned with those in the host country, the US. If, on the other hand, the US's risk premiums *did* go down, Mexican interest rates could well go down as well, which would boost investment and growth there. It could be that with dollarization, the interest premium owing to devaluation risk would disappear, but this would not necessarily mean the disappearance of sovereign risk. In any case, because of the former (currency risk), interest rates would significantly decrease in any country wishing to dollarize, Mexico included.[4]

In addition to promoting financial integration, greater price stability, and lower interest rates, Mexican dollarization might contribute to trade integration with the US and the rest of the world, to a degree that would not be possible otherwise. Mexico could achieve significant savings in transaction costs (similarly demonstrated in Europe by countries that have already developed extensive trade and other economic ties through the euro).[5] Dollarization, then, could lead to further increases in trade and investment between countries that are already integrated to a substantial degree. This appears to be the case with the NAFTA countries; so, by this logic, Mexico (and Canada, for that matter) might seriously consider dollarization, as about one-fifth of all Mexican production (and roughly one-third of total Canadian output) is exported to the US. Again, the experience of some southern European countries could offer a useful comparison.

Regarding the costs of dollarization for Mexico, we must consider certain income losses, the loss of economic policy tools (such as the exchange rate), and the surrender of a national monetary policy. The fact is that any country dollarizing must first lose the annual earnings from its stock of international reserves, which must be exchanged for the dollars in cash to be used as the new national currency. The dollarizing country would relinquish forever the so-called "seigniorage" of its own currency, that is, the difference between what it costs to print money and its purchasing power. Seigniorage is the profit a government makes from printing money (for example, it costs three cents to print a $100 bill, but that bill buys $100 worth of goods). In this case, Mexico's loss would be the US's gain—hence the suggestion that the US should share seigniorage with dollarizing countries according to some agreed formula.

After all, the loss of economic policy tools are most important; and any country wishing to dollarize loses the exchange rate as an economic policy tool in addition to losing its own monetary policy. With regard to the exchange rate in particular, the problem comes when the competitiveness of a dollarized country begins to suffer. This may result from excessive wage increases or because the dollar itself becomes overvalued, relative to the currencies of other important trading partners of the dollarized country. This is a problem of overvaluation of the real exchange rate. In such a case, competitiveness cannot be improved through a simple devaluation, but rather through a fall in wages and prices. Experience has shown that these declines are often achieved only at the cost of economic recession, because of the resistance to nominal wage and price reductions in the absence of productivity improvements.

The complete loss of Mexico's monetary policy under dollarization would also include the loss of the lender-of-last-resort function provided by central banks. As lenders of last resort, central banks stand ready to provide liquidity to the banking system in the case of a systemic bank run. Something very similar could happen under a currency board arrangement, where, as noted above, the only way to create base money is through accumulation of foreign reserves. (Countries with currency board arrangements can, however, retain some capacity to create money not fully backed by reserves, as the Argentineans did in 1995 during the "Tequila Crisis" by temporarily reducing their reserve requirements.) The point is that under a dollarized situation, such events need not occur. On the contrary, as some have argued, by dollarizing a country can better prevent the possibility of bank runs in the first place. By dollarizing, the depositors would have more confidence in the domestic banking system, which would make a bank run less likely. Moreover, if, as a consequence of dollarization, large foreign banks played a bigger role in the banking system, this too would reduce the danger of a bank run. In any event, it must be said that in a dollarized economy, as in an economy with a currency board, the authorities always have the option of obtaining lines of credit from external sources that might be used in the event of a crisis.

Mexico could well take some cues from its neighbor to the south— Argentina, where we can see the problems, benefits, and mechanics of dollarization in action. Argentina has, at present, a currency board arrangement with $15 billion in reserve and 15 billion pesos in circulation as its money base. Reserves earn 5% annually, thus yielding $750 million per year. The Argentinean strategy is to sell the reserves for cash dollars, and use the proceeds to retire the entire money base in pesos. As a consequence of this, however, Argentina loses $750 million a year, so they must negotiate with the US to secure an annual transfer flow of $600 million. This is used as collateral for Argentina to borrow in case of a banking crisis. As a result, the US fiscal position increases by $150 million per year. This amount equals exactly the Argentinean annual fiscal cost; but there are other clear benefits for both countries. For Argentina, currency crises can be totally eliminated. For the US, not only is that county better off fiscally, but the arrangement does not necessitate the provision of additional credit lines or even a seat for Argentina on the US Federal Reserve Board— even though the plan allows for the extension of US supervisory powers over banks operating in Argentina, as well as the management of any crisis fund by a committee involving both Argentinean *and* US authorities.[6]

Dollarization from a US Perspective

The advent of euroization is likely to inaugurate a competitive phase between the euro and the dollar. In this context, dollarization will mean that foreign countries will demand even more dollars than the large amounts they already use. But these amounts are still very modest in the aggregate, roughly $300 billion. This figure represents only about 5% of the gross US external liability of more than $6 trillion, and only about 20% of the net US external debt of around $1.5 trillion.

Consequently, overall US liability is small; it will probably never be converted, and if so, surely not precipitously. At the same time, the US would gain substantial seigniorage from a much wider use of its currency in the Western Hemisphere. Naturally, any increase in financial stability in the region would be particularly beneficial for the US. Moreover, as the case of Germany within Europe demonstrates, the processes of dollarization in the Western Hemisphere would clearly enhance the economic role of the US in the region, only at the cost of its accepting a more participative role in the macroeconomic interdependence between richer and poorer countries. As Bergsten points out, Germany found itself in a similar position "vis-à-vis the rest of the European Union" during the formalization of "its de facto 'Deutschmark Zone'" within, first, the European Monetary System and, latterly, the euro.[7] For the US, all of these factors presuppose that only a handful of countries will dollarize (say, Argentina and Ecuador); but if the move is followed by more and larger countries (Mexico, or even Canada) the situation would alter significantly, as economic developments in these countries would have a greater impact on overall monetary conditions in the US. As Bergsten admits on behalf of the US, in such a case "we would have to contemplate accepting those countries as new Federal Reserve Districts and giving them seats on the Fed's Open Market Committee," as well as "devising some form of fiscal federalism to provide an alternative adjustment device to compensate for the abolition of the exchange rate instrument between them and us."[8]

The Euro vs. the Dollar: How Important Will the Euro Be?

Having explored the issue of dollarization, which could conceivably end up creating a dollar bloc in the whole of the Western Hemisphere, we can now consider the prospects for the euro to as a great international currency in competition with the dollar. As Robert Mundell and Jeffrey Frankel argue separately, there are 4 major factors that determine whether a currency is, or can be, a great international currency. The first is a large transaction area. The US economy is still the world's largest in terms of output and trade; but if the United Kingdom and the other non-euro countries ultimately join up with "euroland," the area will be virtually equal in economic size to the US. The second factor is, put plainly, history—what Mundell calls "a sense of permanence" gained through looking into the future. As there is normally a strong inertial bias in favor of whatever has been the vehicle currency in the past, this factor clearly favors the dollar. The third factor has to do with the country's own financial markets. Capital and money markets must not only be open and free of controls, but also well developed, deep, and liquid. In this sense, Frankfurt and the other financial centers in continental Europe will take some time to catch up with New York. The fourth factor is a stable monetary policy and confidence in the value of the currency. The key currency is the form in which assets are held, and here confidence in the stable value of the currency is critical, in the knowledge that it will not be inflated away in the future. It seems clear that both the Federal Reserve Board and the European Central Bank currently have strong non-inflationary reputations. (Some might even argue that at the time of this writing, the European Central Bank, with its reiterated strong monetary policy, surpasses even the Federal Reserve Board in its commitment to a stable currency.[9]) So, two of the four determinants of reserve currency status—developed financial markets and historical inertia—support the dollar over the euro. In terms of the other two criteria—economic size and the reputation for stability—the dollar and the euro could well be tied.[10]

All the above having been said, the euro will soon be a very important reserve currency. Frankel, for one, goes so far as to predict that the euro will eventually have at least a 32% share of central bank holdings, as opposed to the dollar share of 48%.[11] Mundell is similarly confident in his own projections. Presently, there are global foreign exchange reserves of about $1.2 trillion held in dollars and about $0.4 trillion held in other currencies. Assuming that reserves double every 10 to 12 years, Mundell estimates that by 2010, global reserves will grow to approximately $3.2 trillion. He assumes that the demand for dollars in 2010 will be the same, with the demand for euros equaling that for dollars. If these predictions prove correct, then in 2010 global foreign exchange reserves will consist of $1.2 trillion in dollars, $1.2 trillion in euros, and $0.8 trillion in other currencies. In such a scenario, while US dollar reserves would remain stagnant in the next 10 years, euro reserves would increase by about $100 billion a year.[12]

The Dollar-Euro Exchange Rate and the Transatlantic Agenda
Why has the euro been so weak recently and the dollar so strong? Frankel offers several explanations. First, the general upward swing of the dollar over the last 5 years can be explained because the dollar was clearly undervalued in mid-1995. Second, and more importantly, US economic performance throughout the last 5 years has been noteworthy, based in part on the short-term and medium-term factors of good fiscal and monetary policy, but also on favorable long-term structural trends. Among the latter, Frankel cites:

- deregulation (trucking, airlines, natural gas, and banking in the late 1970s, telecommunications in the 1980s, and electricity at present);
- globalization;
- technological innovation (especially information technology);
- business innovation, in the form of more competitive goods and labor markets (corporate restructuring, the move toward managed health care, and flexible labor markets);
- public sector reform.

Frankel concludes that this strong American growth has raised the global demand for US money, and that the dollar will not depreciate until the US economy slows down.[13]

There are, however, credible reasons to expect a major appreciation of the euro against the dollar in the foreseeable future. The first is the expected and important portfolio diversification into euros, ranging from $500 billion to $1 trillion. The second is that the US external economic position will continue to raise doubts about the future stability and value of the dollar. The US has run major current-account deficits for the last 18 years, and its net foreign debt—already huge—is rising annually by 15-20%. This clearly calls for a substantial dollar depreciation. Finally, and very importantly, the policy mix lately implemented in Europe presents a tight monetary policy together with lax fiscal policies in many important countries (France, Germany, Spain), which will demand an appreciated euro. This scenario in Europe may well be analogous to the US situation in the mid-1980s, with the huge budget deficits run by the Reagan administration. There is also a clear analogy in Germany immediately following its reunification, when the Bundesbank produced a strong Deutschmark in the face of large deficits. The dollar-euro exchange rate appears, then, crucial in this streamlined economic scenario of the next century, which will likely include only three major currencies: the dollar, the euro, and the yen.

From the point of view of the transatlantic relationship between the US and Europe, it is clear that much attention will have to be paid to this issue in the near future. As the Nobel Prize-winning Mundell has said, "The dollar-euro exchange rate is going to become the most important price in the world." He points in his writings to 2010, and a situation in which "we will probably be back to a world where we get more fixed exchange rates, and [where] the IMF will be dragged back to its original function."[14] The euro will be instrumental in converting the international monetary system into a *de facto* bipolar regime. This will require—from both sides of the Atlantic—much closer cooperation to ensure the least painful transition to this new regime.

---

[1] C. Fred Bergsten, "Dollarization in Emerging Market Economies and Its Policy Implications for the US," Institute for International Economics Statement (April 1999) at http://www.iie.com/PAPERS/bergsten0499.htm.

[2] Possible reasons include the overvaluation of a currency; the speculation that such schemes produce; the volatility of exchange rates under such schemes; and igniting inflation in emerging market economies. See Sebastian Edwards, "What Is the Right Exchange Rate Regime?" *Deutsche Bank Research* http://www.anderson.ucla.edu/faculty/sebastian.edwards/sebdb.pdf (April 1999); and Edwards, "The IMF Is Panama's Lender of First Resort," *Wall Street Journal* (24 September 1999) at http://www.anderson.ucla.edu/faculty/sebastian.edwards/editorials.htm.

[3] See Rudi Dornbusch, "The Euro: Implications for Latin America" (March 1999) at http://web.mit.edu/rudi.

[4] Other possibilities for interest-rate reduction through dollarization, as opposed to a mere currency board arrangement, have been helpfully quantified. See, for instance, Jeffrey Frankel, S. Schmukler, and L. Servén, "Verifiability and the Vanishing Intermediate Exchange Rate Regime," *Brookings Trade Forum* (April 2000) at http://www.worldbank.org/research/bios/schmuklerpdfs/IASE-8.pdf.

[5] In possibly similar fashion, the volume of trade *between* Canadian provinces is more than 20 times greater than that between Canada and the US, despite 10 years of a free trade area, geographic proximity, and a shared language and culture (with regard to Anglophone Canada). The use of a common currency may well be an important factor in explaining this pattern of national market integration. See Bergsten.

[6] Guillermo Calvo, "Argentina's Dollarization Project: A Primer," Address before a Joint Hearing of the Subcommittees on Economic Policy and International Trade and Finance, Washington DC, February 1999 at http://www.bsos.umd.edu/econ/ciecpn6.pdf.

[7] Bergsten, http://www.iie.com/PAPERS/bergsten0499.htm.

[8] Ibid.

[9] This paper was written in the summer of 2000.

[10] Robert Mundell, "The Euro: How Important?", *Cato Journal*, 18, no.3 (Winter 1999) at http://www.cato.org/pubs/journal/cj18n3-13.pdf; and Jeffrey Frankel, "EMU and the Euro: An American Perspective," June 2000 at http://ksghome.harvard.edu/~jfrankel.academic.ksg/americanviewofemu&euro.pdf.

[11] Frankel, http://ksghome.harvard.edu/~jfrankel.academic.ksg/americanviewofemu&euro.pdf.

[12] Mundell, http://www.cato.org/pubs/journal/cj18n3-13.pdf.

---

13 Frankel, http://ksghome.harvard.edu/~jfrankel.academic.ksg/americanview ofemu&euro.pdf. At the time of going to press, the US economy has faced a slowdown (eds.).

14 Mundell, http://www.cato.org/pubs/journal/cj18n3-13.pdf.

Part Five
Politics, Philosophy, & Security:
Revisiting International Relations

Chapter 14

Atlantic Corridors: Schiller, Papini, and the Americanization of Pragmatism

Anthony Marasco

> At all events I did not invent this faith [in democracy]. I acquired it from my surroundings as far as those surroundings were animated by the democratic spirit (John Dewey).[1]

> It is only when you take your ethics for granted that all problems emerge as problems of technique (Louis Hartz).[2]

Pragmatism, far from being the philosophic formalization of the American democratic experience, had its origins in a transatlantic movement of ideas before being thoroughly "Americanized" by John Dewey.[3] Such a distinction is crucial, not only to correctly place this philosophic position within its historical setting, but also to properly understand its theoretical underpinnings. Seen as the philosophic formalization of the American democratic experience, pragmatism is often put under severe strain when it is claimed that its premises rationally justify democratic theory. But once seen as an attempt to deal with the shifting challenges posed by the diffusion of irrationalism in a transatlantic setting, the connection between pragmatism and democracy may be more exactly appreciated as an American attempt to deal with that context of discourse. Never an easy translation of democracy in theory, pragmatism nonetheless inspired generations of American intellectuals by furnishing alternative ways of rationally grounding human knowledge in the face of irrationalism. As such, pragmatism was not essentially *other* to irrationalism, but an attempt to ply its radical critique of reason within the Enlightenment framework of the American democratic tradition.

My argument, then, rests on two seemingly counterintuitive propositions: first, pragmatism was not at its origins an essentially American philosophic position, but rather the American aspect of a wider European situation, "irrationalism"; and second, only when seen as an American response to irrationalism does the nature of the connection between pragmatism and democracy become fully graspable. In light of this reading, one might suggest that those who still propose to use pragmatism to ground democratic theory today should be careful never to erase its contingent aspects if they wish to avoid turning it into a dogmatic position on what democracy should be to all people at all times. Pragmatism was, in fact, an American way of making irrationalism safe for democracy *in a given historical setting* and not the philosophic formalization of democracy as such. Approached in this way, pragmatism has much to offer, especially to those who are interrogating ways of making current democratic theory more open and rationally grounded.

Irrationalism

In his classic 1958 work, *Consciousness and Society*, H. Stuart Hughes embedded the term "irrationalism" within a suite of other similar terms to account for the intellectual climate of the 1890s: the *fin de siécle* "neo-romanticism" (or better still, "neo-mysticism"), "anti-intellectualism," and finally, "anti-positivism."[4] The reason that Hughes needed those other terms to counterbalance the use of the term "irrationalism" came well into focus in the temporization of a distinction:

> Where the writers of the 1890s had restricted themselves to a questioning of the potentialities of reason, the young men of 1905 became frank irrationalists and even anti-rationalists. This crucial distinction, which so often remains blurred in the history of ideas of our century, was largely a matter of contesting age groups.[5]

In Hughes's reconstruction, both the generations before and after 1905 were irrationalist. What divided them was not a fundamental trait, but the degree to which they moved away from the goals of the Enlightenment. Croce, Weber, and Freud, for example (but also quite evidently James), while responding to the full swing of the *fin de siécle* and the pressuring of neo-romantic or neo-mystic sways, were irrationalists only to the extent that they critiqued the application of the logic of the natural sciences to the study of human behavior. In other words, their distrust of the formal logic of positivism never went as far as to renouncing rationality in itself. An abiding, if sober, faith in the goals and values of the Enlightenment distinguished them from the generation to follow, which was, as Hughes believed, "*frankly* irrationalist." Hughes, however, had difficulties in dividing the two age groups too neatly. What came to the fore after 1905 was, in fact, also present in various forms in the work of the preceding generation, at least as a potentiality. But what was only a potentiality at first becomes a palpable reality for the generation of intellectuals operating after 1905.[6]

Following Hughes, then, I would use the term "irrationalism" to denote not a single phenomenon, but that whole network of discourse that went—albeit uneasily—from the questioning of positivist logic to the negation of reason itself. While I agree with Hughes that such a network developed temporally, I also believe that deeper connections had always existed between the two extremes. So in time, one introduced and cast light on the other in ways that were seldom obvious. As we shall see, William James is the perfect example of this.[7]

Pragmatism as an American Response to Irrationalism

The proposition that pragmatism was not, in some way, essentially American may be startling—but only at first. More deeply shocking are the consequences that can be drawn from this proposition. Since the context from which pragmatism originated is the one described above—irrationalism in its wider sense—pragmatism does not only connect with the American democratic experience, but also with some of the origins of European fascism. But how deep were the European roots of pragmatism? Were they deep enough to contaminate, at the source, one thing by its opposite? When studying the literature on the topic, one may come to two preliminary conclusions: First, most scholars diminish, or even dismiss, the relevance of the European influence on pragmatism.[8] Second, the scholars who have found these influences worth studying divide in two camps: those who saw pragmatism connecting to the rise of social-democratic theory on both sides of the Atlantic, and those who also noted troubling connections between pragmatism and fascism.[9]

My approach the problem is from a different angle, one more interested in the gradual development of a temporal differentiation than in the location of pragmatism's immutable position. At first, pragmatism was also open to those segments of the irrationalist context that would go in the fascist direction. After a given moment, however, pragmatism was normatively tied only to the foundations provided by the American democratic tradition. If one were to speculate on the reasons that such a process has escaped later historiographers, one could point to at least two possible explanations. First, the Anglo-American tendency to study philosophy on analytic ideal types has led many historians of philosophy to bypass temporality in building up pragmatism as a stable philosophic position.[10] Second, the liberal imprint of the study of pragmatism in America led many intellectual historians to project backwards in time the democratic restrictions of a later era.[11] Both tendencies, however, find their historical precedent in the way the origins of pragmatism were recast by John Dewey after the death of William James in 1910. It this process of reframing to which I allude when speaking of the "Americanization" of pragmatism.[12]

Before its Americanization, pragmatism was a transatlantic movement of ideas that had found in America one of its nesting sites. Again, such a proposition should appear startling only at first. One may find evidence pointing to the transatlantic origins of what James tentatively called "pragmatism," beginning with the preface of no less a book than his 1907 manifesto on the topic, *Pragmatism: A New Name for Some Old Ways of Thinking*:

> The pragmatic movement, so-called—I do not like the name, but apparently it is too late to change it—seems to have rather suddenly precipitated itself out of the air. A number of tendencies that have always existed in philosophy have all at once become conscious of themselves collectively, and of their combined mission; and this has occurred in so many countries, and from so many different points of view, that much unconcerted statement has resulted. I have sought to unify the picture as it presents itself to my own eyes, dealing in broad strokes, and avoiding minute controversy. Much futile controversy might have been avoided, I believe, if our critics had been willing to wait until we got our message fairly out.[13]

It was for that very reason that *Pragmatism* had been written, at least rhetorically: to give a multifarious and multinational movement some perspective. In private letters, James had clearly stated that he considered the leaders of the movement to be two Americans, John Dewey and himself, and two Europeans, the Oxford philosopher F. C. S. Schiller, and the Florentine *letterato*, Giovanni Papini.[14]

The names of the two European pragmatists are hardly absent from the literature on pragmatism.[15] And yet, outside of the most specialized circles, the proposition that James had more overt admiration for Papini than Dewey in 1906 is seldom articulated, and it would give some pause to all but the most informed readers. Even more shocking would be to learn that the pragmatist Papini became a Futurist just a few years after having met with James's enthusiastic approval, and was to become one of the few Fascist intellectuals with whom Mussolini actually talked from time to time.[16] Equally startling could be the proposition that James had closer and more frequent contacts with the eugenicist-to-be, F. C. S. Schiller, than with John Dewey the democrat. Schiller not only encouraged James to continue his research at a time when very few professional philosophers in America acknowledged the relevance of his work, but he also turned Oxford University into a veritable hotbed of debate over it. With the temporal dimensions of the connection between pragmatism and democracy repressed for so long, some of the early features of that historical sequence now come back to haunt the model that strictly links pragmatism to democracy in America. This is particularly evident today in the clashes of opinion caused by the arrival in America of less anachronistic ways of researching the history of philosophy.

The clash between an older and a newer way of studying ideas in America is well represented by the polemics set up by the historian James T. Kloppenberg against the radical historicism of the neo-pragmatist philosopher Richard Rorty.[17] Opposing Rorty's claim that the connection between pragmatism and democracy is only contingent, and that pragmatism could lead to other political outcomes with equal ease, Kloppenberg radicalized a claim made by Hilary Putnam according to which Dewey's pragmatism accomplished the rational justification of democratic theory. But as Robert Westbrook noted, it still remains uncertain whether Dewey articulated that claim or not. In fact, according to Westbrook, he *could* have articulated it, but did not. Kloppenberg is therefore "absolutely right to say that Dewey asserted [an] analogy between democratic community and scientific communities of inquiry guided by instrumental logic." However, "the analogy is not self-evident (as Weber would say), and we need to know more about the *argument* Dewey offered for it. My own view is that, strictly speaking, Dewey never offered such an argument, though he often seemed to promise one."[18] So in the end, Kloppenberg's argument that pragmatism is indeed capable of grounding democratic theory rests only in a contextual clustering of textual fragments that all seem to have gone in one direction, but that never went there on point of fact. This is why Schiller and Papini now haunt Kloppenberg's contention, and for one fundamental reason. Grounding his claim on inference more than theory, Kloppenberg put too much weight on Putnam's contention while relying only on the contextual—that is, historical—connection between pragmatism and democracy. So once Putnam's claim is destabilized by competing interpretations such as those of the neo-pragmatists, the only evidence Kloppenberg has to support the proposition that pragmatism is essentially democratic resides in its history.[19] But as we have seen, pragmatism was not the product of a social-democratic context, but had its origins in the discursive network of irrationalism (and the entanglement of Papini in those origins is there to remind us, well beyond dispute).[20]

Having come to this nodal point, where the history of pragmatism seems to be imbricated with both the origins of social-democracy and fascism, one may oppose my reading of the early pragmatist movement with a counter-claim—namely, that the mere presence of Schiller and Papini in the early pragmatist movement envisioned by James in 1906 is equally as "contextual" as the scenario envisaged by Kloppenberg. In other words, the co-presence at that point in time of two intellectuals *who were to become full-fledged irrationalists* does not prove that James's pragmatism was co-substantial with their later positions— Futurism and fascism in the case of Papini, and eugenic reform in that of Schiller. And yet, there is evidence in the textual canon of pragmatism showing how close James came to actually endorsing full-fledged irrationalism.

In the June 1906 issue of *The Journal of Philosophy and Psychology and Scientific Methods*, James published an article rarely mentioned today in the survey literature on pragmatism, "G. Papini and the Pragmatist Movement in Italy." In this article, James not only reported on the advances of the movement in Italy, but positively compared the untechnical, almost literary pragmatism of the Italians to the stiffness of the pragmatism practiced by the Anglo-Americans: "To one accustomed to the style of article that has usually discussed pragmatism, Deweyism, or radical empiricism, in this country, and more particularly in this Journal, the Italian literature of the subject is a surprising, and to the present writer, a refreshing novelty." He argues further, "Surely no other country could utter in the same number of months as badly written a philosophic mass as ours has published since Dewey's 'Studies in Logical Theory' came out.

Germany is not 'in it' with us, in my estimation, for uncouthness of form." Indeed, what separated the Italian writings—those of Papini in particular—from the "badly written a philosophic mass" published in the *Journal* (mostly by Dewey, it would seem), was not the writing style *per se* but the thinking style in its essence. Dewey had been trained on German texts as a logician, while Papini was substantially a poet-thinker, a natural: "Signor Papini in particular has a real genius for cutting and untechnical phraseology. He can write descriptive literature, polychromatic with adjectives, like a decadent, and clear up a subject by drawing cold distinctions, like a scholastic."[21] So it should not surprise us if, at the end, the clearest definition of what pragmatism is for Papini must be expressed through a metaphor, that of the "corridor"—a metaphor James liked so much that he would later use it in his own *Pragmatism,* in which a passage from the article is transcribed almost *verbatim.*

> Pragmatism, according to Papini, is thus only a collection of attitudes and methods, and its chief characteristic is its armed neutrality in the midst of doctrines. It is like a corridor in a hotel, from which a hundred doors open into a hundred chambers. In one you may see a man on his knees praying to regain his faith; in another a desk at which sits someone eager to destroy all metaphysics; in a third a laboratory with an investigator looking for new footholds by which to advance upon the future. But the corridor belongs to all, and all must pass there. Pragmatism in short, is a great *corridor-theory.*[22]

If one were to find a term to describe where the appreciation of Papini's pragmatism had led James, one would perhaps be forced to use the term "irrationalism," the refusal to see in the use of formal logic the prime tool of human understanding. Such an impression would be reinforced by what follows in James's article, the endorsement of Papini's overman, the "Man-God." It was such a figure of becoming that stood at the end of pragmatism, once pragmatism was "unstiffened" (another term that James would borrow from Papini in *Pragmatism*) of all residual reliance to formal logic. At that point pragmatism becomes, in James's own words, "instrumental"—that is, creative: "The common denominator to which all the forms of human life can be reduced is this: *the quest for instruments to act with,* or, in other words, *the quest to power.*" It is power, in the end, that makes human beings creative: "Instead of affirming with the positivists that we must render the ideal world as similar as possible to the actual, Sig. Papini emphasizes our duty of turning the actual world into as close a copy of the ideal as it will let us."[23] Using the full power of the human mind as liberated by the pragmatic attitude, Man would become creative in a way not seen before. "As such, man becomes a kind of god, and where are we to draw his limits?"

In an article called "From Man to God" in the *Leonardo* for last February, Sig. Papini lets his imagination work at stretching the limits. His attempts will be called Promethean or bullfroggian, according to the temper of the reader. It has decidedly an element of literary swagger and conscious impertinence, but I confess that I am unable to treat it otherwise than respectfully. Why should not the divine attributes of omniscience and omnipotence be used by man as the pole-stars by which he may methodically lay his own course? Why should not divine *rest* be his own ultimate goal, rest attained by an activity in the end so immense that all deniers are satisfied, and no more action is necessary? The unexplored powers and relations of man, both physical and mental, are certainly enormous; why should we impose limits on them *a priori*? And, if not, why are the most utopian programs not in order?[24]

James concludes his estimation of Papini's pragmatism with a very unambiguous endorsement: "The program of a Man-God is surely one of the possible great type-programs of philosophy":

I myself have been slow in coming into the full inwardness of pragmatism. Schiller's writings and those of Dewey and his school have taught me some of its wider reaches; and in the writings of this youthful Italian, clear in spite of all their brevity and audacity, I find not only a way in which our English views might be developed farther and with consistency—at least so it appears to me—but also a tone of feeling well fitted to rally devotees and to make of pragmatism a new militant form of religious or quasi-religious philosophy[25] (340).

We have thus come to a very delicate point. What in his own thinking allowed James to endorse Papini's "Man-God"? Any reader of James cannot believe, not even for a moment, that in endorsing the Man-God James had stepped out of his Yankee habit of mind—his proud, unbreakable belief in the primacy of democratic freedom.[26] In this, Kloppenberg is absolutely right. So how could he endorse something that to us smacks immediately of fascism in the make? To answer this question, I believe we must learn to see how the very inclination that led James to endorse the Man-God also kept him apart from it. What attracted him was that Papini's keen poetic eye had discerned neo-romantic, or better, neo-mystic origins similar to those within James's own anti-intellectual positions, which is why he endorsed Papini's position. James believed that Papini had found a way of collating his own divided self, the scientist and the would-be mystic.[27] At the same time, however, James was protected from the authoritarian consequences of the Man-God theory by his life-long reliance on the method of science in adjudicating claims. If, in time, humans would become creative gods, then positive evidence would be produced to corroborate Papini's theory. If not, the theory would have to be revised, if not abandoned. This said, however, it is indisputable that in endorsing Papini, James came close to crossing the divide that H. Stuart Hughes was to locate between the older anti-positivists and the "generation of 1905." In that near slip, however, James revealed something about his pragmatism that is well worth remembering when his ideas are "contextually" conflated with those of Dewey, on the assumption that both lead inevitably to the rational justification of democratic theory.

Pragmatism and American Democracy

After having examined James's reception of Papini's pragmatism, should we conclude that the distance between James's and Dewey's pragmatism proves that Rorty was right? Is the connection between pragmatism and democracy only a fact of contingency? Indeed, the historical process that assisted Dewey's restriction of pragmatism to the premises of the American democratic tradition seems to prove Rorty right. The connections between pragmatism and irrationalism point to the fact that Papini's pragmatism was imbricated at some level with the origins of fascism. But those like Kloppenberg who only see the connections between pragmatism and social-democratic theory forget a fundamental aspect of the European context that also envelops the American tradition. As the revolutionary syndicalism of Sorel well indicates, at a crucial juncture fascism and socialism entangled *their* discursive origins in ways that were never clear cut or uncomplicated.

American intellectual historians have been able to study pragmatism in isolation from its European origins largely because of the presumed "exceptional" nature of American history. In doing so, they forget that James operated in a transatlantic rather than in a strictly national setting. It is a peculiarity of the current debates on pragmatism that the widely accepted critique of "exceptionalism" has not led to the full reconsideration of the transatlantic origins of pragmatism, but—if anything—to a further negation of the role that European irrationalism played in its shaping. By simply suppressing the relevance of the term "American" in statements such as "pragmatism may rationally justify (American) democratic practices," theoretical foundations are seen as existing where only normative restrictions applied. So it was not pragmatism that grounded democracy, but the other way around. It was the American democratic tradition that came to ground pragmatism on its ethical foundations.[28] Those ethical premises were already present in James's pragmatism as the embedded premises of his scientific ideal. In that direction, Dewey's contribution to the development of pragmatism was precisely to transfer back those embedded tenets from the scientific to the democratic ideal.

Adopting a transatlantic perspective in the study of pragmatism may thus help us to accomplish at least two things. First, such a perspective may help us disarm some of the strictures of the present debates over pragmatism and reconnect both its history and its theory to the full complexity of its origins. Second, by forcing us to adopt a comparative stance, that perspective may help us to explore the national aspects of the discourse without surrendering ourselves to exceptionalism all over again. It is precisely by continuing to repress the crucial transnational dimension of pragmatism that exceptionalism keeps returning in its historical reconstructions. By postulating a strict theoretical dependence of pragmatism and democracy while building that dependence on history alone, pragmatism is made "essentially" democratic only as long as it is can be kept "essentially" American. What the transatlantic perspective does to this fallacy is to remind us that in the past, more than one context assisted in the birth of pragmatism, and that in the present, more than one democratic tradition exists to enlarge the dialogue on what democracy really is or ought to be. Democracy, after all, was never essentially American—only contingently so.

---

[1] John Dewey, "Creative Democracy: The Task Before Us" (1939), *The Later Works* (Carbondale, IL: Southern Illinois University Press, 1988), 14: 230.

[2] Louis Hartz, *The Liberal Tradition in America: An Interpretation of American Political Thought Since the Revolution* (San Diego: Harcourt and Brace, 1955), 10.

[3] The "pragmatism" to which I allude is the movement of ideas initiated by William James, and not that element of the philosophy of Peirce that is also labeled "pragmatism." As Peirce himself admitted, James kidnapped Peirce's term, giving it different meaning. Thus, "pragmatism" here refers specifically to the movement of ideas initiated by James around the turn of the century.

[4] H. Stuart Hughes, *Consciousness and Society: The Reorientation of European Social Thought, 1890-1930* (New York: Alfred A. Knopf, 1958).

[5] Ibid., 338.

[6] It was after the first Moroccan crisis of 1905 that the French and the British military began to draw common contingency plans in the event of a clash with the German Empire.

[7] Throughout Hughes's book, William James is a constant presence. "In the course of the present study we shall find the name of William James bobbing up again and again" (112). Such a recurrence was justified by the fact that it had been James who had "acted as the revivifying force in European thought in the decade and a half preceding the outbreak of the First World War" (397). "For with the advent of James—with the publication of his *Varieties of Religious Experience* in 1902, and more particularly with the *pragmatism* of 1907—the intellectual horizon suddenly seemed to clear: everything become simple, direct, unequivocal" (112). Especially evident was James's "anti-intellectualism." In his view, that term "is virtually equivalent to Jamesean pragmatism" (36). And yet, the very fact of its constant "bobbing up" also shows the extent to which James's thinking was entangled with all that made up the evanescent intellectual situation Hughes so admirably tried to define.

[8] The literature on pragmatism is immense and varied. Nevertheless, the assertion that pragmatism is "American" crosses many of its component parts and reduces European pragmatism to an instance of American influence on European thinking. Such a model of reception has structured most scholars' approaches to the transatlantic question. In particular, see H. S. Thayer, *Meaning and Action: A Critical History of Pragmatism* (Indianapolis: Bobbs-Merrill, 1968); Charles W. Morris, *The Pragmatic Movement in American Philosophy* (New York: Braziller, 1970); Garry M. Brodsky, "The Pragmatic Movement," *Review of Metaphysics* 25, no. 2 (1971): 262-291. For earlier work on this idea, see John Dewey, "The Development of Pragmatism," in his *Studies in the History of Ideas* (New York: Columbia University Press, 1925); and Dewey, "William James," *Journal of Philosophy* (September, 1910). See also Ralph Barton Perry, *The Thought and Character of William James* (Cambridge: Harvard University Press, 1948). Perry recognized all the "foreign" aspects of pragmatism but oriented his reconstruction to center the contextual origins of pragmatism almost exclusively in America.

[9] In recent scholarship, the most notable book in the first vein is certainly James T. Kloppenberg's *Uncertain Victory: Social Democracy and Progressivism in European and American Thought, 1870-1920* (New York: Oxford University Press, 1986). Among those who have explored the "darker" side of pragmatism, see John Patrick Diggins, "Flirtation with Fascism: American Pragmatic Liberals and Mussolini's Italy," *American Historical Review* 71, no. 2 (1966); and Diggins, *The Promise of Pragmatism: Modernism and the Crisis of Knowledge and Authority* (Chicago: University of Chicago Press, 1994).

[10] Again, the first instance of an ideal-typical reconstruction of pragmatism can be detected in Dewey's eulogy of William James, (1910), and in his subsequent 1925 reconstruction of the theoretical origins of pragmatism. Later ideal-typical reconstructions have sought to include aspects of pragmatism in the genealogy of analytic philosophy in America. Such a move most often located the pivotal element in the work of the logician Charles S. Peirce. Early instances of such a drive, however, can be already found in Arthur O.

Lovejoy's and Bertrand Russell's negative reception of James's pragmatism. See Arthur O. Lovejoy, "Thirteen Pragmatisms," *Journal of Philosophy* 5 (1908): 5-12; Bertrand Russell, "Pragmatism," *Edinburgh Review* 59 (April 1909): 365. The tendency to amend pragmatism in the interests of more sober analysis can be examined in Stanley Cavell and Alexander Sesonske, "Logical Empiricism and Pragmatism in Ethics," *Journal of Philosophy* 48 (1951): 5-16; Herbert Spiegelberg, "Husserl's and Peirce's Phenomenologies: Coincidence Or Interaction?", *Philosophy and Phenomenological Research* 17 (1956): 164-185; and finally in A. J. Ayer, *The Origins of Pragmatism: Studies in the Philosophy of Charles Sanders Peirce and William James* (London: Macmillan, 1968).

[11] The process of "Americanization" that equated pragmatism with democracy found perhaps its first historiographic canonization in the intellectual history written in the wake of World War I by James's first biographer, Ralph Barton Perry. See Perry, *The Present Conflict of Ideals: A Study of the Philosophical Background of the World War* (New York: Longmans and Green, 1918); see also his *Characteristically American* (New York: Alfred Knopf, 1949). The same identification of pragmatism with democracy can be found in a classic work of intellectual history of the 1950s: Henry Steele Commager, *The American Mind: An Interpretation. Thought and Character Since the 1880s* (New Haven: Yale University Press, 1950).

[12] Dewey radically reconstructed the genealogy of pragmatism after James's death in 1910. As David A. Hollinger noted in 1980, the influence of Dewey and of his followers on the reconstruction of pragmatism has scarcely been registered in the literature. In a note he estimated that "what deserves more attention is the process by which the idea of a single 'American Pragmatism' was kept alive after James's death, especially during the 1920s and 1930s. Dewey and Dewey's followers played a very large role in this process and helped to persuade most Americans who took an interest in the matter that Dewey's work was the logical culmination of the pragmatism of Peirce and James." Hollinger, "The Problem of Pragmatism in American History," *Journal of American History* (June 1980): 88-107.

[13] William James, *Pragmatism: A New Name for Some Old Ways of Thinking* (New York: Longmans, Green, 1907), vii.

[14] Letters written by James shortly before the publication of *Pragmatism* in 1907 show that his notion of what represented the pragmatic movement are vastly different from the ones we have grown accustomed to. In a letter to John Jay Chapman in 1906, for example, James wrote the following revealing statement: "The leaders of the new movement are Dewey, Schiller of Oxford, in a sense Bergson of Paris, a young Florentine named Papini, and last and least worthy, H. G. Wells ought to be counted in, and if I mistake not, G. K. Chesterton as well." Elizabeth Hardwick, ed., *The Selected Letters of William James* (New York: Doubleday, 1961), 226.

[15] For discussions of this aspect in the bibliography of pragmatism, see, for Schiller: Reuben Abel, *The Pragmatic Humanism of F. C. S. Schiller* (New

York: King's Crown Press, 1955); Kenneth Winetrout, *F. C. S. Schiller and the Dimensions of Pragmatism* (Columbus: Ohio State University Press, 1967). For Papini, see Carlo Golino, "Giovanni Papini and American Pragmatism," *Italica* 32, no. 1 (1955): 33-48; Giovanni Gullace, "The Pragmatic Movement in Italy," *Journal of the History of Ideas* 23 (1962): 91-106; G. Snichelotto, "Il pragmatismo irrazionalistico di G. Papini," in *Storiografia e filosofia del linguaggio* ed. C. Giacon, (Padova: Antenone, 1975), 150-66; Gerald E. Mayers, "The Influence of William James's Pragmatism in Italy," in *The Sweetest Impression of Life: The James Family in Italy*, ed. James W. Tuttleton and Agostino Lombrado (New York: New York University Press, 1990), 162-181; E. Paul Colella, "Philosophy in the Piazza: Giovanni Papini's Pragmatism and Italian Politics," *Journal of Speculative Philosophy* 11, no. 2 (1997): 125-142.

[16] See Roberto Ridolfi, *Vita di Giovanni Papini* (Milano: Arnaldo Mondadori, 1957).

[17] James T. Kloppenberg, "Pragmatism: An Old Name for Some New Ways of Thinking?", *Journal of American History* 83, no. 1 (1996): 100-138. By reversing the title James had given to his book—*Pragmatism: A New Name for Some Old Ways of Thinking*—Kloppenberg signaled from the outset that indeed today pragmatism has become a blanket term also used to designate some of the "postmodern" positions the linguistic turn introduced in America.

[18] Robert Westbrook, "Pragmatism and Democracy: Reconstructing the Logic of John Dewey's Faith," in *The Revival of Pragmatism: New Essays on Social Thought, Law, and Culture* ed. Morris Dickstein, (Durham: University of North Carolina Press, 1998), 130.

[19] One of Kloppenberg's main preoccupations in *Uncertain Victory* had been to foreground the way James and Dewey connected their respective positions, especially because his model grounded Dewey's pragmatism on the epistemology provided by James. Kloppenberg's narrative is as follows: At first, James had been alone in questioning the epistemic foundations of positivist science. Then, "James found himself riding the crest of the *Zeitgeist*. James recognized as clearly as Dewey that a process of intellectual convergence was transforming the transatlantic world of ideas" (27). Thus it is within that wider context of transatlantic agreement that the interconnection between the ideas of William James and John Dewey must be placed. And yet, "to leave the world of William James and enter the world of John Dewey is to experience a peculiar sense of dislocation: the landscape seems familiar, yet the atmosphere is strangely different" (41). So in the end, the connection between James and Dewey is more in the wider context than in the concrete body of work they produced.

[20] Like Hughes, Kloppenberg employs the generational model to explain the way their object of study changed in time.

[21] William James, "G. Papini and the Pragmatist Movement in Italy," *Journal of Philosophy and Psychology and Scientific Methods* (June 1906): 337-38.

[22] Ibid., 339.

[23] Ibid.

[24] Ibid., 339-340

[25] Ibid., 340

[26] On the topic of James's reliance on the institutions of the American democratic tradition, see George Cotkin, *William James: Public Philosopher* (Urbana: University of Chicago Press, 1989).

[27] See Howard M. Feinstein, *Becoming William James* (Ithaca: Cornell University Press, 1984); also Kim Townsend, *Manhood at Harvard: William James and Others* (Cambridge, MA: Harvard University Press, 1996).

[28] One of the most consistent proponents of "exceptionalism," Louis Hartz, clearly saw how the American democratic tradition grounded Dewey's pragmatism. "American pragmatism has always been deceptive because, glacierlike, it has rested on miles of submerged conviction, and the conformitarian ethos which that conviction generates has always been infuriating because it has refused to pay its critics the compliment of an argument" (Hartz, 59). One can refer to the fallacy of "exceptionalism" to see that—in this case at least—Hartz was exactly right.

Chapter 15

Old Orders, New Orders and Third Ways: Trends in Anglo-American Party Politics

Philip John Davies

In the introduction to our book, *Political Parties and the Collapse of the Old Orders*, John White and I pursued the idea that the years leading into the start of the 21st century hosted a change in the central foci, and the institutional structures, of political parties on an international scale.[1] These changes have not all been the same, nor have they followed a single pattern, but traditional forms of control have proved less reliable. National governments are less capable of exerting control in a globalized economic world, and have increasingly accepted their altered role as actors alongside multi-national corporate concerns in an international economy. Successful agents and managers of change have become highly valued in this altered world of business and commerce.

Political parties have likewise found themselves looking for leaders and institutional forms that could exercise control in an environment typified by change. In some cases the collapse of old institutional orders and their trappings is readily apparent: Russia, South Africa, and Canada fall into this category. In other places, change resembles a shift in the conceptual structure of the Cold War-era parties that are changing in form, if not in name. The United Kingdom and the United States are key examples where the major parties are altering their ideas and their plans for implementing them, and struggling with the consequences in terms of policy, presentation, party organization and electoral coalition.

While the foundations of this modern change may be unique, this turn of the century era is not the only period of party flux and instability that has happened in either country. In the US in particular, the theory of party political realignment has been used to impose a conceptual pattern on generational change in American political life. Analysts are relatively united in the acceptance of 5 political systems, covering the period from the late 18th century to the 1930s.[2] Thereafter the received wisdom falters. A generation after 1932 came the volatile election year of 1968. Political commentators, and increasingly, political activists, have been examining the entrails of elections ever since in the attempt to determine whether the US has entered a sixth party political system, and inevitably, debate will soon be engaged as to whether the indicators in 2000 and 2004 suggest that the sixth system, if it ever started, is being superseded by a seventh.

A number of political characteristics have generally been associated with earlier realignments. These include an associated weakening of party political attachments; growth of independence and split-ticket voting among the electorate; a rapid growth of the electorate; increases in minor party activity as disaffected voters search for new ways to express their political wishes; and significant changes in party structure and style. Ultimately, a shift of support that changes the balance of party political power for a political generation is, in hindsight, the best evidence of a realignment having happened, but few political scientists are content to wait for hindsight, and even then they are likely to disagree on who has 20/20 vision.

Evidence can certainly be found in the late 20th century. There has been an increase in African American and Hispanic voting, and a continued entry of substantial populations of immigrants to the US electoral system. The proportion of the electorate claiming to cast their votes independent of party influence rose to almost 40% in the late 1970s; by the 2000 presidential election, 27% of voters reported themselves as independents, and a further 9% reported voting against their usual party preference.[3] The two major parties are institutionalized within the US electoral system to a degree unusual in Western democracies. Nevertheless, minor parties have been active throughout the period of the late 20th century. George Wallace's American Independent Party took 5 states in 1968, John Anderson's National Unity Coalition attracted almost 7% of the vote in 1980. Neither the Libertarian Party nor the Green Party has gained large proportions of the vote, but in the close election of 2000 Ralph Nader's Green Party candidacy impacted very strongly on the presidential election. For the lack of a few hundred votes in Florida, Al Gore's Democratic candidacy failed to gain the presidency. Ignoring the question of whether hundreds of voters in West Palm Beach misunderstood the ballot and accidentally voted for the Reform Party candidate, Pat Buchanan, over 97,000 Florida voters chose Nader and the Green Party, votes that are likely to have split to the benefit of Gore had Nader not been running in Florida. Greens and Libertarians have also influenced local elections in states where their messages have proved attractive. Ross Perot attracted almost 19% of the presidential vote in 1992 using the "United We Stand America" banner, and 8.5% in 1996 as the candidate of the subsequent Reform Party. The Reform Party candidate Jesse Ventura took the governorship of Minnesota in 1998.

Previous eras have been typified by unified party control across the branches of federal government, but this pattern has not been evident in the late 20th century (see Table 1).

Table 1
Presidential Party Domination of US Congress, 1789-2000:
the Proportion of Election Years

	1789-1824	1826-1858	1860-1894	1896-1930	1932-1966	1968-2000
Presidential Party Controls Senate & House	95%	59%	50%	83%	78%	24%
Presidential Party Controls Senate or House	5%	23%	39%	11%	0%	18%
Divided Control	0%	18%	11%	6%	22%	59%

In an attempt to encompass this, different authors have identified the contemporary party political system as realigned, but "hollow," "weak," "casual," "soft," "rolling" or "by default." Others have argued that the realignment concept has outlived its usefulness, and that this is demonstrated by an era which has shown a public commitment to divided government.[4] The reasons posited have varied. It may be that the electorate wants different attributes represented in the different branches and chambers of government, and recognizes these attributes as best represented by different political parties. It may be that voters have a sense of "cognitive Madisonianism"—a belief in the value of maximizing the oppositions that are already institutionalized within the checks and balances system. The latter seems an unlikely starting point, but it is clear that the US electorate—increasingly suspicious of all institutions of authority over the last part of the 20th century—is generally comfortable with divided government. This knowledge has underpinned campaigns by both parties that have leaped to defend their candidates for one branch by arguing the dangers of handing "unlimited" power to a single party.

It is not clear that the party leaders were trying to "win realignment," but the need to respond to changes both in electoral behavior, and in the legislated structure of the elections process, meant that they certainly had to think of doing more than the short-term aim of winning the next election. For example, while he was Republican Party chairman in the 1980s, Frank Fahrenkopf's "1991 Plan" injected resources into local party organizations around the country, in an attempt to stimulate realignment from the grass roots. At the national level the Republican Party began generic television advertising in 1980. The Democratic Party, having spent years devoting some effort to reducing the power of its Southern conservative wing in order to develop a progressive civil rights policy, in the last quarter of the 20th century thought it necessary to give more weight to the South in its presidential selection process in order to produce candidates acceptable to the national electorate—to the point where 1992 produced an Arkansas/Tennessee ticket. Both the significance accorded to realignment, and the extent to which it had impinged on the consciousness of political leaders, was signally indicated in 1984, when, upon winning re-election, President Ronald Reagan himself declared that "realignment is real."[5]

The transformed party system of the late 20th and early 21st century US has in some ways been an increasingly competitive context. The Democrats maintained their leadership in Congress most of the time, but lost that advantage in 1994. The Republicans have dominated but not monopolized presidency, but failed to unify their party control of government during the last years of the 20th century by losing the executive precisely as they gained the legislature. The Republicans may feel justified in seeing the election results of 2000 as their opportunity to bring to an end the post-New Deal era of party competition, and instituting an era of Republican party control more akin to earlier party alignments—bringing to a conclusion the "interrupted realignment."

In 2000 the Electoral College gave the presidency to Republican George W. Bush by 271 to 266 votes, with one abstention, while the popular vote went to Democrat Al Gore by a margin of over half a million votes—about 0.5% of the total votes cast nationally. Similar divisions between the popular and Electoral College vote have occurred previously in US history, in 1876 and 1888. Gore's popular vote plurality was larger numerically than in any of these previous cases, but not in percentage terms, since these earlier losing candidates received pluralities of 3.0% and 3.1% respectively of the total votes cast. In 1824 Andrew Jackson had achieved a 10.4% plurality in the popular vote, and a lead, but not an absolute majority, in the Electoral College, only to have the US House of Representatives deliver the presidential victory to his opponent. The authors of the Constitution deliberately built this complexity into the presidential election system, but, in spite of close shaves in several years, the electoral system had not been subject to this stress for 112 years. The 2000 result hung on a tiny margin in Florida; that state's care in running the elections was brought into question, and the election was not brought to conclusion until the slimmest 5-4 majority on the US Supreme Court effectively closed the opportunities to re-count votes in Florida by its decision in *George W. Bush, et al., petitioners v. Albert Gore, Jr., et al.* on December 12, 2000, which allowed Bush to assume the presidency.[6]

In the other federal elections of 2000, the Republicans retained their control of the House of Representatives, but with a reduced majority. With 221 Republicans, 212 Democrats, and 2 Independents who could usually be relied on to divide between the two major parties, the GOP had a working majority of 9 seats. In the election for US Senate, the Republicans also lost ground in 2000, and when, 4 weeks after the close of voting, the state of Washington confirmed that Democrat Maria Cantwell had unseated republican incumbent Slade Gorton, the final tally lay at 50 Senators for each of the major parties. After the January 20, 2001 presidential inaugural, Vice President Dick Cheney could take his post as President of the US Senate, giving the Republicans control of that body by the thinnest of margins—his casting vote—a margin particularly susceptible to the vagaries of Senatorial mortality.[7]

The Democrats, deeply frustrated by their failure by such paper-thin margins in the 2000 races for presidency, US Senate, and the US House, still take comfort in the Clinton election victories of the 1990s, and in the difficulty that the Republicans have had in establishing a clear and strong margin of control in Congress. Reapportionment of House seats in the light of the 2000 census results should help the Republicans, as they hold the majority of state governorships and will therefore have a strong say in the remodeling of constituency boundaries, but the mid-term elections, traditionally difficult for the party of the incumbent president, still give the Democrats an opportunity to strike back. The 2000 election did not provide a strong personal mandate for George W. Bush, and a poor performance in office would lay the foundation for a strong challenge to his re-election. Each of the candidates gaining the presidency in 1824, 1876 and 1888 stayed in office for just one term, and the Democrats will be looking to help Bush to continue that tradition. In principal the balance is close enough that Democrats can still see the opportunity to rebuff Republican efforts, and to lay the foundation for Democratic strength in the new century.

Some interpretations of the 2000 result stress the point that "the country overall seems to be moving toward a balanced middle," evenly divided, but, in Morris Fiorina's words, "not that committed, one way or the other." In this vision regional differences still exist, but there is a convergence as national cultural influences and demographic mobility spread modernization and diversity to all parts of the nation. Other analysts see a very different picture, one of "Two Nations, Four Parties," in which the cultural politics of voters split the electorate deeply, and the parties' internal debates over "new politics" (Third Way/Compassionate Conservatism) and traditional liberal/conservative agendas create an extra tension between branches of government. An even result can be the basis on which one party builds a subsequent period of domination, but tight electoral margins, whether based on a close balance of centrism, or on confrontation between competing cultural nations in the US, could bed in to have a long term effect.[8]

In the UK the Labour and Conservative parties similarly face each other across an altered political landscape. The factional battle within the Labour Party heightened after the 1979 election victory by Margaret Thatcher's Conservative party. At the time of Thatcher's massive re-election victory, Labour moderate Gerald Kaufman MP called Labour's left-driven, and detailed, manifesto for that campaign, *New Hope for Britain*, "the longest suicide note in history." The Social Democratic Party, many of its leadership nurtured by American support, broke from Labour, but in the end did not break the mould, eventually merging with the Liberal Party. Charles Kennedy, first elected to parliament 1983 as a 23 year old MP for the Social Democratic Party, symbolized the impact, and perhaps the failure, of that party when he won the leadership election for the Liberal Democrat Party in 1999.

Neil Kinnock, elected Labour party leader in 1983, tackled the need to change the Labour party. During the 1980s and early 1990s, as Tim

Hames reports, "Neil Kinnock had engaged in a ruthless reassessment of party policy. Unpopular commitments had been abandoned and the left wing of the party firmly crushed."[9] Regardless of this, the Conservatives, led by Prime Minister John Major, won re-election again in 1992. John Smith took the helm of the Labour Party, and modernized further—especially in shifting the party away from its traditional financial and membership dependence on the trades unions—but Smith's early death in 1994 left the party in shock. Tony Blair won the subsequent leadership contest, and pressed forward the modernization of the party with a remarkable dedication and firmness, in one particular strike at the symbolic heart of the old party, persuading it to abandon "Clause Four," its age-old core commitment to national ownership of primary industries.

At the center of the debate on party and policy modernization at the end of the 20th century in the UK and the US has been the Third Way. The Democratic Leadership Council and the Progressive Policy Institute have provided the US location for the generation and debate of third way ideas. They claim that Bill Clinton, at the beginning of the final decade of the 20th century, then governor of Arkansas and early in his process of policy positioning for his first presidential campaign, made the first mention of the third way in its current political context. Tony Blair was then a Member of Parliament in a Labour Party early in its second decade of opposition. It was Blair, though, who wrote that, "I have always believed that politics is first and foremost about ideas ... Furthermore, ideas need labels ... The 'Third Way' is to my mind the best label for the new politics which the progressive centre-left is forging ..."[10]

Whatever its origins, "Third Way" seems neither to have entered very successfully the public awareness in the US, nor to have leaped across the linguistic barrier presented by Washington DC's Beltway. In the UK the term is more accepted as part of the language; the debate as to what the Third Way really means is live enough that the media can assume public recognition and reaction. When the Prime Minister and his family took a holiday in Tuscany in August 1999, Italian security arrangements raised eyebrows and hackles locally, and the subsequent negotiation of final arrangements attracted media attention. *The Times* reported the fuss and the compromises under the headline "Third Way to Beach."[11] The joke in this headline, however weak, gives some evidence of the recognition of the term in the UK. When in summer 2000 a pressurized government faced public and party revolts on fuel taxes and pension provisions, the Labour leadership's pronouncements at that year's annual party conferences were interpreted in terms of their evidence of a return to Old Labour rhetoric, and at least a slight step to the side of the Third Way.

While the rhetoric of pensions support, education and health spending may have the ring of Old Labour, and of electoral pandering, it is less clear that they are antagonistic to Third Way thinking. While the Third Way may be looking for alternative funding streams, increased quality control and accountability, partnership in the creation of ideas and resources, and the implementation of policy, it sets its face neither against spending nor social engineering. More evidently, in the style of Bill Clinton's guru Dick Morris, it is looking for a triangulated position, not denying that existing competing ideologies of the left and right already require expenditure and (however much they deny it) involve social engineering through policy. Tony Blair argues that the Third Way "is about traditional values in a changed world ... uniting great streams of left-of-centre thought—democratic socialism and liberalism." The values he lists are "equal worth, opportunity for all, responsibility and community." The main features of change he highlights are globalization of markets and culture, technological advance, the transformed role of women, radical changes in the nature of politics—including the loss of popular faith with distant, unresponsive and often ineffective political institutions. These lead Blair to identify the task of the Third Way as meeting 4 broad policy objectives:

- A dynamic knowledge-based economy founded on individual empowerment and opportunity, where governments enable, not command, and the power of the market is harnessed to serve the public interest;
- A strong civil society enshrining rights and responsibilities, where the government is a partner to strong communities;
- A modern government based on partnership and decentralization, where democracy is deepened to suit the modern age;
- And a foreign policy based on international co-operation.[12]

In the US the DLC/PPI homepage encapsulates the Third Way as seeking

to adapt enduring progressive values to the new challenges of the information age. It rests on 3 cornerstones: the idea that government should promote equal opportunity for all while granting special privilege to none; an ethic of mutual responsibility the equally rejects the politics of entitlement and the politics of social abandonment; and, a new approach to governing that empowers citizens to act for themselves.[13]

Tony Blair insists that the Third Way is "not just the lowest common denominator between left and right. It is a genuine attempt to address the problems of the future according to the principles of justice ... it offers a new, different, radical, and better way forward for politics in the 21st century."[14] This comes close to claiming that the Third Way at least realigns political ideas. For example, both Blair and Clinton declared an end to "big government," and admitted that their parties' traditional ideas on taxing and spending have had to alter. Reagan and Thatcher both made the rhetoric of tax and spend/big government into formidable electoral tools. Reagan's success in instilling the rhetoric while actually leading an administration that saw an unprecedented acceleration in national debt came home to haunt President George H. W. Bush, whose inability to maintain his "no new taxes" pledge while in office contributed to his 1992 defeat. In the 1997 UK election New Labour felt confident enough in its new image to attack the John Major Conservative government for an alleged 22 separate increases in taxation. New Labour, in its turn, promised specifically that there would be no increases in tax rates, and more efficient delivery of health care (reduced waiting lists), and education (smaller classes). The specific language of such promises leads to difficulties. On petrol, for example, the overall percentage tax rate declined marginally between 1997 and 2000, but unpredicted and large price rises increased the total tax take considerably. In an example of the globalization of protest, UK truckers and farmers (the latter of whom are actually already able to claim substantial relief from high petrol prices) decided to emulate the direct action of their French counterparts in challenging fuel prices, blocking the exit of fuel from refineries throughout Britain. Similar protests took place in other countries as the owners of heavy equipment realized that the tools of their trade were potentially valuable in pursuing a campaign of disruption. The British government, and most others, took a strong line against the protesters, but no amount of pointing to the honoring of the government commitment on tax rates could undermine the general public sympathy with the protesters, or shake the opinion of 91% of those polled in the UK that the government was mishandling the situation. In an age when a president can argue that "it all depends on what your definition of 'is' is," the public's patience in listening to arcane deconstruction of political rhetoric is tested to the limits.

If the fuel crisis shook the Blair government, it was only part of the problem in the UK in the delivery of the different parts of the Third Way agenda. The Third Way as interpreted by Blair calls for decentralization and "deepened democracy," but the perceived need to deliver policy designed to underpin a generation of future New Labour election victories inclines the party in many ways to a more centralized operation. With the enactment of the Labour administration's reforms, this has introduced deep and abiding tensions.

New Labour has certainly instituted a set of constitutional reforms that are unprecedented in recent British politics. A Scottish parliament and a Welsh Assembly have devolved political authority regionally within the UK to a greater degree than has been known in centuries. In the name of deepening democracy and catering to community, New Labour introduced to the UK, through the Welsh and Scottish elections, a proportional representation system based on constituency elections plus at-large members chosen on a party list basis. The resulting system made it difficult for Labour to win an overall majority in either Scotland or Wales (something they would very likely have achieved with a non-PR system). It gave the Conservatives, reduced to the status of an England-only party in the 1997 General Elections, the opportunity to regain an electoral foothold in Scotland and Wales— mainly through their now salaried at-large members, with no constituency responsibilities.

Proportional representation in the European elections (introduced in this case by European regulation) reduced the ability of either main party to dominate those results. The reform of the House of Lords, launched but still ongoing, has initially stepped down the numbers of Lords, promising later to replace the chamber with one chosen by a different, but so far not completely explained method. London has gained an elected Mayor, possibly to be followed by a similar reconstruction of local government in other major cities. At the same time Blair has adopted an inclusive approach. Northern Ireland policy has been conducted in co-operation with the Republic of Ireland, and the relationship between Prime Minister Blair and Taisoaech Bertie Ahern appears constructively close. Liberal Democrat Leader Paddy Ashdown was formally included in certain government discussions (a link that Charles Kennedy has undertaken to maintain), and Conservative former MP and Governor of Hong Kong, Chris Patten, accepted appointment from Blair, in spite of being accused by the late Lord Beloff of being traitors to their political allies.

These major ventures into "partnership and decentralization" have been paralleled by accusations of increasingly authoritarian use of power within the party and the government administration. The New Labour government appears to use personal political advisers more than any previous administration. While an increase in reliance on temporarily appointed advisers, rather than on the established civil service leaders, was noted throughout the previous Conservative administrations, New Labour arrived with a larger cadre of advisers than had been experienced before. These personnel increasingly handle public relations as well as direct policy advice; the relationship between policy initiation, development, presentation and spin has never been so close, as New Labour has launched into an administration of permanent campaigning on issues and policies.

There has been immense constitutional reform under the Blair government—much of which fits well within the parameters of the Third Way aims to created an enabling, empowering, stakeholder democracy. These reforms attempt to deliver, in a fundamental way, the decision-making structure that the Third Way envisages as healthy and democratically reinvigorating. In policy terms, however, these reforms have consistently made more difficult the Blair administration's ability to deliver the policies it wishes to embed. Candidate choice battles emerged in the European elections, the Welsh and Scottish elections, and the campaign for the mayoralty of London, and in each case critics observed the heavy hand of New Labour central control. Least favored Labour Members of the European Parliament were listed low on the party's lists, which, with the introduction of PR, ensured their departure from office. After the London HQ's favorite for the Welsh leadership, Ron Davies, fell foul of scandal, New Labour worked hard, and ultimately successfully, to insert Blair favorite Alun Michael into the leadership position. But this proved only a temporary success, and in 2000, Michael's inability to maintain the loyal backing of the Welsh Assembly led to his resignation, and the selection of Rhodri Morgan—all along the favored leader within the Principality. Failing to win the anticipated sweeping victory in the Scottish elections, Labour also failed very publicly to hammer home its coveted Third Way policy regarding the financing of higher education students. The untimely death of Labour stalwart, and Scottish First Minister, Donald Dewar, took a strong and powerful Blairite voice from that parliament. Early in 2001 Prime Minister Tony Blair admitted that the heavy-handed attempt to control the choice of a Welsh leader had been an error, but by the time of this admission, the logic of devolution was proving a strong counter to party centrism, and both Wales and Scotland were governed locally by Labour/Liberal Democrat coalition administrations.

These constitutional reforms have produced some notable and valuable results. In terms of empowerment and stake-holding, it is worth noting that 37% of Members of the Scottish Parliament are women, as are 42% of the Welsh Assembly. This compares very favorably with the 18.5% female House of Commons, and the 13% female US House of Representatives.[15] New Labour's aims for a devolutionary structure of government fall clearly within its Third Way principles, regardless of the tensions and difficulties that this presents for a political party with aims to control and deliver policy in a "responsible party" manner. Whether New Labour realized how far their structural changes would make more complex their policy environment is not at all clear. The Third Way and "triangulation" appear to aim at a kind of conciliated policy creation and delivery, and it is planned that access and enabling structures feed into this process. However, devolutionary political structures are not necessarily conciliatory, at least in the short term, providing, as they do, more forums to engage in confrontation, and more power loci in which non-conciliating regional and ideological oppositions may gather authority.

Whether the policies of New Labour fall as comfortably within its Third Way principles as its devolutionary aims for government has been debated with some heat. After the unexpectedly large losses suffered in the June 1999 European elections, John Monks, General Secretary of the Trades Union Congress, complained that the party was in serious danger of becoming distant from its core support while in pursuit of a broader middle class base. "I always understood the new support was meant to be an addition ... Labour too often seems embarrassed by its traditional supporters and what they believe."[16] The warning was all the more telling for the fact that Monks is a Blair ally and friend. An alternative perspective was that "the tendency to 'talk right and act left' was turning off party activists. Many of them did not know of the measures the Government had taken to help the 'core vote.'"[17] As Andrew Rawnsley points out,

A Conservative Government would not have introduced the minimum wage, nor the maximum working week. There would not have been a New Deal for the unemployed, tax credits to improve the incomes of the low paid, or the largest ever increases in child benefit. There is a long list of things that Labour could boast it has done for its old voters—but it doesn't for fear of alienating its new voters. Gordon Brown has been as redistributionist as any Labour Chancellor.... [but] it remains a secret to [Labour] supporters."[18]

Old Labour suspects the Third Way of being conservatism in new clothing. The Conservatives, on the other hand, would like to convince the electorate that the Third Way is Old Labour in new clothing.

New Labour, therefore, has a number of serious difficulties in moving comfortably to a party system defined by majority support for the Third Way. The very decentralization that is part of the Third Way makes it more difficult for the major party to deliver policy effectively. Insofar as policy results may be similar to old policies, credit may only be claimed carefully for fear of undermining the attraction to voters pulled to the party by the claim to be "new." Gains that should appeal to traditional supporters may therefore be unclear and unrecognized, leading to a perception that that the party has, in the wake of Thatcherism's shifting of the policy agendas, become Tweedledee to a conservative Tweedledum. Weakness on single salient issues can damage the party in elections even when its overall popularity remains high. In this political structure New Labour has shown a willingness and ability to use many mechanisms to drive on with its policies. Those mechanisms include party sanctions unavailable in the US, but, as decentralized political forms take shape, there has been a real increase in the use of permanent policy campaigning—to influence the policy debate within the party, the political media, the politically-aware public, and even in the international community.

This is a form of politics perhaps better known in the US where decentralization is a fact of political life, where policy negotiation within government is necessitated by the system of checks and balances, and where there is limited party control over candidate choice. Political leaders in this environment have, for a long time, had to exert their authority by showing an ability to negotiate, cajole, and lead their fellow politicians to recognize their right to exercise power. Even with this historical background, Charles O. Jones has expressed the opinion that President Clinton expanded the notion of the permanent campaign to that of campaigning to govern, as well as to win elections. At presidential level his victory in 1992 was a triumph of focused effort. Leading up to the re-election, the 1995 so-called "stealth campaign" designed to put Clinton into an unbeatable position was ground-breaking, and may have changed the shape of campaigning in terms of finances and advertising practice.[19] Jones has argued that Clinton has also adopted a strategy of campaigning on issues while in office, using this approach to close the gaps in the separated system, and involving the executive, congress, different groups within the parties, and the politically-aware electorate in a relatively constant debate.[20]

The process of permanent campaign and the policy of the Third Way may well go closely together. *Permanent Campaign* author Sidney Blumenthal is the Clinton adviser who liaised with Tony Blair on Third Way matters, and stimulated the transatlantic conferences that brought the Clinton and Blair administrations together to discuss and promote the adoption of Third Way ideas. Anthony Giddens considers that "the Third Way is now the centre of a really global dialogue."[21] Much of the writing about the Third Way remains around its definition and is operationalization, both within nations and on the international scene. Robert Reich sees the Third Way as a moral crusade that Clinton failed successfully to articulate, and that now depends on European leadership.[22] *The Wall Street Journal* called George W. Bush's "compassionate conservative" approach "Third Way Republicanism," and William Hague visited Bush in Texas to see if a little could rub off on his own leadership of the Conservative Party.[23] Alan Ryan expresses his disappointment in the Third Way, arguing that "to the extent that it is a coherent or acceptable approach to government it resembles the New Liberalism of the beginning of the century."[24] But American promoters of the Third Way approach see a positive comparison with the age of Progressive reform—an era when progressive ideas affected the policy agendas of both US political parties, and whose institutional reforms were having major impact over half a century later, when primaries and referendums came into their own.

Both in the US and the UK, some analysts consider the forces of the Third Way to be in retreat. In May 2000 the Labour Party suffered unexpectedly large reversals in local council elections. The debate grew as to whether the party could manage the Third Way realignment straddle of maintaining the loyalty of its traditional voters, while carving other chunks of the electorate into a New Labour mould. Postmortems of the 2000 presidential election discussed whether Al Gore had spent too much effort appealing to old core Democratic values, and moving away from the modernization brought by Bill Clinton. The 2000 Democratic campaign, eager to liberate Gore from the less-than-virtuous personal shadow of Clinton, stands accused by some of having failed to build a campaign on the political and economic virtues of Third Way approaches, and thereby of having eroded the potential value of retrospective approval of the administration's successes.

What is clear is that the Third Way has shifted the fulcrum of the political debate in both countries. According to Jonathan Freedland, "Clinton's great contribution to modern politics was what he called 'triangulation'—recast by Tony Blair as modernisation and the third way. Clinton realised that Democrats would only win if they moved rightward on welfare, crime and the deficit."[25] In Freedland's opinion the playing field has been re-designed, and the conjuring of "compassionate conservatism" by the George W. Bush campaign is at least rhetorical evidence of this, even if his choice of the very conservative Dick Cheney as his vice presidential candidate is a suggestion that the conversion may not be very deep. Nevertheless, Polly Toynbee wrote, "the *Washington Post* reports that even George Bush was toying with using [Third Way] himself."[26] Within the UK Conservative Party a similar battle appeared to be playing out. While William Hague's meetings with George Bush did not have him coming out as a "compassionate conservative," Michael Portillo, a leading contender for the Conservative leadership in light of Hague's resignation, chose the Conservative Party conference as an opportunity to declare for a more inclusive, multicultural, and accepting vision of the party and the nation.[27]

It was reported that Tony Blair's essay on "Third Way, Phase Two" published in the February issue of *Prospect*, was "spread across the front page of *La Republica* in Italy. *Les Echos* in France has reprinted it, *Die Zeit* in Germany follows. Latin American and parts of Asia are espousing third way political language too."[28] Gratifying though this must be, Third Way adherents think that it is not enough to see its influence as having shifted the debate on an existing political spectrum. It is not clear that the Third Way can have the political impact to underpin a party realignment in either the UK or the US, even if the parties do now want to "win" a realignment. The political landscape has changed both in terms of the issues pushed to the center of debate in the 1980s and the post-Cold War period, and the developing environment of political campaigns. The Third Way attempts to respond to the need for new political structures and ideas while incorporating the permanent campaign as a technique of governing. In the US it has affected at least the rhetoric of current campaigning. In the UK it has rendered constitutional reform unprecedented since the expansion of the franchise beyond a tiny elite. It will continue to have repercussions. It may be the best in terms of realignment that transatlantic social democratic forces can expect.

---

[1] John Kenneth White and Philip John Davies, eds., *Political Parties and the Collapse of the Old Orders* (Albany, NY: State University of New York Press, 1998).

[2] There is a massive literature, stimulated most, perhaps, by V. O. Key Jr., "A Theory of Critical Elections," *Journal of Politics* 17 (1955): 3-18; W. D. Burnham, *Critical Elections and the Mainsprings of American Politics* (New York, W.W. Norton, 1970).

[3] Harold W. Stanley and Richard G. Niemi, *Vital Statistics on American Politics* (Washington, DC: Congressional Quarterly Press, 1990), 144; Voter News Service 2000 exit poll of 13,279 presidential voters.

[4] See, for example, the essays in Byron E. Shafer, ed., *The End of Realignment? Interpreting American Electoral Eras* (Madison, Wisconsin, University of Wisconsin Press, 1991).

[5] Cited in John K. White, "Partisanship in the 1984 Presidential Election: the Rolling Republican Realignment" (paper presented at the Southwestern Social Science Association annual meeting, Houston, Texas, March 1985), 18.

[6] Statistics calculated from *Congressional Quarterly's Guide to U.S. Elections*, 2nd ed. (Washington, DC: Congressional Quarterly Inc., 1985), 329, 339, 342; "2000 Official Presidential General Election Results," from the Federal Elections Commission website, http://www.fec.gov.

[7] And senators changing allegiances, as happened in 2001 (eds.).

[8] Burt Solomon, "Disunity for All," *National Journal*, 16 December 2000, 3870-3876; John Kenneth White, "The Election in Perspective: Two Nations, Four Parties," in *America's Choice 2000*, ed. William Crotty (Boulder, Co.: Westview Press, 2001).

[9] Tim Hames, "The United Kingdom: Change Within Community," in *Political Parties and the Collapse of the Old Orders*, eds. John Kenneth White and Philip John Davies (Albany, NY: State University of New York Press, 1998), 27.

[10] Tony Blair, *The Third Way: New Politics for the New Century* (London: The Fabian Society, 1998).

[11] "Third Way to Beach," *The Times* (London), 7August 1999, 1.

[12] Blair, *The Third Way*, 1-7.

[13] http://www.dlcppi.org/ppi/3way/3way.htm.

[14] Tony Blair, "Turning Ideas Into Action," *The New Democrat* (May/June 1999): 15.

[15] Lucy Ward, "Women Lose Out," *The Guardian*, 19 May 2000.

[16] William Rees-Mogg, "Riding Back to Power," *The Times* (London), 21 June 1999, 20.

[17] Patrick Wintour and Nicole Veash, "The People's Party Loses," *The Observer*, 20 June 1999, 12.

[18] Andrew Rawnsley, "Is Tony's Coalition Cracking Up?" *The Observer*, 20 June 1999.

[19] See, for example, Philip John Davies, chap. 8 in *US Elections Today* (Manchester: Manchester University Press, 1999).

[20] Charles O. Jones, "Clinton and Congress: Risk, Restoration and Re-election" (plenary address presented at the annual meeting of the British Association for American Studies, Glasgow, March 1999).

[21] Anthony Giddens, *The Third Way: The Renewal of Social Democracy* (Cambridge: Polity, 1998); quotation from a letter to the author, 22 March 1999.

[22] Robert B Reich, "We Are All Third Wayers Now," *American Prospect* (March/April 1999): 51.

[23] In the May 2001 elections, Conservatives were again defeated by a significant majority, and William Hague resigned the party leadership. As we go to press, the battle for the new leader is still being fought (eds.).

[24] Alan Ryan, "Britain: Recycling the Third Way," *Dissent* (spring 1999): 80.

[25] Jonathan Freedland, "Trying to Fill Bill's Shoes," *The Guardian*, 16 August 2000, 19.

[26] Polly Toynbee, "This is Blair's New Road Map, But It Leads Nowhere," *The Guardian*, 28 February 2001, 20.

[27] Portillo lost the support of his party and has, he says, now retired from front-line politics. (eds.)

[28] Toynbee, "This is Blair's New Road Map," 20.

Chapter 16

Above the Law? Transatlantic Perspectives on the Development of the International Criminal Court

Roberta Glaspie, Lesley Hodgson, Andrew Thompson, and Donald Wallace

In 1998 the Universal Declaration on Human Rights (UDHR) marked its 50th anniversary. That year also witnessed significant moves towards the creation of an International Criminal Court (ICC) at a special conference in Rome. The period between the establishment of the UDHR in 1948 and the Rome conference has witnessed a growing recognition that human rights must be protected within an international framework. Within this framework the nation-state nevertheless continues to be the principal actor with regard to the legal provisions for the protection of human rights. Moreover, individuals are still very much national citizens bound by national legal entitlements. This chapter examines the development of the ICC, and draws a comparative analysis between the responses of the US and the EU (EU) member states to the prospect of a transnational institution of justice by scrutinizing specific objections to the ICC. It is clear that while nation-states have ceded growing powers to transnational bodies in the economic sphere, they still retain considerable control over the rights of their citizens.

The Development of the International Criminal Court

To discuss the emergence of the ICC, it is necessary to outline the recent developments regarding the creation of the statute establishing the court, the remit of the court, and the role it will play in upholding rights. The need for such a court is evidenced by the fact that, despite having numerous rules and laws defining and forbidding war crimes, crimes against humanity, and genocide, in addition to conventions and protocols banning everything from poison gas to chemical weapons, there continues to be a general disregard for the norms of international humanitarian law. For countless transgressions of international criminal laws there have been comparatively few prosecutions in national courts, despite legal obligations to pursue the violators of legal norms.[1]

The ICC will be a permanent court that will investigate and bring to justice individuals who commit the most serious violations of international humanitarian law. The Rome statute establishing the ICC will enter into force 60 days after 60 states have ratified it. As of December 2000, 122 states have signed up to the Statute and 25 have ratified it.[2] The establishment of the ICC will not be easy. There were various attempts to set up such a court before the outbreak of World War II; however these did not come to fruition as the establishment of such a court was deemed to be untimely.[3] Following the war, the human rights movement displayed "a certain guilt" that so little had been done to stop the mass destruction of peoples and property throughout the war period.[4] The dominant perception of the "Nazi problem" as a domestic affair and a strongly entrenched non-interventionist policy meant that governments felt justified in their inaction. After the war this attitude was questioned from all quarters, as the full magnitude of human rights abuses became apparent. It was in this frame of mind that nations (albeit in the shape of the victorious powers) came together to form the International Tribunals at Nuremberg and Tokyo. Although not strictly "international," these tribunals were to lead to profound changes in the rule of law as they confirmed that a state's treatment of its people was no longer merely a matter of domestic legal concern.[5] They set down historical precedents when it was decided that no longer could individuals plead "obedience to superior authorities" in defense of crimes against humanity, even in times of war. The prosecutors at Nuremberg indicated that these principles would become binding international law and as such would be applied to all states and all world leaders.

In 1947, the United Nations established the International Law Commission (ILC) with the remit of setting up an International Criminal Court, which was at this time deemed to be both a necessary and feasible project. Issues of state sovereignty and national pride, however, were to dominate, as problems concerning the definition of crimes and jurisdiction loomed. The onset of the Cold War was to bring an end to any attempts on the part of the UN to create a permanent international criminal court. There were, however, moves during the post-war period to codify human rights within the Universal Declaration of Human Rights (UDHR) and the subsequent European Convention on Human Rights (ECHR). Increasingly over the years, a number of conventions set up by the UN have had a bearing on this subject. But recent history proves how ineffectual these Conventions are in practice.[6]

The tragic events of the former Yugoslavia and Rwanda were to focus debate on the issue of internal aggression that goes unpunished by the nation-state, rather than upon issues of international conflict. The result was the setting up of *ad hoc* tribunals by the UN Security Council. Both tribunals (ICTY 1993 and ICTR 1994) were drawn up under the auspices of the ILC. A committee established to discuss the statutes and rules of procedure for both tribunals suggested the setting up of an ICC, but several major nations were either opposed or would not commit themselves to such a venture at that time. Despite many obstacles, the Yugoslav and Rwandan tribunals have had some measure of success, although the problem of state sovereignty has once again been raised as issues of jurisdiction have surfaced. To date, some prominent individuals have been arrested although some still remain at large.

It has now become "acceptable" to hold Heads of State responsible for abuses of human rights, as exemplified by the cases of Augusto Pinochet in Chile and Hissan Habre in Senegal, as well as recent investigations into atrocities in Sierra Leone and East Timor. While the punishment of individuals has sent out a clear message that the international community will not tolerate abuse of power, it has also fuelled concerns regarding non-intervention in other areas of the globe. For the most part, it would seem as if non-intervention is still the norm unless political expediency dictates otherwise.

As R. A. Falk suggests, there are two main developments that have kept the Nuremberg ideals alive: first, official moves to convene the *ad hoc* war crimes tribunals, and second, activism by those who have seen the Nuremberg decision as a means of "challenging the state in the war/peace area, validating the emergence of civil resistance."[7] The main driving force behind the recent momentum to set up the court came from a coalition made up of "like-minded states" and non-governmental organizations (NGOs). The like-minded states include such countries as Canada and Sweden, but also groups of small- and medium-sized states that have in recent years undergone transitions from authoritarian rule, and so have first-hand experience of how impunity undermines the rule of law. This group of like-minded states numbered almost 60 at the close of the Rome Conference. The NGO Coalition for an International Criminal Court (CICC) began as a small international gathering of NGOs in the mid-1990s, and grew to encompass some 800 organizations at the time of the Rome Conference; today they number over 1000 groups.[8] NGOs, while having some concerns regarding the ICC Statue (such as the breadth of preconditions to jurisdiction), have been pragmatic, realizing that if the Rome Conference failed it could indefinitely delay the establishment of such a court.

Whilst it is recognized that the ICC will not be a panacea for all human rights abuses, its jurisdiction will encompass 4 core crimes: genocide; crimes against humanity (including enslavement, ethnic cleansing, torture, rape, sex slavery, and enforced pregnancy); war crimes; and the crime of aggression (which was left undefined). There is no hierarchy of crimes within the Statute as there has been in the ICTY.[9] In order to ratify the Statute it is incumbent upon states to change their domestic laws; this will have the effect of "extending the rule of law and bringing national courts up to international law standards."[10] The Rome Conference ended with 122 countries voting for establishing the ICC, which will be situated at The Hague. Although US support for the creation of an international criminal court continued throughout the drafting and revision process, with the US participating in the Preparatory Committee sessions, the US was one of the 7 states to vote against the court. The US has unlikely allies also opposing the court, including China, Iraq, and Iran. Twenty-one states abstained.

The Responses of the US and the EU to the ICC
Governments across the world enter into various levels of international treaties that, while not necessarily having a direct effect on national legislative competency, do carry obligations to abide by the letter or the spirit of those agreements. The EU is the most advanced example of international law, wherein legislation passed by

the EU does have direct effect on the domestic laws of the member states. The institutions of the EU do not have general legislative competency, but instead have specific legislative powers, notably relating to certain aspects of economic and—to a lesser extent—social affairs. Of these powers, arguably the most significant is that of a regulation being "binding in its entirety and directly applicable in all Member States." A regulation does not, then, require action by a national legislature to incorporate it into national law. Two other forms of EU legislative powers, "directives" and "decisions," are also binding on the parties specified in the rulings, but they do require national legislation in order to give effect to them in national courts. The EU, therefore, represents a unique instance in international affairs of an international actor possessing sovereign powers, even if in limited legislative areas. As J. A. Usher argues, reflecting a widely shared view, the EU "constitutes a new legal order of international law for the benefit of which the States have limited their sovereign rights"; moreover, the Treaty of the European Union is "more than an agreement which merely creates mutual obligations between the contracting states."[11] Thus, the situation in the EU is unlike that in any other region of the world.

The EU has been involved at the various committee and preparatory-committee meetings for the ICC and has continually given the court its backing. The European Parliament has called for member states of the EU to take measures for the "speedy ratification" of the ICC Treaty.[12] To date, all 15 member states have signed up to the court, 5 have ratified and the other 10 are at various stages in the process. The extent of states' true commitment to the court and the ratification process can be questioned, however, when the speed of ratification is assessed. For example, some states, such as Italy, ratified the court before changing domestic legislation, whilst others seem to be stalling. By contrast, the UK has been at the forefront of the ICC debate for a number of years and signed up to the court on November 30, 1998, but it will not ratify the statute for some time because of "the complexity of the necessary enabling legislation."[13]

Challenges to the Sovereignty of the Nation-State

There are a host of practical legal problems involved in trying to bring together different national legal procedures and attitudes towards the sovereignty of national law, and to create a forum that will operate at a level above that of the justice systems of individual nation-states. The difficulties in creating an international criminal court are two-fold. First, nation-states are reluctant to yield their preferred status, which allows them to enjoy the priority of jurisdiction over crimes committed within their territories, either by their nationals or against their nationals. As R. Teitel argues, "Few states would volunteer to compromise their national criminal law."[14] Second, the subject-matter jurisdiction of the ICC, although limited to genocide, crimes against humanity and war crimes (with the possible inclusion at a later date of the crime of aggression), involves highly political and sensitive issues.[15] Consequently, they are matters of great concern to the military, politicians, and decision-makers.

The reversal of the US position on the ICC reflects these major objections. The US opposition fundamentally derives from adherence to the inflexible position that no international court has a right to override US law in the trial of US citizens.[16] The US government wanted "to have the right of veto to prevent any of its own nationals being brought to trial," but at the same time did not want that same right extended to other nations.[17] Specific US objections are that:

- the ICC has the inherent potential to become politicized to the point where alleged offenders will be charged by less-than-impartial prosecutors and tried by less-than-impartial judges from hostile nations;
- the differences in legal cultures do not afford defendants the same constitutional protections as seen in American courts;
- the ICC has no jurisdiction over non-ratifying states;
- there is a perceived lack of alternatives to prosecution of human rights violators afforded in the Rome Statute.[18]

These concerns are in fact largely unfounded; as the following discussion shows, they lead to the destruction of a basic element necessary to the Court's ability to function.[19]

The "Politicized Nature" of the ICC

The rejection of the ICC stems, in part, from US fears that American military personnel serving in international peacekeeping forces might be tried on politically-motivated charges.[20] In addition, some have speculated that the real target of the supporters of the ICC is ultimately the President of the United States and his top decision-makers; by targeting these officials, the proponents are trying to create international structures that inhibit the use of American force.[21] One compromise approved in the Rome Statute to allay US fears is the opt-out clause allowing a government to withhold authority from the ICC to prosecute its citizens for 7 years. It would not only exclude the duty of the State Party to cooperate with the ICC, but would exclude the jurisdiction of the court over war crimes committed by a national of that State Party during those 7 years.[22]

The basis of another compromise rests on the principle of complementarity. Under this principle, nation-states have primacy of jurisdiction to prosecute crimes within the jurisdiction of the ICC. Here the jurisdiction of the ICC will only arise if the state holding a suspect in custody is unable or unwilling to prosecute that person. Yet, this attempt to ensure state sovereignty necessarily confers upon the ICC the authority to transgress state sovereignty. The requirement of the ICC to determine "unwillingness" to prosecute implies a value judgment as to the criminal justice system of a state.[23]

The power of the Prosecutor to initiate its own investigation without a referral from either the Security Council or a State has been a contentious issue since the beginning of the 1994 Court negotiations. Opponents of the Rome Statute feared that the Court could become involved in political decision making if the Prosecutor were allowed complete discretion in the decision to open an investigation. The US sought guarantees that the UN Security Council would have final prosecutorial decision-making power through exercise of its veto, thus allowing permanent Council members (like the US) to veto any case against their own citizens. Other countries would be consigned to an inferior status.[24] In response to this opposition, Article 15 of the Rome Statute was modified to allow the Prosecutor to initiate an investigation, but subject it to the approval of the Pre-Trial Chamber. This chamber must in turn conclude there is a reasonable basis to proceed.[25] Presently under the ICC, the Security Council does have a central role. Under Article 13(b) the Court must accept referrals made by the Security Council. Without this provision, the Court would be powerless to prosecute an individual whose country was not a party to the Court, or refused to consent to the Court's jurisdiction. Furthermore, under the Statute, the Security Council is given a form of collective control in that under Article 16; the permanent members can vote to postpone an investigation for up to 12 months on a renewable basis.[26] However, the role of the Security Council is not limitless. Under the Statute, Article 13 permits jurisdiction over a situation that is referred to the Prosecutor by a State Party, and where the Prosecutor has initiated an investigation in respect of one of the ICC crimes. From this lack of complete deference to the Security Council, ICC critics have inferred a disparagement of the UN Charter. Wedgwood asserts that the Security Council is meant to have pre-eminent authority within the UN system on matters of international peace and security.[27] Even with these safeguards in place, opponents of the Statute still fear that a politically-motivated Prosecutor could unfairly target the US. Fears that an independent ICC Prosecutor could turn out to be an international Kenneth Starr are taken seriously by these critics.[28]

Differences of Legal Culture in Constitutional Protections

The US has also objected to the perceived sweeping nature of the offenses over which the ICC has jurisdiction, and the impact on free speech guarantees. Article 25, section 3, of the Rome Statute makes punishable *as* genocide the direct and public incitement *of* genocide. Genocide means any of the several acts committed with intent to destroy, in whole or in part, a national, ethnic, racial, or religious group. These acts reach beyond killing or causing serious bodily or mental harm, to imposing measures intended to prevent group cohesion and the forcible transfer of children from one group to another group (Article 6). Fletcher criticized the breadth of this section, observing that if a person engages in "writing or speaking in favor of population transfer," this in itself renders the speaker liable for the heinous crime of genocide."[29]

A seeming conflict between speech protection in the US and international calls for the criminalization of hate speech are apparent in this portion of the Rome Statute. There is a broad international consensus recognizing freedom of speech as a fundamental human right, but one that is not absolute, in that the protection does not include the most degrading and threatening forms of racist speech.[30] For example, Article 4 of the International Convention on the Elimination of All Forms of Racial Discrimination (ICERD) requires the signatories to declare as an "offence punishable by law, all dissemination of ideas based on racial superiority or hatred, incitement to racial discrimination, as well as all acts of violence or incitement to such acts against any race or group of such persons of another color or ethnic origin." Despite Fletcher's concerns, there are limitations in the Rome Statute that require that genocidal speech be "direct" and "public." The Rome Statute's definition of Genocide incorporates verbatim the language of the 1948 Genocide Convention. The Rwanda International Criminal Tribunal (R-ICT) in the Jean-Paul Akayesu prosecution involved the first verdict interpreting the 1948 Genocide Convention rendered by an international tribunal following a trial.[31] According to the R-ICT, the "public" element of incitement focuses on the place where the incitement occurred and could include the means of mass media. "Direct" implies that the incitement assumes a direct form and specifically provokes another to engage in a criminal act. Something more than mere vague or indirect suggestion is necessary to constitute direct incitement. The prosecution, according to the R-ICT, must prove a definite causal link between the act characterized as incitement, and a specific offense. The R-ICT found that these elements could be satisfied if a defendant were to play skillfully on mob psychology and create an atmosphere favorable to the perpetration of genocide. Yet, the incitement need not be successful in order to be punished. Fletcher concluded that it is not possible for the US to endorse an international tribunal that would punish conduct constitutionally protected in the US.[32] Accordingly, the only way to minimize the conflicts is to require the ICC to punish in cases where genocidal crimes *have been* committed, resulting in a visible cohort of victims.

At the same time, US jurisprudence does not follow a course of absolute protection, but displays some conformity with international norms on free speech. The US Supreme Court has upheld the constitutionality of legislative bans on certain forms of expression such as incitement to commit a serious crime; incitement to violate public order; the dissemination of knowingly slanderous or libelous information about government officials and private individuals; the use of so-called "fighting words"; and calls for subversive activities against the state.[33] The views of the R-ICT in the Akayesu prosecution would not appear to contrast sharply with these approved legislative bans.

Jurisdiction Over Non-Ratifying States

The US insisted that the ICC not prosecute citizens of states that have not signed and ratified the treaty, yet this would devastate the Court's legitimacy. As Bickley notes, such a condition would prevent the prosecution of Saddam Hussein for war crimes committed by his forces in Kuwait unless he consented.[34] Presently, Article 12 requires the consent of the state of nationality of the accused, or of the state on whose territory the crime in question was committed. Furthermore, the complementarity provision of the Rome statute provides a safeguard to non-party states that is not customarily afforded in domestic judicial systems. This measure of jurisdiction over nationals of states that have not ratified the ICC treaty is not novel. International law has long recognized that states may prosecute foreign nationals under the principle of territoriality (for matters that occur within their state territories), the principle of passive personality (for matters that that affect their citizens as victims), and the principle of protective jurisdiction (for matters that merely affect state interests).[35]

One argument viewing as novel the jurisdiction of the ICC over third parties identifies a difference between exercising jurisdiction as part of national criminal justice authority, and surrendering a defendant to an international body in which his or her own state is a non-participant. If the hallmark of the ICC Treaty is the consent of nation states, this foundation is undermined by the exercise of third-party jurisdiction. This argument's call for consent is based on a desire for the continuing dominance of the Westphalian architecture for nation-states,[36] and stems from the predominant pre-World War II jurisprudence that nations are bound to international obligations only if they consent. This traditional premise, in which all states are bound to respect the domestic governance of other countries, includes their legitimate exercise of pubic authority over criminal acts.[37]

Alternatives to Prosecution

A further US justification for its rejection of the ICC is the Rome Statute's failure to acknowledge the legitimacy of local amnesties.[38] Application of the principle *ne bis in idem*, as defined in Article 20 of the Statute and its lack of double jeopardy protection, is problematic for truth commissions and amnesties which may attempt to shield an offender from criminal responsibility. Accordingly, a strategy of amnesty for national reconciliation in new democracies will not prevent prosecutions of officials of a prior regime in the ICC.[39] Article 53 of the Rome Statute does allow the Prosecutor to decline the review of a case where a "prosecution is not in the interests of justice, taking into account all the circumstances." Wedgwood argues that the lack of clarity of the term "justice" provides no principled means to accommodate the danger for democratic transitions posed by the prosecutions of deposed leaders of former autocratic regimes. The omission from the Rome Statute of alternatives to criminal prosecutions was most likely intentional. Recognition exists that international law obliges nation-states to prosecute humanitarian offenses, which would deny the possibility of respect for amnesties.[40]

The less noble, but admitted, goal of protecting the confidence of "economic investors" through the "regularization of government" succession has been suggested as another reason to provide alternatives to prosecution, such as amnesty.[41] The ICC's prosecution of human rights violators is criticized as being too financially and politically disruptive transitions to democracy. Undoubtedly this alternative goal to criminal prosecutions merely fuels the suspicion that "[c]orporate capitalism may simply be legitimized genocide by economic means."[42] Fears have been raised about the ICC regarding corporate criminal liability for the funding of Saddam Hussein's forces in the genocidal activities committed against the Kurds in 1988. The critics foresee pressures to expand the ICC's jurisdiction "to encompass corporate actors who are alleged to be depriving indigenous citizens of their human rights, who are alleged to be in cahoots with regimes."[43] However, concern over corporate criminal liability under the ICC is grounded, at best, only upon speculation over future amendments to the Rome Statute. The concept was entertained in the Draft Statute that went forward to Rome and included, as a possibility, the imposition of criminal liability of juristic persons, for instance corporations, but during the Conference this provision was dropped. Therefore, the jurisdiction of the ICC is confined to the principle of individual responsibility of only natural persons [ICC Statute, Art. 25(1)].[44]

The creation of the ICC demonstrates two contradictory views on the realities of globalization and the resulting modern international society. While the rest of the world appears willing to consent to have its actions judged by the rule of law, the US acknowledges globalization but wants it to proceed independently, based upon its own theory of vital interests.[45] Roth characterized the US objection to the ICC on the grounds of US contention that "we have special responsibilities for global security and therefore we deserve a special break." Unfortunately, this argument appears to conclude that the Americans deserve the right to commit war crimes or crimes against humanity. This impression is strengthened when the opposition states that Americans will never submit to an international court and have their actions judged by the rule of international law.[46] The American delegation argued unsuccessfully at the Rome conference that US citizens should be allowed to stand outside this evolving framework of international law, and that the US should pursue its policies with impunity, unhindered by the rule of law that other nations accept.[47]

This view should be contrasted to the one exemplified by US participation in Nuremberg. Justice Jackson, the US prosecutor at the Nuremberg trial, declared that if certain offenses are crimes, "they are crimes whether the US does them or whether Germany does them, and we are not prepared to lay down a rule of criminal conduct against others which we would be unwilling to have invoked against us."[48] Despite this historical sentiment, it should not be surprising that the US rejected the ICC. American exceptionalism is not a new phenomenon. History is replete with instances of the intransigence that has prompted American political policy-making, particularly with human rights accords. The US has used its very powerful global voice to raise transparent objections to the ICC. Instead of exercising a role as a moral leader of the world, the US instead prefers to preserve its pre-eminence through military and economic might.

Still, opponents should observe the ICC as part of the continuing development of human rights legislation since World War II. Gradually over the years, there has been a growing definition of crimes and a readiness to set up tribunals and legislation to deal with those crimes. This has been a step forward in extending the scope of international responsibility for violations of rights. The ICC still, however, has many hurdles to cross before it becomes a reality—not least of which is the objection raised by certain powerful states that such a court would be a threat to their national integrity and sovereignty. The greatest fear of human rights activists is that the ICC will become so watered down in the effort to appease national governments that it will not have the "force" that was intended at the outset. The work of ratification of the court has yet a long way to go.

The closing decade of the 20th century witnessed growing speculation on the future of the nation-state. Even allowing for the perils of political punditry, one could not be accused of throwing caution to the wind in suggesting that this discussion will intensify in the opening decade of the current century. At the heart of this debate is the matter of whether the nation-state, as it is conventionally perceived, will continue to have any meaningful status in domestic and international affairs. If the reaction of the US to the ICC is indicative of the present status of the nation-state, then some caution may be advisable. It is clear that, while governments are prepared to be party to treaties that will either have a direct effect on national legislation (as in the case of some EU law) or will involve compromise with regard to national policy—or even, as in the case of some regulatory regimes, lead to changes in national legislation—they are less willing to allow interference in the relationship between state and citizen. The problems facing those charged with the establishment of a permanent International Criminal Court are considerable. The tide of political change over the past 50 years shows that states are willing to cooperate, compromise, and even, as in the case of the EU, transfer law-making powers in certain areas to a higher legislative body; but they continue to remain wary of significant alterations to the balance of power in the state-citizen relation.

[1] R. Teitel, "The International Criminal Court: Contemporary Perspectives and Prospects for Ratification," *New York Law School Journal of Human Rights* 16 (2000): 505-551.

[2] For a continuous update see http://www.iccnow.org.

[3] Teitel, 505-551.

[4] Ambassador P. Kirsch, "Background: Creation of the Court" (speech at the Irish Centre for Human Rights, Galway, Ireland, August 2000).

[5] R. Falk, "Taking Rights Seriously at Home," *Political Quarterly* 68, no. 2 (1997): 179-187 (180).

[6] L. Bickley, "US Resistance to the International Criminal Court: Is the Sword Mightier Than the Law?" *Emory International Law Review* 14 (2000): 213-276.

[7] M. C. Bassiouni, "Accountability for International Crime and Serious Violations of Fundamental Human Rights: Searching for Peace and Achieving Justice: The Need for Accountability," *Law and Contemporary Problems* (Fall 1996): 9.

[8] R. Falk, *On Humane Governance: Toward a New Global Politics* (Cambridge: Polity Press, 1995).

[9] This came about in ICTY largely because of the various backgrounds and legal systems within the states from which the judges at ICTY originated. See J. Pejic, "The International Criminal Court Statute: An Appraisal of the Rome Package," *International Lawyer* 34 (2000): 65.

[10] W. Schabas, "Subject Matter: Jurisdiction" (speech at the Irish Centre for Human Rights, Galway, Ireland, August 2000).

[11] J. A. Usher, *Plender and Usher's Cases and Materials on the Law of the European Communities* (London: Butterworths, 1993), 73.

[12] European Parliament, *Resolution on the International Criminal Court* (1998), at gopher://gopher.igc.apc.org/00/orgs/icc/natldocs/prepcom6/eurparl.res.

[13] D. Fatchett, British Member of Parliament, quoted in "ICC Now in Sight," *Amnesty* (January-February, 1999).

[14] Teitel, 508.

[15] Van Der Vyver, "Personal and Territorial Jurisdiction of The International Criminal Court," *Emory International Law Review* 14 (2000): 1-103.

[16] Bickley, passim.

[17] Robin Cook, then British Foreign Secretary, quoted by British Information Services (New York, August 1998).

[18] See Bickley.

[19] M. D. Mysak, "Judging the Giant: An Examination of American Opposition to the Rome Statute of the International Criminal Court," *Saskatchewan Law Review* 63 (2000): 275-299.

[20] W. Schabas, "The International Criminal Court Is Into the Home Stretch," *Human Rights Tribune* 5 (April 1998): 1-2.

[21] Bolton, "Symposium: Toward an International Criminal Court? A Debate," *Emory International Law Review* 14 (2000): 159-197.

[22] See Bickley, and Van der Vyver.

[23] See Van der Vyver.

[24] J. Seguin, "Denouncing the International Criminal Court: An Examination of US Objections to the Rome Statute," *Boston University International Law Journal* 18 (2000): 85-109; Bickley, passim.

[25] See Seguin; Mysak, 286.

[26] See Seguin.

[27] R. Wedgwood, "The International Criminal Court: An American View,"*European Journal of International Law* 10 (2000): 93-107.

[28] See Seguin.

[29] See Teitel.

[30] F. Kubler, "How Much Freedom for Racist Speech? Transnational Aspects of a Conflict of Human Rights," *Hofstra Law Review* 27 (1998): 335-376.

[31] Prosecutor v. Jean-Paul Akayesu (1998). Case No. ICTR-96-4-T, Trial Chambers Judgement, International Criminal Tribunal for Rwanda, 2; D. F. Orentlicher, "Genocide," in R. Gutman and D. Rieff, eds., *Crimes of War: What the Public Should Know* (New York: W. W. Norton, 1999), 153-57.

[32] Teitel, passim.

[33] A.Vasiliy, "Legal Theory: Political Rights and Freedoms in the Context of American Constitutionalism: A View of a Concerned Soviet Scholar," *Northwestern University Law Review* 85 (1990): 257-289.

[34] Bickley, passim.

[35] Wedgwood, 93-107.

[36] Mark W. Janis, *An Introduction to International Law* (New York: Aspen Law and Business, 1999).

[37] Wedgwood, 99.

[38] Wedgwood, 93.

[39] Van der Vyver, 103.

[40] Wedgwood, 107; D. Orentlicher, "Settling Accounts: The Duty to Prosecute Human Rights Violations of a Prior Regime," *Yale Law Journal* 100 (1991): 2537- 2569; G. Hafner et al., "A Response to the American View as Presented by Ruth Wedgwood," *European Journal of International Law* 10 (2000): 108-123.

[41] Wedgwood, 95.

[42] J. B. Gerald, "Is the US Really a Signatory to the UN Convention on Genocide?" (1995), at http://serendipity.magnet.ch/more/genocide.html.

[43] Bolton, 181-82.

[44] Van der Vyver: 1-10.

[45] Bickley, passim.

[46] Bolton, 176

[47] Bickley, 213.

[48] Bickley, 238

Chapter 17

The Trauma of a Nuclear Pearl Harbor: Transatlantic Relations, Fortress America, and the Loss of Nuclear Invulnerability

Susanna Schrafstetter

> Shall we expect some transatlantic military giant to step the Ocean and crush us at a blow? Never! All the armies of Europe, Asia and Africa combined, with all the treasure of the earth (our own excepted) in their military chest, with a Bonaparte for a commander, could not by force take a drink from the Ohio or make a track on the Blue Ridge in a trial of a thousand years.[1]

In 1836, Abraham Lincoln was convinced that the New World, due to its geography and vast resources, was a safe haven from foreign invasion. More than 100 years later his assessment was still valid. The US had remained a sanctuary during two world wars—Pearl Harbor notwithstanding—while Europe and Asia lay in ashes. For many Americans, the experience of World War II reinforced President Washington's conviction that America should avoid entangling alliances. The fear of international communism, however, signaled the end of isolationism. In 1949, the US entered into a transatlantic alliance to protect Western Europe from Soviet domination. Less than a decade later, American invulnerability was over. Soviet nuclear missiles could turn the state of Ohio into a wasteland and wipe the Blue Ridge Mountains off the map.

This chapter examines how the geo-strategic position of the US influenced the nature of the North Atlantic Alliance. While the North Atlantic was the uniting element that gave the alliance its name in 1949, it also set its members apart: two *trans*-Atlantic members in a safe-haven from nuclear attack, and 10 European states threatened with invasion by the conventional forces of the Warsaw Pact. The loss of US-invulnerability—or at least the perception of it—marked the turning point in relations between America and Western Europe and the real beginning of the globalization of conflict. To counter loss of invulnerability, the US administrations explored a variety of schemes that promised a return to fortress America. Initial attempts focused on non-proliferation—if not to regain invulnerability, at least to limit the number of states capable of dragging the US into a nuclear war, reducing them to a single one: the Soviet Union.

In contrast to the US, which is bound east and west by oceans, Russia possesses the longest land border of any state and has been repeatedly invaded by foreign powers throughout its history. Fear of invasion, rather than loss of invulnerability, has been (and remains) the nightmare that haunts the Kremlin. Soviet measures designed to reduce the threat of invasion were habitually interpreted by the US as a prelude to imminent Soviet attack. The resultant security dilemma led to an arms race that further increased US vulnerability *to* an attack. In common with the Soviet Union, the countries of Western Europe also had a history of invasion. This, coupled with the threat of living under constant nuclear annihilation, led to the development of different "strategic cultures" within the Transatlantic Alliance that resulted in considerable tensions between the allies.[2] The erosion of American invulnerability brought into question the military concept underpinning the defense of the alliance: massive retaliation by US nuclear forces. The ensuing debate between Europe and America was often heated and acrimonious, and has been characterized by one author as the "Transatlantic Cold War."[3]

The Alliance has survived this crisis as well as the transition from a bipolar to a multipolar world. The recent admission of states from Eastern Europe has added a further connotation to the term "transatlantic partnership." The emergence of new nuclear powers and nuclear rogue states is a stark demonstration that the international non-proliferation regime is a paper tiger. In a multipolar nuclear world, America feels increasingly exposed to new nuclear threats. To deal with these new threats—and the old ones—the US administration aspires to return to the golden age of fortress America. What consequences does this hold for the transatlantic partnership?

With the formation of NATO in April 1949, the US entered into a commitment to defend Western Europe against Soviet attack. Article 5 of the NATO Treaty enshrined the principle of collective defense: an attack on one member would count as an attack against all. The US nuclear guarantee was never made explicit, but it was clear that in response to an attack against Western Europe, alliance strategy would be based on massive nuclear retaliation by the US. Indeed, with the US mainland invulnerable to Soviet attack, the avowed purpose of the transatlantic alliance was the defense of Western Europe. Soviet aggression, it was anticipated, would not be directed against America but against Western Europe. Military planners feared that with its massive superiority in conventional forces, the Red Army would be capable of reaching the French coast in a matter of weeks. For the US, a commitment to deter the Soviets from invading Europe did not involve the excessive provision of blood or treasure: America still had a nuclear monopoly. It was clear that this status would not last forever, but it was assumed that for many years to come, the Soviet Union would not be able to reach the continental US with nuclear weapons. The West believed that this realization would deter the Kremlin from invading Western Europe for fear of triggering a massive nuclear assault on the Soviet urban population. Thus, the transatlantic alliance exhibited structural characteristics similar to those of the wartime alliances: Uncle Sam was prepared to defend Europe but without the danger of direct attack on the US homeland. Or, as one US general put it, speaking in the 1980s: "We fought World War I in Europe, we fought World War II in Europe, and if you dummies let us, we'll fight World War III in Europe."[4]

The role of the Atlantic as a physical barrier against attack worked in both directions. For America, this meant that before the advent of intercontinental delivery systems, Moscow could only be attacked from bases in Western Europe. Thus, for nuclear retaliation to be credible, front-line US bases in Europe were required. Consequently, US nuclear weapons were deployed in Europe in great numbers under US control. The importance of Europe as one big US forward base was reflected by the key position of NATO's Supreme Allied Commander in Europe (SACEUR)—stationed in Paris but always an American. To maximize the strength of the alliance, the Eisenhower administration was willing to grant allies considerable control over nuclear weapons. In 1956, talks began on the deployment of *Thor* and *Jupiter* missiles in the UK and Turkey under the "double key" system. In this system, the host country's key was required to fire the missile, and the US key was required to arm the nuclear warhead. To fire the weapon, both keys needed to be turned simultaneously. The West German *Bundeswehr* was soon equipped with tactical nuclear weapons under the same system. Recent research by Marc Trachtenberg suggests that the ability of the host country to fire the missiles deployed in Germany and Britain during the 1950s amounted to *de facto* nuclear control.[5] In other words, US forces subordinated unilateral control to the overriding concern of maintaining alliance cohesion. In 1958, the Eisenhower government amended the McMahon Act so as to allow the US to share nuclear information and technology with Britain. Nuclear collaboration, which had been ended abruptly by the McMahon Act in 1946, was resumed.[6] If it had not been for the negative position of Congress, Eisenhower would have extended this bilateral collaboration to include France.[7] The Eisenhower administration was willing to actively participate with the Europeans in nuclear defense: military strength assumed a clear priority over the danger of nuclear proliferation. The Europeans, in turn, facing the prospect of nuclear warfare unleashed on their homelands, did not wish to be completely dependent on the Americans. "No annihilation without representation"—paraphrasing the slogan of the Boston tea party—summed up European fears that the invulnerability of the US would make their distant allies too adventurous. The Europeans might have to pay the price for an itchy US finger on the nuclear trigger. In the event of hostility with the Soviet Union, nuclear attacks would destroy Whitehall, not the White House. Prime Minister Winston Churchill reminded his government that "by creating the American atomic base in East Anglia, we have made ourselves the target, and perhaps the bull's eye of a Soviet attack."[8]

The launch of *Sputnik*, the first Soviet satellite, in October 1957 signaled the end of US invulnerability: it demonstrated that American cities were now within reach of Soviet intercontinental missiles. Although in retrospect the threat was more apparent than real, it nevertheless made a profound psychological impression on the American public. The episode led to panic about a "missile gap" and fear that the Soviet Union might actually be ahead in missile technology.[9] Under the shadow of Sputnik—almost literally—the Gaither Committee, a panel of experts originally commissioned to examine fallout shelters, turned to the question of how to protect the nation against nuclear surprise attack. In its final report it concluded that the Soviets had almost certainly surpassed the US in rocket development and recommended a massive increase in defense spending.[10] In response to the report, the American intercontinental ballistic missile (ICBM) program and the deployment of American nuclear weapons in Europe were accelerated. Before the ICBM program was complete, the only way for the US to credibly attack the Soviet Union with missiles was to station Intermediate Range Ballistic Missiles (IRBMs) in Europe. In short notation, IRBM + Europe = ICBM. Such measures could only be a short-term solution. Sputnik marked the most important turning point for the alliance during the Cold War. By overcoming the geographic distance from Europe to America, Sputnik brought into question the credibility of the American nuclear guarantee, and exposed a rift in the alliance that has remained unresolved to the present day. In short, would a US government risk the destruction of Boston for the defense of Berlin, or Los Angeles for London?

The question is not just academic: this issue almost brought the world to the brink of nuclear war. In October 1962, the Soviet Union deployed IRBMs in Cuba. The deployment of Soviet nuclear missiles 100 miles from the coast of Florida placed American cities under the threat of nuclear annihilation and forced the US leadership to share the same experience faced by the Europeans.[11] According to one American presidential aide, the British Prime Minister, Harold Macmillan, summed up the situation succinctly:

> His [Macmillan's] first reaction ... was to the effect that the British people, who had been living in the shadow of annihilation for the past many years, had somehow been able to live more or less normal lives, and he felt that the Americans, now confronted with a similar situation, would, after the initial shock, make a similar adjustment. "Life goes on somehow."[12]

The Europeans were accustomed to living with a certain degree of vulnerability, but US public opinion could not accept it.

The panic over Sputnik, the alleged missile gap, and the Cuban crisis were all emblematic of a deep psychological malaise within US society that stemmed from the realization that America was no longer invulnerable. America no longer enjoyed the status of a sanctuary that would be spared in a future war. It also rekindled the trauma of Pearl Harbor, when US forces had been destroyed in a surprise attack during the World War II. If the US administration could not regain invulnerability, it could at least ensure that US nuclear forces were not destroyed in a surprise Soviet attack. Avoiding a nuclear Pearl Harbor became a major objective for the Kennedy administration that came to power in 1961. Missiles were placed at constant readiness, with a proportion of the B-52 bomber forces airborne and armed with nuclear weapons at all times. Taken together, Sputnik and Cuba changed the entire nature of the Cold War. With the end of US vulnerability, the confrontation shifted from a military to a politico-economic struggle.

Sputnik and Cuba vividly brought home to US military planners the prospect of imminent Armageddon: the experience altered US nuclear policy and NATO strategy dramatically. To avoid nuclear confrontation between the superpowers and maintain the delicate balance of terror, the concept of mutual assured destruction (MAD) was developed. To add substance to the concept, the Kennedy administration proclaimed a new defense strategy: America would no longer automatically react with a full-scale nuclear strike in response to attack by the Warsaw Pact, a concept that later became known as "flexible response." Europe was faced with a massive dilemma: in the absence of automatic massive retaliation, the Soviets might become more adventurous in their dealings with European governments. Could a war in Europe be fought and won? The battlefield shifted away from the Soviet Union and into *Mitteleuropa*. At the same time, the NATO headquarters in the US, located in Virginia, was strengthened considerably. It was only in the late 1960s that the tasks and responsibilities of NATO's Supreme Allied Commander Atlantic (SACLANT) were clearly defined. While all were equally vulnerable, the superpowers now had a shared interest: to avoid the nuclear extinction of their respective populations by limiting conflict to the territories of their smaller allies.

The delicate balance of terror could only be maintained, however, if the superpowers had full control over the use of nuclear weapons within their alliances. In the absence of such control, both could be unwillingly dragged into a nuclear war by an ally. In fact, France's nuclear strategy was partially based on that principle.[13] The wheel had turned full circle. While in the 1950s the US had been willing to strengthen the nuclear defense of Europe, Washington was now anxious to halt proliferation, even among allies. Robert McNamara, Secretary of Defense in the Kennedy administration, called small, independent nuclear forces—such as the British and French arsenals— "dangerous, expensive, prone to obsolescence and lacking in credibility as a deterrent."[14] The message was clear: the US wanted to be the only nuclear power within the Transatlantic Alliance. Similarly, the Soviet Union felt increasingly threatened by Peking's nuclear potential. Fear of Chinese nuclear weapons developed into such paranoia that by the late 1960s, the Soviets were willing to take part in joint military action with the US to destroy the Chinese stockpile before it grew too large.[15] Both superpowers shared an interest in controlling the military forces of established nuclear powers and halting the spread of nuclear weapons. This led to the successful conclusion of the nuclear Non-Proliferation Treaty (NPT) in 1968. The desire of the US to increase its control over nuclear technology resulted in a number of transatlantic clashes, in particular German-American arguments over the NPT, and the crisis within NATO caused by the withdrawal of France in 1966. While the US and the Soviets could impose a certain discipline on their allies, they failed to exert influence over states outside their respective alliances. Countries such as China, India, Pakistan, Israel, and North Korea abstained from the NPT. As it will be shown below, in the post-Cold War nuclear world, American concern about nuclear blackmail and a nuclear Pearl Harbor focused on these countries.

During the 1970s, while the relative geographic distance separating the North Atlantic allies was effectively reduced, the political distance between America and her European partners increased. Disagreements centered on both security and economic issues. The discussion on the deployment of the neutron bomb and the NATO double-track decision reflected these growing tensions, and a "Transatlantic Cold War" came hand-in-hand with the "Second Cold War" of the 1980s.[16] The European allies were not willing to support President Reagan's hard-line approach towards the Soviet Union unconditionally. They were unwilling to sacrifice economic interests, namely trade with the Soviet Union, to satisfy American domestic objectives.[17] Reagan's desire to revive and win the Cold War was reflected in the decision to establish a strategic missile defense system, the Strategic Defense Initiative (SDI), also known as "Star Wars." The desire to regain the strategic status of the 1950s—American invulnerability—had found a new champion.

Even without the deployment of SDI, the Soviet Union crumbled, leaving the Western alliance to tread warily into the post-Cold War environment. Some analysts claimed that the demise of the bipolar world would herald the end of the Manichean alliance system. Transatlanticism would be dead: a new unified Europe would emerge from the Cold War.[18] The Western European Union (WEU) would be dragged kicking and screaming from its shadowy existence and proclaimed the future core of an independent European defense policy. But the "end of history" never materialized. Like a stage-struck actor, the Transatlantic Alliance refused to leave the stage. Indeed, it was given new tasks: peacekeeping and out-of-area operations. President

George Bush even sought a "New World Order," with America leading the UN as "world-policeman." Western Europe would provide the military (via Britain) and financial (via Germany) support to the American political lead.[19] Former foes turned friends. The admission of Poland, Hungary, and the Czech Republic has shifted the center of the alliance further away from the Atlantic. Geographically, it includes *Mitteleuropa*, with the US now—at least, on paper—committed to the defense of these countries. The attempt to inject new life into the WEU did not succeed in creating a European defense identity. Neither the WEU nor the EU's nascent Common Foreign and Security Policy (CFSP) has been able to fulfil more than symbolic functions. Neither has been able to respond effectively to the Bosnian and the Kosovo conflicts or to enhance the profile of the European security and defense policy.

Even more importantly, despite the dependency and the insecurity of relying on the US, the Europeans appear unable or unwilling to provide for their own nuclear defense. The possession of nuclear weapons is tied too deeply to national prestige. The integration of defense policy has proved even more difficult than economic convergence. National possession of Polaris and the *force de frappe* appear to be more important than keeping the British pound or the French franc. Similarly, there is no genuinely European defense industry. European defense companies are dominated by national interests, heavily protected and uncompetitive.[20] Two additional factors contribute to NATO's continued attractiveness: first, the ever present threat resulting from the spread of nuclear and biological weapons, and second, Russia's increased emphasis on the use of nuclear weapons in its military doctrine. In relation to the former, the indefinite extension of the nuclear Non-Proliferation Treaty in 1995, with 179 states adhering to the treaty, was considered a great success in the struggle against proliferation. However, a significant number of crucial states remain outside the international non-proliferation regime, and considerable doubts remain as to whether certain countries will honor their pledges. Russia's nuclear policy continues to cause concern. Despite (or because of) immense financial difficulties, Russia has ordered the development of a new generation of nuclear missiles capable of attacking Europe. More worryingly, Russia has disavowed her "no first use" pledge that ruled nuclear forces during the Cold War. Clearly, some of the old problems continue.

A "Second Nuclear Age" has emerged, no longer dominated by the superpowers but shaped by new nuclear powers in Asia, such as India and Pakistan; by the growing sophistication of the Chinese nuclear technology; and by the prospect of rogue nuclear states such as North Korea and Iraq.[21] During the Cold War, the US and Europe were united against one single threat. In the Second Nuclear Age, both face a multitude of new problems ranging from the eruption of violent nationalism to the challenges caused by religious fundamentalism. America's willingness to play the role of world policeman, however, is not a role that US public opinion is happy to sanction. The death of a few GIs rapidly revives isolationist sentiments. In a multipolar nuclear world, the US faces challenges from a multitude of "restive Ruritanias" and—far more critically—the nuclear potential of China, a great power with global aspirations.

To meet these (alleged) threats, the US administration has started to think about national missile defense (NMD), a defensive missile shield intended to protect America from nuclear attack. NMD is yet another attempt to return to the age of invulnerability, with the Atlantic barrier replaced by a system of anti-ballistic missiles. For the postmodern critique, the contradictions are all too apparent: in an age of globalization, the US retreats into isolation. However, while the Atlantic provided safety only for a certain period of time, the national missile defense is unlikely to guarantee 100% safety against nuclear attack. NATO's campaign in Kosovo demonstrated the difficulties of relying on technological fixes and so-called "clinical air-strikes." Deployment of such a system could also prove counterproductive in arms control negotiations. For the US to opt for NMD would reveal a considerable lack of faith in international arms control agreements and non-proliferation efforts, and would send signals to other states. An American unilateral reaction to the global problem of proliferation would give states such as North Korea or Iraq a very good excuse to abstain from the international non-proliferation regime.[22]

Western Europe does not support this initiative. Unlike the US, the Europeans do not regard the risk of vulnerability as unduly worrisome. Camille Grand points out how geo-strategic differences between the alliance partners have influenced their attitudes towards NMD:

> Over the centuries Europeans have learned to live with a certain degree of inescapable vulnerability. Having survived 40 years under the threat of an overwhelming Soviet conventional and nuclear threat that could have obliterated most of Western Europe in a matter of minutes, the growing but limited missile capabilities of a few so-called states of concern do not raise intense public anxiety.[23]

Once again, the Europeans worry that US invulnerability will lead to adventurism in US foreign policy. There is suspicion over the role that

America wishes to play: is it world policeman, guardian angel, or global gangster? Indeed, given US relative invulnerability, Europe is concerned that it might become the *ersatz* target for potential retaliation or aggression directed against the US. Churchill worried that the US bases in East Anglia would be "the bull's eye of a Soviet attack"; with NMD, US troops or interests in Europe could become prime targets for rogue states or terrorists. The worries of the early 1950s have returned. Whether NMD is realized or not, the transatlantic marriage is unlikely to end in divorce. Despite renewed calls for a European defense policy, it is debatable whether the European countries will be able to produce either the required resources or unity.[24] Indeed, recent EU plans for a European Security and Defence Initiative (ESDI) accept that a European security profile can not and should not replace the North Atlantic Alliance. As NATO's Secretary General Lord Robertson explained:

> For the foreseeable future, Europe's strategic independence is simply not feasible. Not many people may say that, but everybody knows it. Only NATO has the assets and capabilities that are necessary for larger scale operations. That is why ESDI is being developed to complement NATO, not to replace it.[25]

For the present, ESDI is confined to crisis management and humanitarian missions drawing on NATO assets and capabilities. ESDI takes over the modest responsibilities of the WEU, which will gradually be dissolved.[26] To add life to the ESDI, a European Rapid Reaction Force (RRF) has been created, which gives the EU "military muscle."[27] This, however, is a long way from the creation of a European army; troops will not be deployed anywhere without the explicit consent of their national governments, so without this caveat, the RRF will end up fighting political rather than military battles. The constant difficulty for the Europeans is to establish a sense of unity. As Anthony Gardner put it, transatlantic relations from an American perspective still resemble "shaking hands with a multiheaded octopus."[28] Thus, the reality vividly contrasts with the ideal that ESDI is striving for—the transatlantic alliance as a bridge resting on two pillars.

The Europeans are still dependent on the US for the strategic defense of their homelands, a situation that will remain for the foreseeable future. The US needs the Europeans in addressing global challenges such as the spread of nuclear weapons, organized crime, and, increasingly, environmental tasks such as dismantling Chernobyl-type nuclear plants. The New Transatlantic Agenda (NTA), signed at the

US-EU summit in December 1995, reflected not only the joint interest in addressing these problems, but also confirmed NATO's role as the centerpiece of transatlantic security, and indicated where future NATO tasks are likely to lie. Consequently, to paraphrase Voltaire, "if NATO did not exist, one would have to invent it." Or, to return to a geographical image: the American and the European plates may be drifting apart—but very, very slowly.

---

[1] Walter McDougall, *Promised Land, Crusader State: The American Encounter with the World Since 1776* (Boston: Houghton Mifflin, 1997), 52.

[2] For the concept of strategic cultures, see John Baylis and Russell Trood, eds., *Strategic Cultures in the Asia-Pacific Region* (London: Macmillan, 1999), 3-27.

[3] For the term "Transatlantic Cold War," see David Reynolds, *One World Indivisible: A Global History Since 1945* (New York: Penguin, 2000), 481-93.

[4] D. Campbell, *The Unsinkable Aircraft Carrier* (London: Paladin, 1984), 23.

[5] Marc Trachtenberg, *A Constructed Peace: The Making of the European Settlement, 1945-1963* (Princeton: Princeton University Press, 1999), chaps. 5 and 6.

[6] See Jan Melissen *The Struggle for Nuclear Partnership* (Groningen: Styx, 1993), 38-42.

[7] Trachtenberg, 193-209.

[8] Campbell, 1.

[9] On Sputnik, see Robert Divine, *The Sputnik Challenge* (Oxford: Oxford University Press, 1993).

[10] Divine, 57.

[11] For a recent assessment see Len Scott, *Macmillan, Kennedy and the Cuban Missile Crisis* (London: Macmillan, 1999).

[12] Ibid., 49.

[13] For French nuclear strategy, see Beatrice Heuser, *NATO, Britain, France, and the FRG: Nuclear Strategies and Forces for Europe 1949-2000* (London: Macmillan, 1998), 93-123.

[14] Robert McNamara's Ann Arbor Speech, June 16, 1962.

[15] See Raymond Garthoff, *Detente and Confrontation: American-Soviet Relations from Nixon to Reagan* (Washington DC: Brookings Institute, 1994), 236-37.

[16] Fred Halliday, *The Making of the Second Cold War* (London: Verso, 1983).

[17] On the "Gas Pipeline Row," see Angela Stent, *Technology Transfer to the Soviet Union. A Challenge for the Cohesiveness of the Western Alliance* (Bonn: Europa Union, 1983).

[18] See Ronald Steel, "NATO's Last Mission," *Foreign Policy* 79 (1989): 83-95.

[19] Ken Booth, "Liberal Democracy, Global Order and the Future of Transatlantic Relations," *Brasssey's Defence Yearbook 1993*, 360-61. President Bush claimed that the Gulf War was a successful realization of this concept.

[20] See Anthony Gardner *A New Era in US-EU Relations?* (Aldershot: Ashgate, 1999), 30.

[21] For the concept of the Second Nuclear Age, see Paul Bracken," The Second Nuclear Age," *Foreign Affairs* 79 (2000): 146-156.

[22] Camille Grand, "Missile Defense: The View from the Other Side of the Atlantic," *Arms Control Today*, (2000): 12.

[23] Ibid., 14.

[24] *The Guardian*, 4 August 2000.

[25] Lord Robertson's Speech at George Washington University, Washington DC, April 4, 2000.

[26] *Sueddeutsche Zeitung*, 14 November 2000.

[27] *The Guardian*, 21 November 2000.

[28] Gardner, 25.

Chapter 18

The European Union and Defense: Autonomy within the Bounds of Transatlantic Solidarity

Sven Biscop

The Cold War demonstrated broad consensus among the NATO allies over their security strategy, which was dominated by the division between East and West. Under American leadership, NATO was to protect Western Europe from the perceived Soviet threat, in particular through the presence of large numbers of US troops in Europe, with the American nuclear weapons as deterrent and ultimate guarantor of security. Although there were exceptions, such as France's withdrawal from the alliance's integrated military structure in 1966 and European protest against the deployment of missiles in Europe in the 1980s, the presence of a common enemy ensured that a consensus was essentially maintained and that American leadership and the predominance of NATO as a security organization were not fundamentally questioned.[1] Gradually, however, the European allies began to strive for a greater degree of autonomy in the field of security. Original plans to create a European Defence Community failed in the 1950s because of internal divisions among the European countries and a lack of confidence in the ability of Europe to provide for its own security. As a result, the collective defense of Europe was organized in an Atlantic framework.

The Move towards a European Security and Defense Policy

In the developing Atlantic framework, the European security organization, the Western European Union (WEU), founded in 1954, delegated all operational matters to NATO. It remained dormant until 1984, when it was reactivated in an attempt to develop security strategies in the context of European integration.[2] There were several reasons for these developments.[3] In 1970, the member states of the then European Economic Community (EEC) instigated the phase of European Political Cooperation (EPC), which provided for mutual consultation on foreign policy. They recognized that the economic giant that the EEC was and would further become could not do without some degree of foreign policy coordination. Although formally EPC could only touch upon the economic and technological aspects of security, in practice it was soon found that foreign and security policy could not be separated. This became clear during the negotiations for the framework of the Conference on Security and Cooperation in Europe (CSCE), the "three-basket" structure proposed by the EEC, which included a "basket" dealing with security matters and confidence-building measures. The member states ultimately found no consensus, however, to widen the scope of EPC so as to include security and defense.

Moreover, it had been realized that European and American interests did not always necessarily coincide. For example, the EEC attached much more importance to the maintenance of good relations with the Mediterranean states than the US did, because of close economic ties and the presence of large numbers of Europeans in these countries. For geopolitical and economic reasons, the EEC was also more inclined to maintain dialogue with the countries of Eastern and Central Europe, regardless of the state of affairs between the two superpowers. The US, on the other hand, obviously had greater interests in Latin America than the European allies did. This divergence of interests necessitated a certain degree of European autonomy in policy-making.

The European allies were also aware that, in the long term, the US might not be willing to continue bearing the burden of European defense, and might call for larger contributions from the Europeans themselves. Those wishing to maintain the strong transatlantic link saw the necessity of increasing the European defense effort in order to convince the Americans to maintain their contribution to European security. Arguably, the Atlantic-minded countries conceded to the reactivation of the WEU in 1984—rather than maintain security and defense within the terms of EPC—because the WEU had been closely connected to NATO but had played only a minor role. Therefore it could hardly pose a threat to transatlantic solidarity.

European public opinion had also contested American supremacy in the field of foreign affairs and defense. The deployment of nuclear weapons in Europe, which many perceived to be a unilateral American decision against European wishes, provoked severe protests and mass demonstrations. European policymakers, too, were sometimes annoyed by the American disregard for their allies' opinions. A notable example was the unilateral announcement by President Reagan in 1983—without any prior consultation—of the Strategic Defense Initiative, commonly known as the "Stars Wars Program." This incited the European allies to strengthen the European pillar within the NATO alliance. Economic crises had also forced European countries to cut their defense budgets. Research and development of high-technology weapons and equipment became ever more expensive and therefore difficult for the individual states to bear. This, in turn, increased the need for multinational cooperation, which encouraged member states to coordinate other aspects of their security and defense policies as well.

During the Gulf War, the EEC proved itself capable of efficacious action within the limits of its authority, notably in the field of humanitarian aid. The limited security dimension of EPC, however, and the lack of instruments and supportive structures for common action, rendered diplomatic and military action impossible. Thus the limitations of EPC and the requirements of an effective foreign and security policy corresponding to the Community's economic power became clear. On the other hand, the WEU did play its part in the naval operations of the war, contributing a fleet of 45 ships to enforce the embargo against Iraq, and 25 ships for minesweeping operations in the aftermath of the conflict. The WEU thus demonstrated its ability to execute military operations, although the Gulf War also demonstrated the deficiencies in its operational capacity. Most importantly, the WEU acted in close coordination with the EEC.[4]

Subsequently, because of American unwillingness to intervene in the Balkans, the EEC took the lead in the attempts to resolve the conflict that erupted in Yugoslavia in 1991. Initially, member states were able to act unanimously, approving a number of common measures; but very soon it became clear, yet again, that the limited scope, instruments, and structures of EPC could not meet the requirements of an effective foreign policy, which could not be separated from the security dimension. It further appeared that the EEC needed a military capacity as a necessary instrument of foreign policy. If the EEC had been able to use credible military pressure or deploy peacekeeping forces in the early stages of the conflict, it might have taken a completely different course. To some, a European military capacity seemed all the more necessary, given that initially the Americans were unwilling to intervene in what they considered to be a European problem, one in which no American interests were directly at stake and which therefore should be dealt with by the Europeans themselves. The WEU staged another naval operation, this time in close cooperation with NATO, but again it was forced to acknowledge its lack of structures for the execution and command of large-scale military operations.[5]

All these factors combined convinced the European member states of the need for an enhanced foreign and security policy dimension, which eventually led to the creation of the Common Foreign and Security Policy (CFSP) through the 1991 Maastricht Treaty. The CFSP envelops all aspects of security, including common defense, and the European Union (EU) can make use of the WEU as its operational capacity. The WEU greatly expanded its operational capacity, creating a Planning Cell, which included an intelligence unit, a Situation Centre, a Satellite Centre and additional military staff organs, while multinational military units such as the Eurocorps were put at its disposal. Armaments cooperation was enhanced by creating the Western European Armaments Group (WEAG) which, in due course, should evolve into a European armaments agency.[6] Through the 1997 Amsterdam Treaty, the so-called "Petersburg Tasks" were incorporated into the EU domain: peacekeeping, peace enforcement, humanitarian operations, and rescue operations.

The Kosovo crisis and, in particular, Europe's meager performance in the military field proved to be another major incentive for the further development of an operational military capacity for the EU. As NATO Secretary-General Lord Robertson put it, it was unacceptable that Europe—by its sheer lack of cooperation—should have such difficulties in deploying 50,000 troops, considering that European armed forces totaled over 2 million.[7] The lesson was that in order to be able to perform in the field, the European allies must coordinate their defense efforts and urgently redirect their defense budgets towards force-projection and sustainability.

At the Cologne European Council in June 1999, it was decided that the EU should have an autonomous capacity to make military decisions and, without prejudice to NATO, launch and conduct EU-led military operations in response to international crises.[8] The Helsinki European Council in December 1999 adopted a concrete plan to realize this operational capacity.[9] Member states set themselves the so-called "headline goal": by the year 2003, through voluntary cooperation, they should be able to rapidly deploy forces capable of executing the full range of Petersburg Tasks to the level of peace enforcement. Within 60 days member states should be able to field a unit of army-corps size (50-60,000 troops) and the necessary support units in the fields of logistics, intelligence, and other relevant arenas. This deployment should have a sustaining capability of at least one year.

According to the terms of the Helsinki plan, the decision to mount an operation is taken unanimously by the Council, comprised of the various Ministers of Foreign Affairs, who are joined by the Defense Ministers when dealing with security and defense. A new Political and Security Committee deals with all aspects of the CFSP including security and defense and (under the authority of the Council) exercises political control and strategic direction of operations. It is advised by a Military Committee comprised of the Chiefs of Defense Staff. A Military Staff within the Council structures is now responsible for early warning, situation assessment, and strategic planning. The other existing organs of WEU will gradually be integrated into the EU. Deficiencies in the fields of transport, intelligence, command, and control have yet to be filled; but the ultimate goal is to enable the EU to assume the great tasks of European crisis management.

A Threat to Transatlantic Solidarity?

NATO recognized European security aspirations at an early stage. At the June 1991 Copenhagen Summit, NATO principally accepted that the so-called European Security and Defence Identity (ESDI) would reflect greater responsibilities. At the same time, it was stressed that, considering its broad membership and its military capacity, NATO should remain the essential forum for consultations on and definition of the security and defense policy of the alliance. In its Rome Declaration on Peace and Cooperation of November 1991, NATO expressed its support for the reinforcement of the European pillar of the alliance and the WEU's role therein, which was seen as a process of mutual reinforcement between the alliance and the European partners. This was also reflected in the revised Strategic Concept, which was adopted at the same summit. Again the indivisibility of security was emphasized. Support for the European initiative has been reiterated at every summit since 1991. At the 50th Anniversary Summit in Washington in April 1999, the alliance acknowledged "the resolve of the European Union to have the capacity for autonomous action so that it can take decisions and approve military action where the Alliance as a whole is not engaged."[10]

The US has repeatedly voiced its wish for a greater European defense effort. Especially after the air war over Kosovo, Washington urged its European allies to bear a larger share of the security burden. According to the US, Europe should spend more on defense so as to increase the output of its armed forces and close the technology gap with America. It is hoped that this will relieve the US of some defense burdens in Europe, which would allow resources to be reallocated to security threats in other regions of the world. A Europe with more autonomous defense capabilities might even join the US in crisis-management operations outside of Europe. A more self-reliant Europe might also be less resentful towards American predominance within the alliance. The result would be a stronger NATO consisting of equally contributing partners.[11] However, at the same time, there is considerable concern in the US over the possible damage that greater European autonomy could do to transatlantic solidarity. American fears can be summarized in the "3 D's" as expressed by the former Secretary of State, Madeleine Albright: *duplication, decoupling*, and *discrimination*.[12]

The US sees *duplication* of what is already being done in NATO as a waste of resources, with European defense budgets as low as they currently are. Instead, the US would prefer the European allies to make use of the Combined Joint Task Forces concept (CJTF) as agreed at the June 1996 Berlin summit, which allows for NATO assets to be made available for European-led operations. Europe should focus on improving projectability and sustainability as recommended by the alliance's Defence Capabilities Initiative (DCI), and on closing the technology gap with the American military. In fact, the US has doubts about whether the Europeans' declared intentions can result in the actual reform of defense spending, as most EU governments are still reducing defense budgets.

Washington wants to avoid *decoupling* or de-linking the US from Europe through the lack of coordinated defense efforts on both sides of the Atlantic. In the American view, the ESDI should be a strengthened European pillar within the alliance. The European defense effort and European integration in the field of security should be enhanced in order to improve performance, but the definition of security and defense policies should remain the prerogative of NATO. As Strobe Talbot, the former Deputy Secretary of State put it, the US does not want to see ESDI grow out of NATO and then away from it, ending up duplicating and competing with NATO. The US fears that European policy will focus on institution building; Washington wants to see additional capabilities, not new institutions, which, from the American standpoint, would only serve to jeopardize coordination.[13]

The Americans insist that there should be no *discrimination* against those allies who are not members of the EU (Iceland, Norway, Turkey, Poland, Hungary, and the Czech Republic, all of whom are Associate Members of the WEU) including, of course, Canada and the US itself.

All alliance members are to be involved in possible EU operations, from decision-making to operations in the field, and there should be full consultation between all members at all times. For its part, Turkey indeed proved to be dissatisfied with EU intentions, claiming that the plans for an autonomous European security capacity disregarded the status of non-EU allies.[14]

In response to the negative approach that appeared to dominate American policy, Lord Robertson attempted to reformulate its concerns in a more positive way, introducing the "3 I's": *improvement* of European defense capabilities, *indivisibility* of transatlantic security, and *inclusiveness* for all Allies. Essentially, however, these do not diminish US fears.

Autonomy within the Bounds of Solidarity

Arguably, the creation of an autonomous European defense and security capacity need not affect transatlantic solidarity at all. The EU asserts that it has taken into account the concerns of all the allies.[15] At the Feira European Council in June 2000, it was decided that in the course of each European presidency, there shall be regular meetings with the non-EU European members of NATO and the candidates for accession to the EU (the "EU+15" format), and at least two meetings with the non-EU European members of NATO alone (the "EU+6" format). These meetings will deal with all aspects of security and defense policy, in particular the establishment of an EU capability for crisis management ("routine phase"). In the event of a crisis ("pre-operational phase") consultation will be intensified. Once the Council decides to launch an operation ("operational phase"), the non-EU European members of NATO can participate in any operation having recourse to NATO assets. The Council can also invite them and other countries that are candidates for EU accession to participate in operations that do not make use of NATO assets. They will have the same rights and obligations as the EU member states in the day-to-day conduct of the operations, through an ad hoc committee of contributors. The political control and strategic direction of the operation remain with the Council and the EU's Political and Security Committee.

The European Council has further provided for consultation between the EU and NATO. As an interim measure, 4 working groups have been created to deal with the following subjects: preparation of an EU-NATO security agreement to allow exchange of information; coordination of the EU's efforts to meet the headline goal and NATO's Defence Capabilities Initiative; preparation of an agreement on the modalities for EU access to NATO assets in a CJTF-framework; and the definition of a permanent agreement "which would formalize structures and procedures for consultation between the two organizations in times of crisis and non-crisis."[16] These working groups were convened for the first time under the French Presidency, which began on July 1, 2000.

All of these arrangements are designed to ensure that all allies will be maximally involved in EU operations without discrimination, and that EU and NATO policies will be coordinated, while at the same time respecting the autonomy and institutions of the EU. There is to be no "decoupling," since NATO remains the framework in which the collective defense of all allies is organized. Of course the Modified Brussels Treaty (MBT), which founded the WEU, comprises a collective defense guarantee as well (Article V), but this is unlikely to be included in the Treaty on European Union (TEU) and so will only be binding on the WEU's current 10 full members. In any event, implementation of Article V has been delegated to NATO since the creation of the WEU, and there appears to be no intention of changing this.[17] Granted, one might indeed prefer to see Article V incorporated into the TEU, if only because this would symbolize solidarity between all member states of the EU, whereas now only 5 of them have Observer status in the WEU (Denmark, Austria, Finland, Ireland and Sweden). Only the first of these belongs to NATO. In order to achieve full transparency in the security architecture and, perhaps, to avoid freeloading, it would be preferable that the other 4 join the alliance as well, since currently they do not contribute to the collective defense effort. Unfortunately, this does not appear to be feasible for the near future.[18]

Under the latest arrangements, the EU will only assume tasks in the field of crisis management and will conduct operations "where NATO as a whole is not engaged." This clause is often interpreted as NATO having a "right of first refusal," although this has never been declared so explicitly. In fact, it is expected that a division of labor between the two organizations will develop gradually through the practice of actual consultations and cooperation. Considering the American demands for a greater European defense effort after Kosovo, it seems reasonable to expect that in future crises on the European continent, NATO will welcome European initiatives and will only act if European means appear to be insufficient. Such expectations are further supported by America's past unwillingness to intervene in what Washington deems to be "European problems," such as during the early stages of the conflict in the former Yugoslavia or after the eruption of violence in Albania in 1997. Of course, it is another question entirely whether the US would also accept, say, a greater European political and military profile in the Middle East, which would be wholly relevant to the Euro-Mediterranean Partnership.

It is precisely because of the possibility that NATO and the US might not be willing or able to intervene in a crisis on the *periphery* of the EU that the Union needs the capacity to act autonomously if necessary. This implies a redirection of European defense budgets towards deployable forces and the capability to sustain deployments over a longer period of time, which means that further efforts will have to be made in the field of transport and logistics. Coordination and pooling of the means of the individual member states—in other words, moving European integration into the field of security and defense—is the best way to achieve a higher degree of efficacy and efficiency. An autonomous European capability also implies the creation of decision-making structures, the capacity to gather intelligence, and the means of planning and conducting military operations. Hence the new organs provided for by the European Council and the integration of WEU organs into the EU.

Applying the CJTF concept in itself would not be sufficient to provide the EU with the capacity to act autonomously. First of all, it is often forgotten that the common assets belonging to NATO are, in fact, rather limited, these being mainly confined to the alliance's planning organs and command structures, as well as a few dozen AWACS airplanes. All other means are provided by the member states separately. Second, the North Atlantic Council (NAC), which makes decisions by consensus, would have to authorize the use of NATO assets on a case-by-case basis. Organizing the EU capacity on the sole basis of the CJTF concept would thus make European operations dependent on the agreement of non-EU countries. Furthermore, security and defense are an integral part of the EU's CFSP, with all its decision-making organs from which the EU should not be separated. The conclusion must be that some degree of duplication is inevitable, notably where planning and decision-making structures are concerned, to allow autonomous EU operations when necessary. This is indeed recognized by the European Council, which decided that the creation of a European capacity should avoid "*unnecessary* duplication" (my emphasis). The regular consultation between the EU and NATO, as provided for by the Feira European Council, will ensure that full coordination is maintained.

It is clear that the US cannot, on the one hand, demand that Europe bear a larger share of the burden, and on the other hand, retain full and exclusive control over the use of all military means. If Washington expects Europe to do more on defense, it should also allow the EU a reasonable degree of autonomy.[19] The autonomous European capacity and NATO are, in fact, mutually reinforcing: an effective European capacity for crisis management can be used in both EU and NATO operations, and relieves the US of a significant burden. Other promising areas of cooperation present themselves as well, such as in civil crisis management, a field in which NATO is mostly absent and in which the EU is building a pioneering capacity.[20]

Immediately after the end of World War II, the countries of Western Europe attempted to establish some form of military integration, to protect themselves against the possibility of renewed German aggression and, more importantly, to counter further Soviet expansion. Circumstances dictated that the collective defense of Western Europe would be organized in a transatlantic framework, while the process of European integration focused on domestic and economic concerns. Quite soon, however, the need for foreign policy cooperation arose because an economic power such as the EEC—now the EU—simply could not (and cannot) do without it. Then, as now, foreign policy could not be separated from security policy; the threat or use of military action must sometimes be used as an ultimate instrument to guarantee peace and security, one of the objectives of the EU's CFSP. Because the US is not always able or willing to intervene, an autonomous European capacity for crisis management is clearly necessary, so that Europe can act when its interests are at stake. The reasons for the creation of a "military arm" for the EU are thus highly pragmatic. It is not a matter of prestige or megalomania, but the obvious need for the ability to act when necessary—a realization that led even the UK, the most "Atlanticist" of the EU's member states, to consent to the creation of an EU capacity for crisis management.[21]

If handled sensibly there is no need for these developments to conflict with the interests of NATO and transatlantic solidarity. The arrangements decided upon by the European Council ensure that European and American policy will continue to be closely coordinated. The creation of an effective European capacity will enhance the efficacy of NATO, and will reduce the weight now carried by the US. Of course frictions between allies on either side of the Atlantic will arise. The current debate on the US National Missile Defense project—the "Son of Star Wars"—is a prominent example. Essentially, however, the existence of NATO is not under threat. It remains the basis of the collective defense of all allies, and is designing a new role for itself in the field of crisis management, a role that it will rightfully share with the EU.

---

[1] Michael J. Brenner, "Multilateralism and European Security," *Survival* 35 (1993): 138-155.

[2] See Sven Biscop, *De integratie van de WEU in de Europese Unie. Europa op weg naar een Europese defensie organisatie* (Leuven: Acco, 2000).

[3] William Wallace, "European Defence Cooperation: The Reopening Debate," *Survival* 26 (1984): 251-261; David Greenwood, "Constructing the European Pillar: Issues and Institutions," *NATO Review* 36, no. 3 (1988): 13-17.

[4] *Consequences of the invasion of Kuwait: Operations in the Gulf. Report submitted on behalf of the Defence Committee by Mr. De Hoop Scheffer, Rapporteur* (WEU Assembly Document 1243) (Paris: WEU Assembly, 1990); *Consequences of the invasion of Kuwait: Continuing operations in the Gulf region. Report submitted on behalf of the Defence Committee by Mr. De Hoop Schepper, Rapporteur* (WEU Assembly Document 1248) (Paris: WEU Assembly, 1990); *The Gulf crisis – lessons for Western European Union. Report submitted on behalf of the Defence Committee by Mr. De Hoop Scheffer, Rapporteur* (WEU Assembly Document 1268) (Paris: WEU Assembly, 1991).

[5] *WEU's operational organization and the Yugoslav crisis. Report submitted on behalf of the Defence Committee by Mr. Marten, Rapporteur* (WEU Assembly Document 1337) (Paris: WEU Assembly, 1992); *Lessons drawn from the Yugoslav conflict. Report submitted on behalf of the Defence Committee by Sir Russel Johnston, Rapporteur* (WEU Assembly Document 1395) (Paris: WEU Assembly, 1993); James Gow, "Deconstructing Yugoslavia," *Survival* 33 (1991): 291-311; Nicole Gnesotto, *Lessons of Yugoslavia* (Chaillot Paper 14) (Paris: WEU Institute for Security Studies, 1994).

[6] Anon., *WEU Today* (Brussels: WEU Secretariat, 1997).

[7] Luc Rosenzweig and Daniel Vernet, "George Robertson, secrétaire général de l'OTAN: "Sans capacités militaires, l'Europe serait un tigre de papier," *Le Monde*, 4 November 1999.

[8] European Council, *Conclusions of the Presidency. Cologne, 3-4 June 1999*, http://www.europa.eu.int.

[9] European Council, *Conclusions of the Presidency. Helsinki, 10-11 December 1999*, http://www.europa.eu.int.

[10] North Atlantic Council, *Rome Declaration on peace and cooperation. Issued by the Heads of State and Government participating in the meeting of the North Atlantic Council in Rome on 7th-8th November 1991* (Brussels: NATO Office of Information and Press, 1991); North Atlantic Council, *Washington Summit communiqué issued by the Heads of State and Government participating in the meeting of the North Atlantic Council in Washington, DC on 24th April 1999* (Brussels: NATO Office of Information and Press, 1999).

[11] Stanley R. Sloan, *The United States and European defence* (Chaillot Paper 39) (Paris: WEU Institute for Security Studies, 2000).

[12] William Drozdiak, "US Seems Increasingly Uncomfortable with EU Defence Plan," *International Herald Tribune*, 6 March 2000; see also Sloan.

[13] David Buchan, "US Diplomat Warns Europe Over Defence," *Financial Times*, 19 May 2000; Daniel Vernet, "Paradoxes euro-américains sur la défense," *Le Monde*, 2 June 2000.

[14] Pierre Bocev, "Les Quinze et les 'six furieux': Aigreur turque après le Sommet de Feira," *Le Figaro*, 22 June 2000; Matthew Kaminsky, "Turkey Threatens to Block NATO from Providing Assistance to EU," *Wall Street Journal Europe*, 24 May 2000.

[15] European Council, *Conclusions of the Presidency. Santa Maria da Feira, 20 June 2000*, http://www.europa.eu.int.

[16] Ibid.

[17] It should be noted that the MBT stipulates stricter obligations on mutual assistance than the North Atlantic Treaty in the case of armed attack on a member state. The former obliges all contracting parties to afford "all military and other aid in their power," whereas the latter only obliges them "to take such action as they deem necessary."

[18] Jean-François Gribinski, "L'Union européenne face aux défis de la neutralité," *Défense nationale* 52 (January 1996): 85-102.

[19] Charles Barry and Sean Kay, "America Needs a Strong Europe," *Wall Street Journal Europe*, 2 June 2000.

[20] Luke Hill, "EU Unveils Plan for Rapid Reaction Disaster Force," *Defence News*, 1 May 2000.

[21] Sven Biscop, "The UK's Change of Course: A New Chance for the European Security and Defence Identity," *European Foreign Affairs Review* 4, no. 2 (1999): 253-268; Sven Biscop, "Le Royaume-Uni et l'Europe de la défense: de l'opposition au pragmatisme," *Revue du Marché commun et de l'Union européenne* 43 (2000): 73-77.

Selected Bibliography

Andrews, Kenneth R. *Trade, Plunder, and Settlement: Maritime Enterprise and the Genesis of the British Empire, 1480-1630.* Cambridge: Cambridge University Press, 1984.

Blackburn, Robin. *The Making of New World Slavery: From the Baroque to the Modern, 1492-1800.* London: Verso, 1997.

Burk, Kathleen, and Melvyn Stokes, eds. *The United States and the European Alliance since 1945.* Oxford: Berg, 1999.

Castillo, Susan, and Ivy Schweitzer, eds. *The Literatures of Colonial America.* Oxford: Blackwell, 2001.

Cervantes, Fernando. *The Devil in the New World: The Impact of Diabolism in New Spain.* New Haven: Yale University Press, 1994.

Falk, Richard. *On Humane Governance: Toward a New Global Politics.* Cambridge: Polity Press, 1995.

Fisher, J. R. *Silver Mines and Silver Miners in Colonial Peru, 1776-1824.* Liverpool: Liverpool University Press, 1977.

Forbes, Jack D., *Africans and Native Americans: The Language of Race and the Evolution of Red-Black Peoples.* Urbana: University of Illinois Press, 1993.

Ford Foundation. *Crossing Borders: Revitalizing Area Studies.* New York: Ford Foundation, 1999.

Garber, Marjorie et al., eds. *Field Work: Sites in Literary and Cultural Studies.* New York: Routledge, 1996.

Gardner, Anthony. *A New Era in US-EU Relations?* Aldershot: Ashgate, 1999.

Garthoff, Raymond. *Detente and Confrontation: American-Soviet Relations from Nixon to Reagan.* Washington, DC: Brookings Institute, 1994.

Geographical Review 89, no. 2 (April 1999). [Entire issue devoted to Duke University's *Oceans Connect* project.]

Giddens, Anthony. *The Third Way: The Renewal of Social Democracy.* Cambridge: Polity Press, 1998.

Giles, Mary E., ed. *Women in the Inquisition: Spain and the New World.* Baltimore: Johns Hopkins University Press, 1998.

Giles, Paul. *Transatlantic Insurrections: British Culture and the Formation of American Literature, 1730-1860.* Philadelphia: University of Pennsylvania Press, 2001.

Gilroy, Paul. *The Black Atlantic: Modernity and Double Consciousness.* Cambridge: Harvard University Press, 1993.

Greaves, Thomas, and William Culver, eds. *Miners and Mining in the Americas.* Manchester: Manchester University Press, 1985.

Gregory, D. *Brute New World: The Rediscovery of Latin America in the Early 19ᵗʰ Century.* London: British Academic Press, 1992.

Griffiths, Nicholas, and Fernando Cervantes., eds. *Spiritual Encounters: Interactions between Christianity and Native Religions in Colonial America.* Lincoln: University of Nebraska Press, 1999.

Halliday, Fred. *The Making of the Second Cold War.* London: Verso, 1983.

Heuser, Beatrice. *NATO, Britain, France, and the FRG: Nuclear Strategies and Forces for Europe 1949-2000.* London: Macmillan, 1998.

Hugh, Honour. *The New Golden Land: European Images of America from the Discoveries to the Present Time.* New York: Pantheon Books, 1975.

Jara, René, and Nicholas Spadaccini, eds. *Amerindian Images and the Legacy of Columbus.* Minneapolis: University of Minnesota Press, 1992.

Kaufman, Will, and Heidi Slettedahl Macpherson, eds. *Transatlantic Studies.* Lanham: University Press of America, 2000.

Kloppenberg, James T. *Uncertain Victory: Social Democracy and Progressivism in European and American Thought, 1870-1920.* New York: Oxford University Press, 1986.

Lewis, Martin W., and Kären Wigen. "A Maritime Response to the Crisis in Area Studies." *Geographical Review* 89, no. 2 (April 1999): 161-68.

Linebaugh, Peter, and Marcus Rediker. *The Many-Headed Hydra: Sailors, Slaves, Commoners, and the History of the Revolutionary Atlantic.* Boston: Beacon Press, 2000.

Lorimer, Joyce, ed. *English and Irish Settlement on the River Amazon, 1550-1646.* London: Hakluyt Society, 1989.

Lundestad, Geir. *"Empire" by Integration: The United States and European Integration, 1945-1997.* Oxford: Oxford University Press, 1998.

Marks, Shula, and Peter Richardson, eds. *International Labour Migration: Historical Perspectives.* London: Temple Meads, 1984.

Marshall, Oliver, ed. *English Speaking Communities in Latin America.* London: Macmillan, 2000.

McDougall, Walter. *Promised Land, Crusader State: The American Encounter with the World Since 1776.* Boston: Houghton Mifflin, 1997.

Perry, M. E., and Anne J. Cruz, eds. *Cultural Encounters: The Impact of the Inquisition in Spain and the New World.* Berkeley: University of California Press, 1991.

Phillips, William D., and Carla Rahn Phillips, *The Worlds of Christopher Columbus.* Cambridge: Cambridge University Press, 1992.

Pratt, Mary Louise. *Imperial Eyes: Travel Writing and Transculturation.* New York: Routledge, 1992.

Quinn, Patrick F. *The French Face of Edgar Allan Poe.* Carbondale: Southern Illinois University Press, 1971.

Rabasa, José. *Inventing America: Spanish Historiography and the Formation of Eurocentrism.* Norman: University of Oklahoma Press, 1993.

Rediker, Marcus. *Between the Devil and the Deep Blue Sea: Merchant Seamen, Pirates, and the Anglo-American Maritime World, 1700-1750.* Cambridge: Cambridge University Press, 1987.

Reeves, B. O. K., and M. A. Kennedy, eds. *Kunaitupii: Coming Together on Native Sacred Sites.* Calgary: Archaeological Society of Alberta, 1993.

Roach, Joseph. *Cities of the Dead: The Social Foundations of Aesthetic Forms.* New York: Columbia University Press, 1996.

Schwartz, Stuart B., ed. *Implicit Understandings: Observing, Reporting, and Reflecting on the Encounters Between Europeans and Other Peoples in the Early Modern Era.* New York: Cambridge University Press, 1995.

Scott, Len. *Macmillan, Kennedy and the Cuban Missile Crisis.* London: Macmillan, 1999.

Thornton, John. *Africa and Africans in the Making of the Atlantic World.* New York: Cambridge University Press, 1992.

Todd, A. C. *The Search for Silver: Cornish Miners in Mexico, 1826-1947.* Padstow: Lodenek, 1977.

Tompkins, William David. *The Musical Traditions of the Blacks of Coastal Peru.* Los Angeles: University of California Press, 1981.

University of Chicago Globalization Project, *Area Studies, Regional Worlds: A White Paper for the Ford Foundation.* Chicago: Center for International Studies, 1997.

Vines, Lois Davis, ed. *Poe Abroad: Influence, Reputation, Affinities.* Iowa City: University of Iowa Press, 1999.

Volkman, T. A. "Crossing Borders: The Case for Area Studies." *Ford Foundation Report* 29, no. 1 (1998): 28-29.

White, John Kenneth, and Philip John Davies, eds. *Political Parties and the Collapse of the Old Orders.* Albany: State University of New York Press, 1998.

Winand, Pascaline. *Eisenhower, Kennedy, and the United States of Europe.* New York: St. Martin's Press, 1993.

Zamora, Margarita. *Reading Columbus.* Berkeley: University of California Press, 1993.

INDEX

About the Contributors

Saturnino Aguado is a Professor of Economics in the Department of Economics of the University of Alcalá, Madrid, Spain, and the Director of the Institute for North American Studies. He received his MA in 1981 from The University of Chicago and has been a Visiting Scholar at Harvard University (1986-87) and a Research Associate at the University of California-Berkeley (1995).

Sven Biscop is attached to the International and European Research Unit at Ghent University, where he is writing a Ph.D. thesis on the Common Foreign and Security Policy of the European Union and security in the Mediterranean. His latest book is *Integratie van de WEU in de Europese Unie. Europa op weg naar een Europese defensie-organisatie* (Acco Publishers, 2000).

Lars Ivar Owesen-Lein Borge studied social anthropology at the University of Oslo, and is a Ph.D. candidate in Mexican Ethnohistory at the University of Frankfurt. He is currently working on the impact of the Catholic Reformation on popular culture and beliefs among different groups in New Spain, and the development of transatlantic cultures of magic in the colonial society.

Steve Brewer teaches French, German, and European Culture at Staffordshire University, UK. He has recently published a translation of Jean-Paul Sartre's "Situations, V" under the title *Colonialism and Neo-Colonialism* (Routledge, with Azzedine Haddour and Terry McWilliams).

Philip John Davies is Professor of American Studies at De Montfort University, Leicester, UK, and Chair of the British Association for American Studies. He has published widely on American culture and politics; his books include *US Elections Today* (Manchester University Press), *Political Parties and the Collapse of the Old Orders* (SUNY Press), and *The History Atlas of North America* (Macmillan USA).

Roberta Glaspie is currently completing her Masters in Criminal Justice Administration with an emphasis on corrections, legal studies, and inmate rights at Central Missouri State University in Warrensburg, Missouri, USA.

Lesley Hodgson is a Ph.D. candidate at the University of Glamorgan, Wales. She has recently been involved in a European Funded

TEMPUS project with Glamorgan, Lodz University, Poland and Växjö University, Sweden. She attended the Maastricht Center for Transatlantic Studies as an undergraduate and has since delivered two papers at the Center.

Martin Jesinghausen is a Senior Lecturer in Modern Languages and European Culture at Staffordshire University, UK. He has a Ph.D. in cultural theory and has published a monograph on modernist cultural theory in Europe and the US. He has also written articles in the areas of cultural and literary theory.

Richard Milton Juang is a Ph.D. candidate at Cornell University and a graduate member of the university's Women's Studies program. His dissertation explores the role of the transatlantic cultural economy in British literature.

Will Kaufman is a Reader in English and American Studies at the University of Central Lancashire, UK, and a founding member of the Maastricht Center for Transatlantic Studies. He is the author of *The Comedian as Confidence Man: Studies in Irony Fatigue* (Wayne State UP, 1997) and co-editor of *Transatlantic Studies* (UPA, 2000).

Brigitte Leucht is a Ph.D. student of History at the University of Vienna, Austria, and is affiliated with the Austrian-American Educational Commission (Fulbright Commission). She was a Fulbright student in 1998-99. Her research focuses on the history of early European integration from a transatlantic point of view.

Marcia Loo, a native of Peru, is a former Fulbright scholar and a Ph.D. candidate in Ethnomusicology at the University of Maryland, USA. Her area of specialization focuses on Latin American Studies and Critical Theory. At the present, she is conducting a research on the migration of the Andean *Cabana* culture from the Southwestern Andes of Peru to the USA.

Heidi Macpherson is a Senior Lecturer at the University of Central Lancashire, UK. She is the author of *Women's Movement: Escape as Transgression in North American Feminist Fiction* (Rodopi, 2000), and the co-editor of *Transatlantic Studies* (UPA, 2000). Her current research is on women and the law in 20th-century fiction. She is working on a new monograph, *Courting Failure*.

Phillippe Mahoux-Pauzin received his Ph.D. from Université de Bourgogne (Dijon) in 1997. He is currently working as a Maître de Conférence (Associate Professor) at the Université de Nancy, teaching American Studies and English and American poetry. His publications include articles on WWI poetry, AIDS and poetry, polemical poetry and the slavery question.

Anthony Marasco graduated in Anglo-American Literature from the University of Venice, Italy, and is now a Ph.D. candidate in History at the University of California, Berkeley. His research focuses on the early stages of the pragmatic movement in Europe and the US.

Milissa Ellison-Murphree is concluding work on her dissertation for Auburn University, "The East Anglian Witch-Hunts, 1645-1647." She is also pursuing a second doctorate at Auburn, in medieval English literature, as well as teaching at the State University of West Georgia.

María Dolores Narbona Carrión is a teaching assistant at the University of Málaga, Spain. She specializes in American Studies, concentrating on 19th-century women writers; her dissertation is focused on Elizabeth Stuart Phelps (1844-1911).

Melanie Perrault is an Assistant Professor of History at Salisbury University, USA. She received her Ph.D. in History from the College of William and Mary in 1997. Her current research interests include science and gender in the Atlantic world.

Susanna Schrafstetter is a Lecturer in History at the University of Glamorgan, Wales. Her particular areas of interest are nuclear diplomacy and West German foreign policy during the Cold War. She is the author of *Die dritte Atommacht. Britische Nichtverbreitungspolitik im Dienst von Statussicherung und Deutschlandpolitik 1952-1968* (Oldenbourg, 1999).

Sharron Schwartz is a part-time Lecturer in the Department of Lifelong Learning at Exeter University's center in Truro, Cornwall, UK. She is the Director of the Cornish Global Migration Programme, a research project analyzing demographic flows from Cornwall between 1815 and 1930, and is currently completing her doctorate on the socio-economic effects of Cornish migration to Latin America at Exeter University.

Andrew Thompson received his Ph.D. from the University of Wales, and currently lectures in Sociology at the University of Glamorgan, Wales. He is the co-author of *Theorising Nationalism* (Macmillan, 2002) and *Changing Europe* (Routledge, 2002) and the co-editor of *Nation, Identity, and Social Theory* (University of Wales Press, 1999) and *Wales Today* (University of Wales Press, 1999).

Elvira Vilches is an Assistant Professor at North Carolina State University, where she teaches early modern Spanish literature from both Spain and Colonial America. She is currently working on a book manuscript entitled *The Economy of the Marvelous: Transatlantic Values and Fictions in the Spanish Empire (1492-1664)*.

Donald H. Wallace is a Professor of Criminal Justice at Central Missouri State University in Warrensburg, Missouri, USA. He received a Juris Doctorate and a Master of Arts in Law-Psychology Studies from the University of Nebraska, and a Masters of Laws in International Law from the University of Missouri-Kansas City. His research interests include the death penalty and other human rights issues in criminal justice.

Michael C. Wilson has taught at universities and colleges in Canada, the US, Japan, and China. He is at present Chair of the Geology Department at Douglas College, New Westminster, BC. His last book was *Beyond Subsistence: Plains Archaeology and the Postprocessual Critique* (University of Alabama Press, 1995) and he recently completed a new book manuscript, *Antlers in the Land*.